高校英语选修课系列教材

A SHORT STORY OF WESTERN CIVILIZATION

西方文明

胡翠娥　主编

U0367319

清华大学出版社
北京

内 容 简 介

全书分为四个部分，共二十五章，主要从古代世界、中世纪文明、早期现代欧洲和现代西方的兴起四个板块阐述西方文明的简短发展史。本书从西方文明这一概念的起源入手，介绍了对西方文明的形成和发展发挥至关重要作用的各项要素，包括古希腊、古罗马的思想和政治成就，科学、技术和宗教的因素等；还展示了西方文明对世界上其他地区产生的影响，包括亚洲、非洲和美洲。对于重点章节的介绍，本书还提供了相关的权威性引文，为学生提供原汁原味的素材。本书既可用于高校英语专业、翻译专业的课堂教学，又可作为高校英语通识选修课教材。

本书另配有课后练习的答案详解及电子课件，读者可登录 ftp://ftp.tup.tsinghua.edu.cn/ 下载使用。

图书在版编目（CIP）数据

西方文明：英文 / 胡翠娥主编. —北京：清华大学出版社，2022.4（2024.8重印）
高校英语选修课系列教材
ISBN 978-7-302-60401-3

Ⅰ.①西… Ⅱ.①胡… Ⅲ.①文化史—西方国家—高等学校—教材—英文 Ⅳ.① K103

中国版本图书馆 CIP 数据核字（2022）第 048641 号

责任编辑：方燕贝　刘　艳
封面设计：子　一
责任校对：王凤芝
责任印制：曹婉颖

出版发行：清华大学出版社
　　　网　　址：https://www.tup.com.cn，https://www.wqxuetang.com
　　　地　　址：北京清华大学学研大厦 A 座　　邮　编：100084
　　　社 总 机：010-83470000　　　　　　　　邮　购：010-62786544
　　　投稿与读者服务：010-62776969，c-service@tup.tsinghua.edu.cn
　　　质量反馈：010-62772015，zhiliang@tup.tsinghua.edu.cn
印 装 者：天津鑫丰华印务有限公司
经　　销：全国新华书店
开　　本：185mm×260mm　　　印　张：16.25　　字　数：352 千字
版　　次：2022 年 4 月第 1 版　　　　　　印　次：2024 年 8 月第 4 次印刷
定　　价：68.00 元

产品编号：079947-01

"文明"和"西方文明"的定义

按照历史学家的定义,文明最早出现在五六千年前,当时世界各地的人们开始生活在具有不同的政治、军事、经济和社会结构的聚落中。宗教、思想和艺术活动在这些早期社会中扮演着重要角色。

人们通常把西方文明看作是一种与欧洲大陆密切相关的文明。事实上,在过去几个世纪里,西方文明自身已经有了长足的发展。虽然"西方"的概念在美索不达米亚人和古埃及人的时代尚未存在,但他们的文字、法典和基于性别的不同角色发展终究都影响了西方文明的形成。虽然古希腊人并没有将西方文明视为一种文化实体,但他们的艺术、思想和政治贡献却对西方文明的形成至关重要。古罗马人创造了一系列非凡的成就,为西方文明的发展奠定了基础。西方文明主要由古罗马人攻占的欧洲大陆构成,在这片土地上古罗马的文化和政治理想逐渐传播开来。不过,这些早期文明中的人们视自己为城邦或帝国的臣民,而非西方文明中的一员。随着罗马帝国末期基督教的兴起,欧洲各民族开始认识到自己所属的文明不同于其他文明,比如伊斯兰文明,进一步形成了区别于其他文明的"西方文明"的概念。在 15 世纪,文艺复兴时期的知识分子不仅开始将这一文明等同于基督教文化,还等同于古希腊罗马的思想和政治成就。对于发展一个独特的西方文明而言,重要的是与其他民族的接触。从 700 年到 1500 年,与伊斯兰世界的接触帮助定义了"西方"这一概念。

但在 1500 年后,欧洲船舰开始到达世界上其他地区,与亚洲人、非洲人和美洲人相遇,这不仅影响了这些地区的文明,而且影响了西方人对自身的定义。与此同时,随着欧洲人建立起殖民地,他们开始将西方认同感移植到世界上其他地区,尤其是北美洲和拉丁美洲的部分地区,这些地区逐渐被认为是西方文明的一部分。

正如西方文明这一概念经过了几个世纪的发展,与其相关的价值观及特点也在发展。科学对现代西方文明的发展起到了重要作用。古希腊、古罗马和中世纪时期的欧洲社会主要建立在对精神秩序存在的信仰之上,然而,在 17 世纪的科学革命时期发生了向自然或物质宇宙观的剧烈转变。科学和技术对如今现代的、世俗的西方文明的发展十分重要,但宗教仍然是当今西方世界的重要组成部分。

许多历史学家将自由的概念、对个人基本价值的信仰以及基于逻辑分析思维体系的理性展望看作是西方文明的独特之处。当然，西方也见证过对自由、个人主义和理性的严重否定。种族主义、奴隶制、暴力、世界大战、极权主义政权——这些也构成了西方文明复杂进程中的一部分。

本书的编排

本书以可靠的权威素材为编写依据，通过简明扼要和深入浅出的编排方式，为国内学生描绘了一部简短的西方文明发展史。其中，最重要的是介绍了西方文明形成的关键因素以及它与其他文明的关系。鉴于此，我们不认为原创性是本书的最突出特点；相反，为了让学生在日益全球化的教育体系下更好地发展，我们借鉴了国内外学者关于西方文明的可靠著作，对于这些学者我们不胜感激。

本书分为四部分：古代世界、中世纪文明、早期现代欧洲和现代西方的兴起。为了让历史变得栩栩如生，书中包含了第一手文献资料（引文部分），以供学生进行延伸阅读，亲自感受历史学家所描绘的过去景象。每章设有导言和结论板块，以便学生掌握重要的单元主题。每章还配有各种形式的课后练习，不仅帮助学生更好地掌握书中的语言点、知识点，将学习成果以总结或讨论的形式展现出来，还有利于培养他们的批判性思维，形成认识西方文明的正确视角。

党的二十大报告提出"实施科教兴国战略，强化现代化建设人才支撑"，教育要"为党育人、为国育才，全面提高人才自主培养质量，着力造就拔尖创新人才，聚天下英才而用之"。本书以二十大报告强调的"中国式现代化""中国特色社会主义"与"人类命运共同体"等思想为指导，不仅为学生客观地讲解西方文明知识，还在每章的课后练习中设计中西文明比较论题，作为课堂讨论和写作的主题，注重将专业教育与思政教育有机结合，引导学生树立正确的世界观、人生观和价值观。本书旨在培养大学生对西方文化的辨识力、对人类思想与艺术创作的鉴别力，以及对人类文明发展动力的把握与认知。

如果对两种文明的发生与发展有了客观、理性的了解，我们就能确认一条颠扑不破的真理，即人类文明发展的动力来自人民的劳动、创造和牺牲。举凡中西文明发展史上每一次物质繁荣、技术突破、思想创新乃至制度革新，其背后无一不是人民的智慧结晶，无一不体现了习主席所说的"广大人民群众对美好生活的向往"。在发现和了解西方文明的同时，我们也是在发现和了解中华文明的潜能，以更好地把握中华文明未来的发展方向。朝乾夕惕，自强不息，此为本书编写之旨。

本书的框架和编排受到 Jackson J. Spielvogel、Thomas H. Geer & Gavin Lewis 和 Peter Waston 等人相关史书的启发，对此深表感激。本书插图部分购自视觉中国，部分由刘纯玮女士绘制，部分由臧力强先生慷慨赠予，在此谨表谢意！由于编者水平有限，本书难免存在一些不足之处，欢迎各位专家、学者和读者批评指正。

编者

Contents

Part One
The Ancient World
(3000 B.C.–500 A.D.)

Part Two
Medieval Civilization
500–1300

Part Three
Early Modern Europe
1300–1650

Part Four
The Rise of the Modern West
1600–1850

Part One

The Ancient World

•(3000 B.C.–500 A.D.)•

The beginning of Western civilization can be traced back to the ancient Near East, where people in Mesopotamia and Egypt developed organized societies and created ideas and institutions that we associate with civilization. Around 3000 B.C., people in Mesopotamia and Egypt began to develop cities. They invented writing to keep records and created literature; they constructed monumental architecture to please their gods, symbolize their power, and preserve their culture for all time; they developed political, military, social, and religious structures to deal with basic existence and organization. All these allow us to view how they dealt with three of the fundamental problems that humans have pondered: the nature of human relationships, the nature of the universe, and the role of divine forces in that cosmos.

Chapter 1

Civilization in Mesopotamia

1. The Earliest Cities and Empires

Just like later ancient Greece, Mesopotamia was characterized first by the rise of small city-states near the Persian Gulf. During the 3rd millennium B.C., cities such as Ur, Larsa, and Lagash fought for the political control over Lower Mesopotamia for over 500 years until they were conquered by the mighty Sargon of the Semitic Akkadians in about 2350 B.C. About 400 years later, the Akkadian power was overthrown by another group of Semites, the Amorites. Political power now moved to the city of Babylon. By 1800 B.C., the new state was at its acme under the famous king Hammurabi. A Babylonian culture was established common to all Mesopotamia, extending from the north of Babylon to the Persian Gulf. However, the new power was short lived. A wave of invaders of Indo-Europeans upset the entire Middle East, plunging it into an era of political upheaval and cultural darkness.

By 1500 B.C., much of the creative impulse of the Mesopotamian civilization was beginning to wane. The invasion from new peoples known as Indo-Europeans led to the creation of a Hittite kingdom. The invasion from the Sea Peoples around 1200 B.C. destroyed the Hittite Empire and created a power vacuum that allowed a patchwork of petty kingdoms and city-states to emerge, especially in the area of Syria and Palestine. These small city-states did not last with the emergence of empires that embraced the entire Near East in the 1st millennium B.C. Between 1000 B.C. and 500 B.C., the Assyrians, Chaldeans, and Persians all created empires that encompassed either large areas or all of the ancient Near East. Among them, the Persian Empire was perhaps the largest. Under the two great kings Cyrus the Great (559 B.C.–530 B.C.) and Darius (522 B.C.–486 B.C.), the Persian Empire embraced all the land from the Indus River to Europe and from the Caucasus Mountains and Aral Sea down to the Persian Gulf and Indian Ocean. It remained intact for more than 150 years until it was conquered by Alexander the Great.

The Persians excelled in war and political organization. The king held absolute power. The empire was divided into some twenty provinces known as satrapies governed by satraps. Inspectors from the royal court traveled all of the empire checking on the satraps. To secure efficient administration over the sprawling lands, the Persian kings constructed a marvelous system of roads and post houses. The Persian rule was lenient, for as long as their tributary peoples paid taxes and did not revolt, they were treated most leniently and were even allowed to follow their religious traditions. It is no wonder that many peoples owed their gratitude to the Persians, especially the Hebrews.

2. Society, Culture, and Religion in Mesopotamia

The society in Mesopotamia was well stratified. At the top were the kings and their royal families. Next to them were the great landlords and the priests. At the bottom were peasants and slaves. The rights of each class were closely related to their social and economic status.

It was in Mesopotamia that the earliest codes of laws appeared, as early as the 3rd millennium B.C. The most famous is the Code of Hammurabi in the 18th century B.C. (see Figure 1-1).

It survives on an eight-foot column made of basalt. The upper quarter of the column depicts the Babylonian king (standing at left) being vested with authority by Shamash, the god of justice. The lower quarter is the code's text in cuneiform inscriptions.

Figure 1-1   The Code of Hammurabi

Providing for both civil and criminal cases, the law well illustrated ancient man's concept of justice which demanded "an eye for an eye and a tooth for a tooth". The law covered almost all aspects of human life at that time, from penalties for crimes to regulations of marriage, divorce, inheritance, business transactions, and slavery. Most of our knowledge of the early Mesopotamian society comes from this remarkable code.

From ancient Sumerians came the first writing. One thing is sure that writing evolved as a practical recording technology to support economic pursuits. Because it existed to represent real things, its system of symbols—pictograms were also realistic. Over time, however, a symbol might be used not only to represent a physical object but to evoke an idea associated with that object. For example, the symbol for a bowl of food, a *ninda*, might be used to express something more abstract, such as "nourishment" or "sustenance." Pictograms also came to be associated with particular spoken sounds, or phonemes. When a scribe needed to employ the sound *ninda* as part of another word or name, he would use the symbol for a bowl of food to represent that phoneme. Later, special marks were added to the symbol, so that a reader could tell what the writer meant was to represent the object itself, or a larger concept, or a sound used in a context that might have nothing to do with the food. The writing developed into what was known as cuneiform, because the writing tool, a square-tipped stylus can leave an impression on the clay shaped like a wedge (in Latin, *cuneus*). For over 2,000 years, cuneiform remained the principal writing system of the ancient Near East. The development of writing stimulated speculation in all fields of thought, enabled poetry to be created, and initiated business records such as contracts. People even invented double-entry bookkeeping.

The achievements of cities and city-states were astonishing, with a remarkable number of innovations being introduced which created much of the world as we know it and live in it. It was in Babylonia that music, medicine, and mathematics were developed, the first libraries were created, the first maps were drawn, and chemistry, botany, and zoology were conceived. Babylon is the home of so many "firsts" because it was also the place where writing was invented and therefore we know about Babylon in a way that we do not know history before then.

People in Mesopotamia already devised a sophisticated mathematics based on the sexagesimal system, in which the number 60 rather than 10 is the base unit. Our hour of 60 minutes and our circle of 360 degrees derive from this sexagesimal system. With knowledge of reasonably advanced mathematical principles, it was possible to design more advanced irrigation systems and to construct temples, known as ziggurats.

The religion in Mesopotamia was basically polytheism, numerous gods being associated with natural phenomena and arranged according to power and functions as those of the Greeks and Romans. Some deities were only local; others were universal. Religion was a vital force in Mesopotamia. It stimulated architecture, sculpture, literature, astronomy, and cosmology. From Persia during the 6th century B.C. came the new religion of Zoroastrianism named after the prophet Zoroaster. The beliefs of this religion were significant because they paralleled many of those in the Old Testament. Both, for example, forbade the worship of idols, taught an admirable system of ethics, emphasized monotheism, and saw a conflict between the forces of good and evil.

3. The Hebrews and Their Religion

While political and military power in the ancient Middle East was concentrated for approximately 2,500 years between the Two Rivers, there were other areas which made basic cultural contributions to the Western world. The most important was a thin band of land lying along the eastern coast of the Mediterranean Sea. It was inhabited by the Phoenicians and the Hebrews.

3.1　Establishment of Kingdoms and Division

The Hebrews were a Semitic-speaking people who had a tradition concerning their origins and a history that was eventually written down as a part of the Hebrew Bible, known to Christians as the Old Testament. Describing themselves as nomads organized into clans, the Hebrews' tradition stated that they were descendants of the patriarch Abraham, who had migrated from Mesopotamia to the land of Canaan, where they became identified as the "Children of Israel." Again, according to the tradition, a drought in Canaan caused many Hebrews to migrate to Egypt, where they lived peacefully until they were enslaved by pharaohs. They remained in bondage until Moses led his people out of Egypt in the well-known Exodus. According to the biblical account, the Hebrews wandered for many years in the desert before they entered Canaan. Organized into 12 tribes, they became embroiled in conflict with the Philistines, a people who had settled in the coastal area of Canaan but were beginning to move into the inland area.

Scholars today generally agree that between 1200 B.C. and 1000 B.C., the Israelites emerged as a distinct group of people, possibly organized into tribes or a league of tribes. The first king of Israelites was Saul (1020 B.C.–1000 B.C), who initially achieved some success in the ongoing struggle with the Philistines. But after his death in a disastrous battle with this enemy, a brief period of anarchy ensued until one of Saul's lieutenants, David (1000 B.C.–970 B.C), reunited the Israelites, defeated the Philistines, and established control over Canaan. Among David's conquests was the city of Jerusalem, which he made as the capital of a united kingdom. David centralized Israel's political organization and accelerated the integration of the Israelites into a settled community based on farming and urban life. David's son Solomon (970 B.C.–930 B.C.) did even more to strengthen royal power. He expanded the political and military establishments, and he was especially active in extending the trading activities of the Israelites. Under Solomon, ancient Israel was at the height of its power.

After Solomon's death, tensions between the northern and southern tribes in Israel led to the establishment of two separate kingdoms, the kingdom of Israel, composed of the ten northern tribes, with its capital eventually at Samaria, and the southern kingdom of Judah, consisting of two tribes, with its capital at Jerusalem. By the end of the 9th century, the kingdom of Israel was forced to pay tribute to Assyria. In the next century, Israel itself was destroyed. The Assyrians overran the kingdom, destroyed the capital Samaria in 722 B.C. or 721 B.C., and deported many Israelites to other parts of the Assyrian Empire. These dispersed Israelites merged with neighboring peoples and gradually lost their identity. The southern kingdom of Judah was also forced to pay tribute to Assyria, but managed to survive as an independent state before the Assyrian power declined. A new enemy, however, appeared on the horizon. The Chaldeans first demolished Assyria, then under King Nebuchadnezzar Ⅱ, conquered Judah, and completely destroyed Jerusalem in 586 B.C. Many people were deported to Babylonia, but the Babylonian captivity of the people of Judah did not last. Upon the destruction of Chaldean kingdom by the Persians, the people of Judah were allowed to return to Jerusalem and rebuild their city and the Temple. Judah remained under the Persian control until the Persian Empire was conquered by Alexander the Great in the 4th century B.C. The people of Judah survived, eventually becoming known as the Jews and giving their name to Judaism, the religion of Jehovah, the Israelite God.

3.2 Religion—Judaism

Early Israelites, like other ancient peoples in Mesopotamia, were polytheistic. It was among the Babylonian exiles in the 6th century B.C. that Jehovah—the God of Israel—came to be seen as the only God. After the return of these exiles to Judah, their point of view eventually became dominant, and pure monotheism came to be the major tenet of Judaism. According to the Jewish conception, there is but one God, whom the Jews called Jehovah. God is the creator of the world and everything in it. To the Jews, the gods of all other peoples were merely idols. All peoples were God's servants, whether they knew it or not. This God was also transcendent. God had created nature but was not in nature. The stars, moon, rivers, wind, and other natural phenomena were not divinities or suffused with divinity, as other peoples of the ancient Near East believed, but were God's handiwork. All of God's creations could be admired for their awesome beauty but not worshiped as gods.

The chief source of information about Israel's spiritual conception is the Hebrew Bible, which is the Old Testament of the Christian Bible. The Hebrew Bible focuses on one basic theme: the necessity for the Jews to obey their God. According to the tradition, God entered into a covenant or contract with the tribes of Israel, who believed that Jehovah had spoken to them through Moses. The Israelites promised to obey Jehovah and follow his law. In return, Jehovah promised to take special care of his people. All Hebrew history is interpreted by the Old Testament as reward or punishment meted out by Jehovah. When the Hebrew people obeyed Jehovah, they flourished; when they did not, Jehovah punished them and evil times befell them. For the first time, a religion of high ethical principles was closely bound to society, so that religion became an inspiring and deterring force in human conduct. From the vital concepts of this religion arose later the two most widespread modern religions—Christianity and Islam.

4. The Phoenicians

As a Semitic-speaking people, the Phoenicians resided along the Mediterranean coast on a narrow band of land. They were famous for seafaring and trading. Culturally, the Phoenicians are best known as transmitters. Instead of using pictographs or signs to represent whole words and syllables as the Mesopotamians and Egyptians did, the Phoenicians simplified their writing by using 22 different signs to represent the sounds of their speech. Although the Phoenicians were not the only people to invent an alphabet, theirs would have special significance because it was eventually passed to the Greeks. From the Greek alphabet was derived the Roman alphabet that people still use today. The Phoenicians achieved much while independent, but they ultimately fell subject to the Assyrians, Chaldeans, and Persians.

The reason for including the civilization in Mesopotamia, which is geographically east, is not only because Mesopotamia developed the first civilization in human history, but because the Greeks, when increasingly coming into control in the Middle East, fused the culture of Mesopotamia to their own and more importantly, developed a culture and outlook of their own.

Key Terms

city-states → Babylonian culture → Persian Empire → Hammurabi's Code of Laws → first writing (cuneiform) → polytheism → Hebrews and Judaism → monotheism → Phoenician alphabet

Exercises

1 Vocabulary Building

✎ Fill in each blank with a synonym to the word or phrase in the brackets.

1) The Persian rule was _____ (lenient), for as long as their _____ (tributary) peoples paid taxes and did not _____ (revolt), they were treated most leniently and were even allowed to follow their religious traditions.

2) All Hebrew history is _____ (interpreted) by the Old Testament as reward or punishment _____ (meted out) by Jehovah. When the Hebrew people obeyed Jehovah, they _____ (flourished); when they did not, Jehovah punished them and evil times _____ (befell) them. For the first time, a religion of high ethical principles was closely _____ (bound) to society, so that religion became a(n) _____ (inspiring) and _____ (deterring) force in human conduct.

❷ Translation

❧ Translate the following sentences into Chinese.

1) The invasion from the Sea Peoples around 1200 B.C. destroyed the Hittite Empire, and created a power vacuum that allowed a patchwork of petty kingdoms and city-states to emerge, especially in the area of Syria and Palestine. These small city-states did not last with the emergence of empires that embraced the entire Near East in the 1st millennium B.C.

2) To the Jews, the gods of all other peoples were merely idols. All peoples were God's servants, whether they knew it or not. This God was also transcendent. God had created nature but was not in nature. The stars, moon, rivers, wind and other natural phenomena were not divinities or suffused with divinity, as other peoples of the ancient Near East believed, but were God's handiwork. All of God's creations could be admired for their awesome beauty but not worshiped as gods.

❸ Questions

❧ Answer the following questions.

1) How did the Israelites establish a united state, and what did it become eventually?

2) In what ways was the Jewish faith unique in the ancient Near East, and how did it evolve over time?

3) Who were the Phoenicians, and what was their significance?

Chapter 2

The Civilization of the Greeks

Although the first significant steps in civilization were made in the ancient Middle East and ultimately found their way into what is regarded as the Western tradition, it was the Greeks who created a civilization that was truly Western. It is to the Greeks more than to the peoples of the ancient Middle East that the Western world is indebted for its underlying ethical, esthetic, literary, social, and political outlooks.

The story of ancient Greek civilization is a remarkable one that began with the first arrival of the Greeks around 2000 B.C. By the 8th century B.C., the characteristic institution of ancient Greek life, the polis or city-states, had emerged. Greek civilization flourished and reached its height in the classical era of the 5th century B.C., which was closely identified with the achievements of Athenian democracy. It is generally believed that it was the Greeks who created the intellectual foundations of Western heritage. They asked some basic questions about human life that still dominate the intellectual pursuits in the West: What is the nature of the universe? What is the purpose of human existence? What is our relationship to divine force? What constitutes a community? What constitutes a state? What is justice? What is truth, and how do we realize it? Not only did the Greeks provide answers to these questions, but they created a system of logical, analytical thought to examine them. This rational outlook has remained an important feature of Western civilization.

1. Early Greece: Minoan Crete and Mycenaean Civilization

Geography played an important role in the evolution of Greek history. Compared to the landmasses of Mesopotamia and Egypt, Greece occupied a small area, a mountainous peninsula that encompassed only 45,000 square miles of territory. The mountains and the sea played especially significant roles in the development of Greek history. Much of Greece consists of small plains and river valleys surrounded by mountains ranging 8,000 to 10,000 feet high. The mountainous terrain had the effect of isolating Greeks from one another. Consequently, Greek communities tended to follow their own separate paths and develop their own way of life. Thus was born the spirit of particularism that was to be both the nemesis and glory of the Greeks, which ultimately destroyed Greek political life but also nourished the individualism responsible for the supreme creations of classical civilization.

The earliest civilization in the Aegean region emerged on the large island of Crete, southeast of the Greek mainland. A Bronze Age civilization that used metals, especially bronze, in making weapons had been established there by 2800 B.C. This civilization was discovered at the turn of the 20th century by the English archaeologist Arthur Evans, who named it "Minoan" after Minos, a legendary king of Crete. The civilization of Crete was apparently built upon sea power. The quality of the civilization can be seen in the great palace at Knossos built by King Minos about 1600 B.C. After 1500 B.C., the island of Crete was invaded by the Mycenaeans. Mycenaean civilization reached its high point between 1400 B.C. and 1200 B.C. It is especially noted for its fortified palace-centers, which were built on hills surrounded by gigantic stone walls. As the culture of Crete had been partially destroyed and appropriated by the Mycenaeans, the Mycenaeans fell before a new wave of Greek people that began rolling down from the Balkans about 1200 B.C. and by 1000 B.C had swept over the whole peninsula. Some time before 1000 B.C., a group of Greeks known as Dorians coming from the Balkans plunged Greece into a period of darkness which lasted for almost 400 years.

2. The Archaic Age of Greek City-States (c. 750 B.C.–c. 500 B.C.)

In the 8th century B.C., Greek civilization burst forth with new energy, beginning the period that historians have called the Archaic Age of Greece. Two major developments stood out in this era: the evolution of the polis, or city-states, as the central institution in Greek life and the Greeks' colonization of the Mediterranean and Black Seas.

With overpopulation, the Greeks were finding it ever more difficult to make a living from the soil, often stony and unfertile. It was natural therefore when observing their fellow Greeks along the coast making a decent living, those from the interior should seek homes overseas for better opportunities. The 8th to the end of the 6th century B.C. was the great era of Greek expansion and colonization. The Greeks established colonies in Asia Minor, Thrace, the lands ringing the Black Sea, and southern Italy, Sicily. They founded city-states, introduced their culture abroad, and stimulated the economy of Greece. This was an essential step in the cultural exchange between Greece and the Middle East.

2.1 Forms of Government

When Greece was expanding, city-states were undergoing political transformations that were to result in three forms of government that characterized Greek political life in later centuries and subsequently became typical in the Western world.

At its early stage, it was the king who ruled over the city-states. However, where city-states were more agrarian and less commercial, political privileges were restricted to landed aristocrats. That such men should covet more power was natural. Whenever there was an opportunity or excuse, they would overthrow the king and establish themselves as the ruling power. When this occurred, we call the city-state an oligarchy. Therefore, oligarchy was a government ruled by a few wealthy men whose power was ordinarily derived from the land. Oligarchic government was invariably conservative because it existed to preserve the interests of the wealthy few; the masses were ignored.

As another form of government, tyranny came after oligarchy. In some city-states where agriculture was less important and trade provided a living for most citizens, the sailors, merchants, and artisans had an increasing desire for change. Taking advantage of this agitation, a political opportunist with personal appeal could easily exhort people to action and place himself as at the head of a revolution and finally the ruler when the oligarchy was overthrown. The Greeks called such a man a tyrant because his power was illegal and because he usually denied the authority of law but recognized his own. However, a tyrant was not always like a despot in the East, and a tyranny therefore did not always denote despotic government. There were some successful and benevolent tyrants of the 6th century B.C., including Polycrates of Samos, Cypselus of Corinth, and Cleisthenes of Athens who developed the trade of their city-states and made them become powerful political forces. Tyranny in Greece was largely extinguished by the end of the 6th century B.C. Its very nature as a system outside the law seemed contradictory to the ideal of law in a Greek community. Once the tyrants were eliminated, the door was opened to the participation of more people in the affairs of the community.

The city-state of Athens developed a new form of government, democracy. In the civil war between those who desired a return to the oligarchy and those who wanted further political reforms, the latter were victorious under their leader Cleisthenes who at once initiated the democratic government. By limiting the power of the aristocratic organization called the Areopagus, Cleisthenes set up a new Council of the Five Hundred in charge of the legislation. They were elected each year, 50 from each of 10 tribes that were distributed geographically. The Council was divided into 10 committees, each wielding power for a tenth of a year. Each of these executive committees presented legislation to the Assembly of all citizens for approval. Military power was given to a group of 10 generals, also elected annually. In terms of jurisdiction, almost all justice was handled by a huge jury of 6,000. With so large a jury the procedure was slow and hindered efficiency. Small wonder the jury was severely criticized for being inadequate and at times corrupt. Nevertheless, despite the system of democracy, it was the aristocrats who held the most important offices, and many people, including women, slaves, and foreigners residing in Athens, were not given the same political rights. However, it was still a remarkable achievement for the Athenians to develop such a democratic government as early as the 6th century B.C.

2.2 Religion and Philosophy

Religion in early Greece was mainly polytheism. In *The Iliad* and *The Odyssey* of Homer, various Greek gods controlled the life and destiny of man. Woe to the individual who incurred the wrath of a god! In the 6th century B.C., this concept of man's relation to the gods began to change. Retaining their belief in divine punishment, the Greeks began to agree upon some standards of moral conduct. Whoever disregarded accepted moral behavior and ignored the gods tempted fate; he had become too proud and was certain to suffer divine retribution.

Related to the transformation in religious belief was the beginning of philosophic and scientific speculation. Early Greek philosophy was more like science, because questions asked by the philosophers were basically about the world around them. Most of them showed great interest in the primary substance of the universe. They convinced that nature, in its unseen being, was far simpler than it appeared to be—all material things were made up of a small number of basic elements. Around 600 B.C., Thales of Miletus in Asia Minor believed that the primary substance of the universe was water. Heraclitus of Ephesus concluded that the entire world was in constant flux. He declared that a person cannot step into the same river twice—in fact, the river is changing even as one steps into it. This doctrine proved most disturbing, for if everything is constantly changing (including ourselves), how can we gain true knowledge of anything? At about the same time, Parmenides argued that essentially there was no change in the world. "Change requires motion," he reasoned, "and motion requires empty space. But empty space equals non-existence, which by definition does not exist." Therefore, he concluded, "Motion and change are impossible." Parmenides readily admitted that some things appear to move and change; but "This must be an illusion of the senses," he said, "because it is contradicted by logic."

Thales' immediate successor was Anaximander. He argued that the ultimate physical reality of the universe cannot be a recognizable physical substance. Instead of water, he substituted an "undefined something" with no chemical properties. For Anaximander, the primary substance was aer, a form of mist whose density varied. "Winds arise when the aer is dense, and moves under pressure. When it becomes denser still, clouds are formed, so it changes into water. Hail occurs when the water descending from the clouds solidifies, and snow occurs when it solidifies in a wetter condition." There is not much wrong with this reasoning. Leucippus of Miletus and Democritus of Abdera were atomists. They argued that the world consisted of an infinity of tiny atoms moving randomly in an infinite void. These atoms, solid corpuscles too small to be seen, existed in all manner of shapes and it was their motions, collisions, and transient configurations that accounted for the great variety of substances and the different phenomena that people experience. Empedocles of Acragas, a rough contemporary of Leucippus, identified four elements or "roots" of all material things: fire, air, earth, and water. From these four roots sprang all things. But he also thought that material ingredients by themselves could not explain motion and change. He therefore introduced two additional, immaterial principles: love and strife, which induced the four roots to congregate and separate. Different from all other philosophers, Pythagoras believed that essence of the universe was to be found not in the natural world, but in the study of abstracts, so he concentrated on mathematics and musical theory.

3. Classical Greece (500 B.C.–338 B.C.)

Classical Greece is the period of Greek history from around 500 B.C. to the conquest of Greece by the Macedonian king Philip II in 338 B.C. It was a period of brilliant achievement, much of it associated with the flowering of democracy in Athens under the leadership of Pericles. Many of the lasting contributions of the Greeks occurred during this period. The age began with a mighty confrontation between the Greek states and the Persian Empire.

3.1   Persian Wars

By 500 B.C., the Persian Empire included all Asia Minor and the Greek city-states along the coast of Asia Minor had already fallen subject to the Persian. An unsuccessful revolt by the Ionian cities in 499 B.C., assisted by the Athenian navy, led the Persian ruler Darius to seek revenge by attacking the mainland Greece in 490 B.C.

Darius sent a fleet bearing an army across the Aegean Sea. On the plain of Marathon only 26 miles from Athens, the Athenian hoplites, thought outnumbered, charged across the plain of Marathon and crushed the Persian forces. The Persians did not mount another attack against the mainland Greece for 10 years. Xerxes, the new Persian monarch, was bent on revenge and expansion. Under his leadership, the Persians mounted their second invasion in 480 B.C. The Persians crossed the Hellespont by forming a bridge of ships and then moved through Thrace and Macedonia on their way into Greece. A Greek force numbering close to 9,000, under the leadership of the Spartan king Leonidas and his contingent of 300 Spartans, held off the Persian army at Thermopylae for two days. Unfortunately for the Greeks, a traitor told the Persians a mountain path they could use to outflank the Greek force. King Leonidas and 300 Spartans fought to the last man. The Persian army then occupied and burned Athens. In September of 480 B.C. and in the spring of 479 B.C., two sea battles sealed the war. Xerxes and his army were decisively destroyed by the Spartans and Athenians so much that the Persian peril would never again endanger the Greeks.

3.2 Athenian Empire

After the defeat of the Persians, Athens stepped in to provide a new leadership against the Persians by forming a confederation called the Delian League. Organized in the winter of 478 B.C.–477 B.C., the Delian League was dominated by the Athenians from the beginning. Under the leadership of the Athenians, the Delian League pursued the attack against the Persian Empire. Virtually, all of the Greek states in the Aegean were liberated from Persian control, and the Persian fleet and army were decisively defeated in 469 B.C. in southern Asia Minor. Thinking that the Persian threat was now over, some members of the League wished to withdraw. Naxos did so in 470 B.C. and Thasos in 465 B.C. The Athenians responded vigorously. They attacked both states, destroyed their walls, took over their fleets, eliminated their liberty, and forced them to pay tribute. "No secession" became Athenian policy. The Delian League was rapidly becoming an instrument of Athenian imperialism and the nucleus of an Athenian empire.

Athens reached its height under the leadership of Pericles. Athens embarked on a policy of expanding democracy at home while severing its ties with Sparta and expanding its new empire abroad. This period of Athenian and Greek history witnessed the height of Athenian power and the culmination of its brilliance as a civilization.

Athenian domination was ended by the Peloponnesian War that lasted from 431 B.C. to 404 B.C. The immediate causes of the war involved conflicts between Corinth and Athens. Long jealous of her dynamic neighbor, Sparta finally allied herself with Corinth. The Spartans sent an ultimatum to Athens, threatening to have a war if the Athenians did not back down in their disputes with Corinth and Megara. The Athenians refused to compromise, and inevitably, the war broke out. The war drained the resources of both sides, but even worse, the pressures of war destroyed Athenian reason and moderation and led to the disintegration of collective and individual character as portrayed by Thucydides in his *The History of the Peloponnesian War*.

4. Culture in Classical Greece

Classical Greece saw a period of remarkable intellectual and cultural growth throughout the Greek world, and Periclean Athens was the most important center of Classical Greek culture. What is amazing about the ancient Greeks is their unerring concern with the fundamental problems and ideals of human existence. In seeking truth and perfect beauty, they plumbed the depths of human reason. The Athenian feeling for balance and moderation, the sense of proportion, the desire for saneness, the love of beauty, the urge to create, and the free inquiry were evident in much of the architecture, literature, painting, sculpture, philosophy, history, science, and mathematics.

4.1   The Writing of History

History writing was a Greek creation. Herodotus (c.484 B.C.–c.425 B.C.), the author of *The Persian Wars*, is claimed as "the father of history," and his works are commonly regarded as the first real history in Western civilization. The central theme of Herodotus' works is the conflict between the Greeks and the Persians, which he viewed as a struggle between Greek freedom and Persian despotism. Herodotus was a wide traveler and his source of information was mainly dependent on oral history. Although he was a master storyteller and sometimes with considerable fanciful materials, Herodotus' history is an important source of information on the Persians, especially on the Persian Wars.

Thucydides (c.460 B.C.–c.400 B.C.), the author of *The History of the Peloponnesian War*, was a far better historian; in fact, modern historians consider him the greatest of the ancient world. Unlike Herodotus, Thucydides was not concerned with underlying divine forces or gods as explanatory causal factors in history. Instead, he saw war and politics in purely rational terms, as the activities of human beings. He examined the long-range and immediate causes of the Peloponnesian War in a clear, methodical, and objective fashion.

4.2   Drama

Drama was created by the Greeks and clearly intended to do more than entertainment. It was used to educate citizens and supported by the state for that reason. The first Greek dramas were tragedies, plays based on the suffering of a hero and usually ending in disaster. The plots of Greek tragedies were simple, and they were sometime presented in a trilogy (a set of three plays) built around a common theme. Aeschylus (c.525 B.C.–c.456 B.C.) was the first tragedian. Although he wrote 90 tragedies, only seven have survived.

Another great Athenian playwright was Sophocles (c.496 B.C.–c.406 B.C.), whose most famous play is *Oedipus the King*. Oedipus was a tragic king who unknowingly killed his father and married his mother. The Delphic oracle predicted that King Laius of Thebes would be killed by his own son. To save himself, Laius ordered to place his newborn son on a mountaintop and leave him there to starve. The infant was saved by a shepherd and raised in a distant city, where he was given the name Oedipus. Years later, King Laius was killed while on a journey by a stranger with whom he quarreled. Oedipus arrived at Thebes shortly after and saved the city from the ravages of the Sphinx. He was proclaimed king there and he took the dead king's widow as his own wife. They gave birth to two sons and two daughters. After several years, a terrible plague struck Thebes. The Delphic oracle told Oedipus that to end the plague, he must find and punish the murderer of King Laius. In the course of his investigation, Oedipus discovered that he himself was the killer and that Laius had been his real father. Therefore, he had murdered his father and married his mother. In extreme shame, his mother hanged herself, and in great horror, Oedipus gouged out his eyes. Although it appeared that Oedipus suffered the fate determined by the gods, Oedipus also accepted that he himself as a free man must bear responsibility for his action: "It was Apollo, friends, Apollo, that brought this better bitterness, my sorrows to completion. But the hand that struck me was none but my own."

The third outstanding Athenian tragedian was Euripides (c.485 B.C.–c.406 B.C.). He moved beyond his predecessors in creating more realistic characters. Perhaps the greatest of all his plays is *The Bacchae*, which deals with the introduction of the hysterical rites associated with Dionysus, god of wine. Euripides is often seen as a skeptic who questioned traditional moral and religious values. He was also critical of the traditional view that war was glorious. He portrayed war as brutal and barbaric and expressed deep compassion for the women and children who suffered from it.

Greek tragedies dealt with universal themes that are still relevant in our day. They probed such problems as the nature of good and evil, the conflict between spiritual values and the demands of the state or family, the rights of the individual, the nature of divine forces, and the nature of human beings. Over and over again, the tragic lesson was repeated: "Humans were free and yet could operate only within limitations imposed by the gods. The real task was to cultivate the balance and moderation that led to awareness of one's true position."

Greek comedies developed later than tragedies. The plays of Aristophanes (c.450 B.C.–c.385 B.C.) were examples of Old Comedy, which was used to attack or savagely satirize both politicians and intellectuals. In the *Clouds*, for example, Aristophanes characterized the philosopher Socrates as the operator of a thought factory where people could learn deceitful ways to handle other people.

4.3 Architecture and Sculpture

In architecture, the most important form is the temple dedicated to a god or goddess. The temples on the Acropolis in Athens (see Figure 2-1), attributable largely to Pericles who rebuilt the temples, achieve the highest perfection. The most majestic temple must be the Parthenon (see Figure 2-2) in Doric style which was consecrated to Athena, the patron goddess of Athens. It is a monument of beauty and dignity. The Parthenon typifies the principles of classical architecture: the search for calm, clarity, and freedom from superfluous details.

Figure 2-1　The Acropolis

(Source: Visual China Group)

Figure 2-2　The Parthenon

Built between 447 B.C. and 432 B.C. and located on the Acropolis in Athens, the Parthenon was dedicated to Athena, the patron goddess of the city, but it also served as a shining example of the power and wealth of the Athenian Empire.

(Source: Visual China Group)

Unlike later churches enclosing the faithful, the Greek temples are in the open air. The most significant formal element in Greek temples is the shape and size of the columns in combination with the features above and below the column (see Figure 2-3).

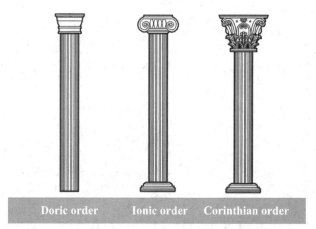

Figure 2-3   Doric, Ionic, and Corinthian orders

The size and shape of a column constitutes one of the most important aspects of Greek temple architecture. The Doric order, with plain capitals and no base, developed first in the Dorian Peloponnesus and is rather simple in comparison to the slender Ionic column, which has an elaborate base and spiral-shaped capitals, and the Corinthian column, which features leaf-shaped capitals.

Greek sculpture also develops a classical style which features both well-proportioned lifelike realism and ideals of beauty. The frieze, the gold and ivory statue of Athena (see Figure 2-4) in the interior of the temple of Parthenon, was a work by sculptor Phidias (490 B.C.–432 B.C.), a friend of Pericles. Later Polyclitus (452 B.C.–412 B.C.) wrote a treatise (now lost) on a canon of proportions that he illustrated in a work known as the *Doryphoros*. His theory maintained that the use of ideal proportions, based on mathematical ratios found in nature, could produce an ideal human form, beautiful in its perfected and refined features. This search for ideal beauty was the dominant feature of the classical standard in sculpture. A comparison between his famous statue *Doryphoros* and the Kouros figure of the Archaic period statues can easily show his talent. In the second half of the 4th century B.C., Praxiteles became famous for the grace of his figures and his rendition of drapery, whose statutes of Hermes with Dionysus and of Apollo have become immortal (see Figure 2-5).

Figure 2-4   Statue of Athena

Figure 2-5   Statue of Hermes

(Source: Visual China Group)

4.4　Philosophy

Philosophy is a Greek word that literally means "love of wisdom." Unlike early philosophers who were more interested in the nature of the universe, philosophers at this time were more attuned to questions of ethics and politics and how to conduct in public and private life. To answer the latter need were a group of teachers known as sophists. They thought the speculation on the nature of the universe was foolish; rather, it was important for human beings to improve themselves. Therefore, they made their living by selling their knowledge to young people, especially those of the Athens. The sophists stressed the importance of rhetoric (the art of persuasive speaking) in winning debates and swaying an audience, a skill that was especially valuable in democratic Athens. To the sophists, there was no absolute right or wrong and this was best exemplified in Protagoras in his famous dictum: "Man is the measure of all things." It means that goodness, truth, and justice are relative concepts, adaptable to the needs and interests of human beings. He concluded that there could be no absolute standards of right and wrong. Empirical facts, established by the perception of the sense, were the only source of knowledge.

In search of truth, no one was more passionate than Socrates (469 B.C.–399 B.C.). For the Greeks themselves, the name of Socrates formed a watershed in the history of their philosophy. The reason they claimed so was that he turned man's eyes from the speculations about the nature of the physical world which had been characteristic of the Pre-Socratic period, to concentrate on the problems of human life. In the most general terms, his message was that to investigate the origin and ultimate matter of the universe, the composition and motions of the heavenly bodies, the shape of the Earth, or the causes of natural growth and decay was of far less importance than to understand what it meant to be a human being and for what purpose one was in the world.

According to one of his most memorable sayings, "The unexamined life is not worth living," he developed a dialectical method of question and answer by which he would stop passers-by and submit every presumed truth to examination in order to establish a firm foundation for further inquiry. His whole aim was to induce his listeners to discover himself ethically for right concepts.

Socrates was credited by Aristotle as the initiator of two things: inductive arguments and general definition. Induction, as Aristotle told us, was the progress from the particular to the universal, and he illustrated it with an example of Socratic type: If the best navigator is the expert and the best driver is the expert, and so on, we infer that in general the expert (or knowledgeable) is the best in every occupation.

The interest of Socrates in definitions is one of the best-attested facts about him. But what was his motive? One feature in the thought and speech of his contemporaries seemed particularly harmful to Socrates. Whether in conversation, in political speeches, or in the oratory of the law-courts, they made constant use of a great variety of general terms, especially terms descriptive of ethical ideas—justice, temperance, courage, and so forth. Yet at the same time, it was being asserted by sophists and others that such concepts had no basis in reality. These terms were not god-given virtues, but only "by convention," varying from place to place and age to age. Serious thought about the laws of human behavior had begun with a radical skepticism, which taught that it rested on no fixed principles, but each decision must be made empirically and ad hoc, based on the expediency of the immediate situation. In such an atmosphere, it was not surprising that there was much confusion in the meanings attached to moral terms. Socrates noted this and disapproved of it. In Socrates' opinion, then, if order is to be restored to thought on the rights and wrongs of human conduct, the first necessity is to decide what justice, goodness, and other virtues are. According to his method, the inquiry consists of two stages. The first is to collect instances to which both parties to a discussion agree that the name under consideration may be applied, e.g. if it is piety, it means to collect instances of agreed pious acts. Secondly, the collected instances are examined in order to discover some common quality in them by virtue of which they bear that name. If they do not share such a common quality, then he claimed it would be improper to go on applying the same word to them all. This common quality is their nature, essence, or "form" considered as pious. It will provide in fact, if it can be discovered, the definition of piety, abstracted from the accidental properties of time and circumstance. As a scientific method, this is of course a necessary basis of any study like botany or zoology whose chief task is classification. Socrates was not interested in botany or zoology but in his fellow men, and what he wanted to see about classification and definition was their actions: "Who is the good citizen in finance, in war, on an embassy, in debate before the Assembly?"; "What is courage?"; or "What is piety?".

The best exposition of the method is in the *Meno*. Without preamble, this impetuous young man bursts out with a burning question of the day: "Can virtue be taught, or how is it acquired?" "How can I tell you that," replies Socrates, "when I don't even know what it is and have never met anyone who does?" Meno is astonished. Socrates then asks him to tell what virtue is. The victim is now in the net, and proceeds to give a string of instances and types of virtue to his own satisfaction, but not to that of Socrates, who complains that he has been given a swarm of virtues when he only wants the one thing, virtue. The process goes on like: "Virtue is the capacity to govern man"; "Then is it virtue in a slave to govern his master?"; and so on.

This "Socratic method," sometimes called the "dialectical method," is simply a procedure for reaching toward truth by means of a dialogue or a directed discussion. Socrates did not believe it is necessary to observe and collect data in order to find absolute knowledge; he had a deep conviction that truth is implanted in the mind but becomes hidden by erroneous sense impressions. The function of the philosopher is to recover the truth that lies buried in the mind. Socrates' theory of knowledge is closely related to his idea of the soul. He believed the soul is immortal, though during life it is hindered by troubles and "foolishness" of the body. Death brings release for the soul and the opportunity to see the truth more clearly than before. And for Socrates, the real aim of life is to know the truth, rather than to seek the satisfactions of the body.

He was accused eventually of corrupting his youthful followers with impiety by the Athenians. Although his friends made arrangements for him to flee the city, Socrates insisted on abiding by the laws. He skillfully defended himself but accepted a verdict of guilty to demonstrate the unreasonableness of a law and people who would support such a charge. By drinking the hemlock, he became the first great martyr for the principle of freedom of thought.

Socrates' brilliant student Plato (427 B.C.–347 B.C.) continued the dialectical method. Plato deemed it is his mission to vindicate Socrates by constructing a philosophical system based on his precepts. He did this in two ways: first by founding an informal school called Academy, and later by writing a series of dialogues with Socrates as the central character. Plato was most famous for his theory of ideal government and of forms or ideas. In *The Republic*, he argued for an ideal city-state by the best, i.e. the philosophers became kings because they excelled in the mind. The other classes included the aristocrats, the guardians, and the workers in a hierarchical order. However, fundamental to an understanding of most of his dialogues is his theory of forms or ideas. He divided the world into two, the unreal world and the real world. According to him, all objects of sense together with their shadows and reflections are unreal and transitory; only general forms or ideas have reality and are unchangeable. Objects are only copies of the form. The supreme idea is the idea of good from which all other ideas emanate.

His theory of ideas can be best illustrated in his three metaphors: the Metaphor of Line, the Sun Allegory, and the Cave Allegory. As we see in Figure 2-6, parts A and B above the line are generally taken as representing the visible world, and C and D as representing the intelligible world. A stands for shadows and reflections of physical things; B for objects themselves. They correspond to two functions of the soul respectively: illusion and opinion. C stands for mathematical objects; D for ideas. They correspond to another two functions of the soul respectively: mathematical reasoning and philosophical understanding.

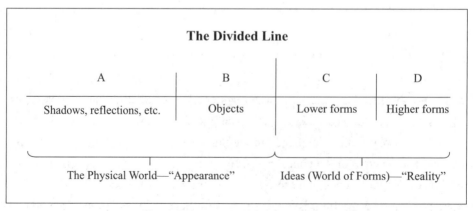

Figure 2-6 Plato's Metaphor of Line

In the Sun Allegory, he compared the supreme idea of good to the sun. As the sun illuminates the visible with light, the idea of good illuminates the intelligible with truth. Also, as the eye's ability to see is made possible by the light of the sun, the soul's ability to know is made possible by the truth of good.

In the Cave Allegory, Plato likened people untutored to prisoners chained in a cave, unable to turn their heads. All they can see is the wall of the cave. Behind them burns a fire. Between the fire and the prisoners there is a parapet, along which puppeteers can walk. The puppeteers, who are behind the prisoners, hold up puppets that cast shadows on the wall of the cave. The prisoners are unable to see these puppets, the real objects, that pass behind them. What the prisoners see and hear are shadows and echoes cast by objects that they do not see. Here is an illustration of Plato's Cave Allegory: Such prisoners would mistake appearance for reality (see Figure 2-7).

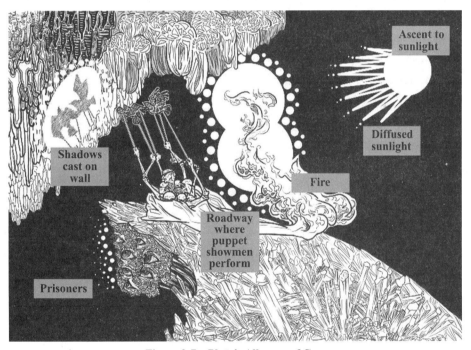

Figure 2-7   Plato's Allegory of Cave

Plato's most distinguished student was Aristotle (384 B.C.–322 B.C.), the tutor of Alexander the Great and possibly the greatest of the Greek philosophers. Unlike his tutor who concerned himself with mathematics and abstract thinking, Aristotle concentrated on factual knowledge. He specialized in natural sciences based on observations. He was a prolific and encyclopedic writer and his writings covered physics, astronomy, biology, psychology, metaphysics, and logics.

The philosopher's object is to explain reality. Plato and Aristotle both set this task for themselves, but the search, conducted according to the dictates of their different philosophical temperaments, led them in the end to make rather different conclusions about where, after all, reality truly lays. Plato reasoned that reality, if it is a possible object of knowledge and not simply of wavering opinions, must be something constant and unchanging. Now the world we live in is subject to continual change, as Heraclitus truly said. Therefore, reality is either unknowable or exists elsewhere than in this world. Plato tended to postulate a transcendent realm of eternal and changeless substances as the only reality and the object of true knowledge. Aristotle rejected Plato's universal ideas and denied that they had a real existence apart from the sensible or individual object that represented them. In fact, Aristotle turned Plato upside-down. Aristotle accepted Plato's general notion of the existence of ideas (forms), but he held that physical matter was also a part of reality and not to be despised. Matter, he thought, constituted the "stuff" of reality, though its shapes and purposes came from the forms that Plato had set forth. For example, for him the existence of musicians does not depend on certain idea called music. Abstractions don't really exist, in the way that trees or animals do. They exist only in the mind. "Musicianship cannot exist unless there are musicians."[1] Suffice it now that he was convicted that reality was to be found within the world of sensible experience.

Another important theory is the four causes. Aristotle used them in his philosophy to include all the factors which must be present for anything to come into being, whether naturally or artificially. These necessary factors are of four kinds: material, formal, efficient (or motive), and final. He insisted that a scientific explanation of any natural product or event (e.g. a man) demanded a statement of all four. Material cause is that out of which a thing comes to be and which persists in it, e.g. the bronze of a statue or the silver of a bowl. The formal cause is the form or pattern, e.g. the design of a statue. The efficient cause is the primary source of a change or state of rest, e.g. the adviser is the cause of an action, a father of his child, and in general the maker or changer of what is made or changed. Lastly, the final cause is the end— what the thing is for, as health is the cause of walking.

Unlike Plato, Aristotle did not seek an ideal state based on embodiment of an ideal form of justice; he tried to find the best form of government by a rational examination of existing governments. In the *Politics*, he examined the constitutions of 158 states and identified three forms of government: monarchy, aristocracy, and constitutional government. But he warned that monarchy can easily turn into tyranny, aristocracy into oligarchy, and constitutional government into radical democracy or anarchy. For him, the government that was workable was one with moderate democracy based on a restricted number of citizens from the middle class. Aristotle had more influence on Western thought than even Plato. Aristotle is the

---

1　Daniel J. Boorstin, *The Seekers: The Story of Man's Continuing Quest to Understand His World,* New York & London: Vintage, 1999, p.69.

colossus whose works both illuminate and cast a shadow on European thought in the next 2,000 years. As Daniel Boorstin also says, "Who would have guessed that Plato's most famous disciple would become the foal that kicks its mother?"

Key Terms

Crete and Mycenaean civilization → city-states → three forms of government → early philosophers → Persian Wars → Athenian imperialism → Oedipus complex → Doric, Ionic, and Corinthian Orders → Kouros sculpture → Socrates, Plato, Aristotle

Exercises

❶ Vocabulary Building

❧ Fill in each blank with a synonym to the word or phrase in the brackets.

1) As the culture of Crete had been partially _____ (destroyed) and _____ (appropriated) by the Mycenaeans, the Mycenaeans _____ (fell) before a new wave of Greek people that began _____ (rolling) down from the Balkans about 1200 B.C. and by 1000 B.C. had _____ (swept over) the whole peninsula.

2) Long jealous of her dynamic neighbor, Sparta finally allied herself with Corinth, a state that _____ (resented) Athenian _____ (encroachment) on her economic _____ (preservation). The war _____ (drained) the resources of both sides but, even worse, it compelled Sparta to ask Persia for assistance and led to political excesses.

❷ Translation

❧ Translate the following sentences into Chinese.

1) Thus was born that spirit of particularism that was to be both the nemesis and glory of the Greeks, which ultimately destroyed Greek political life but also nourished the individualism responsible for the supreme creations of classical civilization.

2) Woe to the individual who incurred the wrath of a god!

3) Whoever disregarded accepted moral behavior and ignored the gods tempted fate; he had become too proud and was certain to suffer divine retribution.

❸ Questions

> Answer the following questions.

1) How did the geography of Greece affect Greek history?

2) In what sense do we say the spirit of particularism was to be both the nemesis and glory of the Greeks?

3) What forms of government were developed by Greek city-states?

4) What were the major philosophical concerns of the Greeks before Socrates?

5) What words would you use to sum up the main characteristics of Greek spirit? And where can you find this spirit?

❹ Term Explanation

> Explain the meaning of the following term in your own words.

Plato's Allegory of the Cave

❺ Topics for Discussion

> Below are two topics related to this chapter. Read them and finish the discussion.

1) Some of Socrates' beliefs are characterized as "paradoxical." For instance, "No one desires evil"; "No one errs or does wrong willingly or knowingly." Develop some point of views and have discussions in groups.

2) Using Aristotle's "Four Causes" theory, clarify the four causes of "dining table" and "man."

❻ Presentation

> In groups, make a presentation on the following topic.

Greek mythology

❼ Writing

> Read the following direction and finish the writing.

One of Socrates' famous sayings is "Know thyself." Write a short essay with the title of "Know Yourself."

Chapter 3

The Hellenistic World

To the north of the weakened Greek city-states, a new power was rising, the kingdom of Macedonia, which would soon put an end to the independence of the city-states. But under Macedonian leadership, the Greeks would enjoy a brief moment of unity that would enable them to replace the Persians as the dominant nation of the international civilized world. Of all the great figures in the ancient world, none, not even Caesar, rivaled Alexander the Great. It was he who changed so profoundly the ideals, values, outlook, and intellectual development of man.

1. Conquest of Alexander

After dealing with disturbances in Macedonia and Greece that had broken out after his father's death, Alexander crossed into Asia Minor to launch the campaign that would make him one of the greatest conquerors in history. In four years, he subdued the Persian Empire and avenged Greece by burning the Persepolis, the capital of Persian Empire. Asia Minor, Syria, Egypt, and Mesopotamia fell before him. It was not enough, however. Alexander pushed east through Afghanistan and into the Punjab where he defeated an Indian army using elephants and captured King Porus. Arriving at the Indus River in 326 B.C., he was forced to stop by his troops. In 323 B.C., Alexander, then only 35 years old, died from a fever at Babylon.

2. Life in Hellenistic World

After Alexander's death, his conquests were fought over and divided into three large kingdoms by his generals. Ptolemy secured Egypt and Palestine over which his successors ruled until the death of Cleopatra in 31 B.C. Seleucus gained control of Asia which his house ruled until 65 B.C., but it was reduced to Asia Minor and Syria because India was lost and the Parthians controlled much of the Persian Empire by the middle of the 3rd century B.C. General Antigonus won Greece. Greek civilization now entered a new era—one for which historians have invented the term Hellenistic (meaning "to behave like a Greek"), so as to suggest a fusion of Greek and non-Greek cultures in which Greek influence predominated. The Hellenistic age is considered to come to an end with the Roman occupation of Egypt, the last of the Greek-ruled states to become subject to them, in 30 B.C. The conquest of Alexander resulted in the emergence of large states and more peace which contributed to the economic development and cultural advance of the Hellenistic world.

Along with Alexander's expansion came thousands of Greeks, inaugurating a new period of Greek colonization that spread Greeks throughout Asia and northern Africa. Widespread trade flourished. Eastern goods from as far as India and China were brought to the Mediterranean world while Greek products went east. Such trade spawned new business and industrial organizations. The vast new market stimulated enterprises: Huge fortunes were made; banking and finance were expanded.

The political forms of the Hellenistic world were different from those of the Greek past. Instead of traditional democracy and oligarchy, absolute rule was accepted as the only effective means of governing large areas, since the fate of the world was now in the hands not of city-states but of great kings.

Instead of small city-states which usually had 5,000 or 10,000 citizens, the metropolis now became the center of social organizations. The largest and most renowned was Alexandria, which had been founded by Alexander near the delta of the Nile River, in Egypt. Its population may have approached one million by the beginning of the Christian era. Alexandria was the economic and cultural hub of the eastern Mediterranean; for centuries, its library and museum were centers of scholarship and scientific study.

The Hellenistic age created social change. With an enlarged economy came greater urbanization which produced an important middle class. Another element of Hellenistic urban life was the individual's loss of identification with the city-state. It was soon evident that all the important decisions were made by a powerful and distant ruler: What the individual did politically on the city level counted little.

If there is a word which can best describe the life in the Hellenistic age, that is blending, either of race or of culture. The Greek city-states were becoming increasingly cosmopolitan; Greeks, Persians, Syrians, Jews, Egyptians, and others lived together and eventually married one another. Perhaps Alexander hoped to blend together the peoples of his empire. According to his biographer Plutarch, "He conceived that he was divinely sent to be the harmonizer and conciliator of Greeks and barbarians alike. He sought to blend as it were in the mixing-cup of good fellowship of all civilizations and customs." This blending explains the development of a feeling of universalism and of syncretic and eclectic trends in culture and religion.

3. Religion and Philosophy

When Alexander began his conquest, he visited Troy because he believed that his ancestor was the great warrior Achilles. In Egypt in 331 B.C., after having founded the city of Alexandria at the mouth of the Nile, he rode 500 miles westward across the desert to a temple of the Egyptian god Ammon, because it was believed to have been visited by Greek mythical heroes Perseus and Hercules to whom Alexander thought himself related. Therefore, by linking himself with heroes and gods, Alexander cultivated the god-king belief. His successors in the three monarchies followed his example. On the other hand, different from the Hellenic period, people in the Hellenistic age lost their identification with the city-states. They came to feel alone and powerless in the vast new monarchies. They desperately needed to believe in some force that would sustain them. Many people turned to the oriental mysterious religions for their promise of eternal life, for example, the Egyptian deities of the underworld and fertility, Osiris and Isis.

For numerous intellectuals and educated people, however, religion was not the only answer. They turned to philosophy. Whereas Plato and Aristotle had been primarily concerned with knowledge and a search after truth, the Hellenistic philosophers were more concerned with immediate human problems. How did a man achieve happiness and find value in his life in the new super states? Different answers were given. The Cynics thought that only by leading ascetic moral life and by being contemptuous of the world and its affairs can man achieve immense satisfaction. The Skeptics went so far as to deny the existence of any knowledge, a belief that could lead to nihilism. However, the philosophies with the largest followers were Epicureanism and Stoicism. The former was propounded by Epicurus (342 B.C.–270 B.C.), who concentrated not on cosmic problems but on ways of achieving individual happiness.

To Epicurus, all forms of existence are temporary combinations of minute, imperishable particles. Only the laws of motion and chance determine the shape and character of things, and there is no governing "purpose" on the earth or in the heavens. In such a universe, Epicurus believed, the only logical aim for the individual is to strive for personal happiness. As a guide in the search of happiness, Epicurus formulated a basic equation: *happiness = pleasure–pain*. He suggested that the major way to secure happiness is by decreasing the pain factor of the equation, rather than by increasing the pleasure factor. According to him, fear, "the ache of mind and heart," instead of body aches, is the deepest source of human pain, and fear feeds on ignorance and superstition. As for the "pleasure" part, he thought that pleasure includes dynamic one (eating, drinking, etc.) and passive one (literature, meditation, etc.). The former is self-defeating, while the latter is positive. He valued above all calmness, poise, and serenity of mind. The power of Epicureanism was immediately felt by the Romans. The Roman poet

Lucretius (1st century B.C.) articulated the doctrines in his poem "On the Nature of Things." This poem is also a hymn to Epicurus himself, whom Lucretius praised for having liberated the human mind from superstitious fears.

The founder of Stoicism was Zeno of Cyprus (335 B.C.–263 B.C.). Unlike the Epicureans, the Stoics declared that harmony and happiness are achieved by striving for virtue rather than pleasure. Virtue, according to their definition, consists of understanding nature through reason, accepting God's purpose by self-discipline, and living in accordance with duty, truth, and natural law (justice). Zeno contended that the world is directed by Divine Reason, or Providence, or God, of which man had only a spark. They regarded all persons as inherently equal, because all share, in common with God, the spark of reason. Stoicism epitomized the universality and cosmopolitanism of the Hellenistic world. Stoicism made a significant mark on Roman times and influenced the future; it offered a noble standard of conduct and its ethics anticipated Christianity. The Christian notions of God and of the brotherhood of man have much in common with Stoic precepts. Perhaps the most direct influence was on Roman legal thought, in which the Stoic idea of "natural law"—law identical with reason and God—was of high importance.

4. Science in Alexandria

By the time of Jesus, Alexandria in Egypt—situated between the west and the east—had been a center of learning. Among the famous scholars who made their names at Alexandria were Euclid, Apollonius of Perga, Archimedes of Syracuse, Aristarchus of Samos, and Eratosthenes who made groundbreaking contributions to mathematics and astronomy.

Euclid (fl. 300 B.C.) may have written his *Elements* during the reign of Ptolemy I (323 B.C.–285 B.C.). The book is widely acknowledged as the most influential textbook of all time. Apollonius (262 B.C.–190 B.C.), "the great geometer," wrote his influential book on conic sections in the city. Archimedes (287 B.C.–212 B.C.) spent time observing the rise and fall of the Nile, and invented the screw for which he became famous. Archimedes also initiated hydrostatics and began his method of calculating area and volume that 1,800 years later, would form the basis of calculus.

In the field of astronomy, Aristarchus (310 B.C.–230 B.C.) developed a heliocentric view of the universe, contending that the sun and the fixed stars remained stationary while the Earth rotated around the sun in a circular orbit. He also argued that the Earth rotated around its own axis. Another astronomer Eratosthenes (c. 275 B.C.–c. 194 B.C.) believed that the Earth was round and all the Earth's oceans were connected, that Africa might one day be circumnavigated, and that India could be reached by sailing westward from Spain. It was

Eratosthenes who calculated the correct duration of a year, and calculated the Earth's diameter to within an error of 50 miles, as 250,000 stades (later amended to 252,000 stades, since it was more conveniently divisible by sixty) was equal to 25,000 miles, not so far from the modern calculation of just under 26,000 miles.

The Hellenistic age saw a gradual withdrawal from reason and belief in man's ability, and a gradual embracing of philosophy and religion that offered extra-human support and hope. Despite the conquest of the Romans, it was here that the Romans found the culture that they were to absorb and pass on to western Europe. Within the Roman Empire, the Hellenistic world remained a distinct cultural region, dominated by Greek civilization. When that empire finally divided, its Greek-dominated eastern half continued for several centuries until the Muslim conquest, and even then, the Hellenistic legacy was preserved by the empire of Byzantium.

Key Terms

Alexander's conquest → Hellenistic world → Cynics → Skeptics → Epicureanism → Stoicism → Euclid → Apollonius → Archimedes → Aristarchus of Samos (Heliocentric) → Eratosthenes (a round Earth, calculation of the Earth's diameter)

Exercises

1 Vocabulary Building

➷ Fill in each blank with a synonym to the word or phrase in the brackets.

The Hellenistic age saw a gradual _____ (withdrawal) from reason and belief in man's ability, and a gradual _____ (embracing) of philosophy and religion that _____ (offered) extra-human support and hope. Despite the conquest of the Romans, it was here that the Romans found the culture that they were to _____ (absorb) and _____ (pass on) to western Europe. Within the Roman Empire, the Hellenistic world remained a(n) _____ (distinct) cultural region, _____ (dominated) by Greek civilization.

❷ Translation

❧ Translate the following sentences into Chinese.

1) He conceived that he was divinely sent to be the harmonizer and conciliator of Greeks and barbarians alike. He sought to blend as it were in the mixing-cup of good fellowship of all civilizations and customs.

2) Virtue, according to their definition, consists of understanding nature through reason, accepting God's purpose by self-discipline, and living in accordance with duty, truth, and natural law (justice).

❸ Questions

❧ Answer the following questions.

1) What were the main features of life in the Hellenistic age?

2) What achievements in science and philosophy were made during the Hellenistic age?

❹ Topic for Discussion

❧ Below is a topic related to this chapter. Read it and finish the discussion.

Based on what you have learned from this chapter, have a discussion about the city of Alexandria and its contribution to Western culture.

Chapter 4

The Rise and Fall of Rome

When the Greeks were engaged in the development of their brilliant civilization, a power was slowly arising in Italy that would ultimately control the Mediterranean world and bring a long era of peace. Roman civilization and Greek civilization were twin versions of a single "Greco-Roman" civilization, in which the Greeks were the originators and the Romans, to begin with, were the followers and later promoters. The Romans absorbed, modified, and spread Greek culture into western Europe. But that is not all. They in turn improved on Greek culture, at least so far as government and warfare were concerned.

1. Roman Republic

Geography had a major impact on Rome's history. Italy is a narrow peninsula extending about 750 miles from north to south but averaging only about 120 miles across. The Apennine Mountains cross the peninsula from north to south. Nevertheless, Italy has some fairly large fertile plains ideal for farming. Most important are the Po Valley in the north, probably the most fertile agricultural area, and the plain of Latium, on which Rome was located. Italy also possesses much more productive farmland than Greece, enabling it to support a large population. From a geographic point of view, Rome's location was favorable. Located 18 miles inland on the Tiber River, Rome had access to the sea but was far enough inland to be safe from pirates. Built on hills, it was easily defended, and because it was situated where the Tiber could be readily forded, Rome became a natural crossing point for north-south traffic in western Italy.

From the 7th century B.C., the region of Latium was ruled by the Etruscans who had come to Italy from Asia Minor or Lydia early in the 9th century B.C. According to the legend, in 509 B.C. some aristocratic Roman families led a revolt against the Etruscans and ousted the Etruscan king. This date marked the independence of Rome and its dominance over Latium as well as the beginning of its expansion.

1.1　Political Development

Roman government was republican in form, dominated by patricians, who belonged to the oldest and noblest Roman families. The mass of ordinary people, called plebeians, included everyone who did not have the hereditary status of patricians, consisting of workers, small farmers, and even quite wealthy citizens. The plebeians had few civic rights, which led to constant class struggle. Among the chief complaints from the plebeians was that they lacked legal protection. Before the 5th century B.C., there had been no written code of law to which an accused person could turn for guidance or defense. By 450 B.C., the plebeians had forced the patricians to draw up a written code of law known as the Twelve Tables. These Twelve Tables served as the foundation for the elaborate system of Roman law that grew up in the centuries to come. The plebeians began to win the main objectives in their contest with the patricians: eligibility for all public offices, the right to marry into the patrician class, and admission to the Senate itself. Citizen assemblies played an important role in legislation, as well as in electing the consuls, tribunes, praetors (judges), pontiffs (priests), and other magistrates for one-year terms. The assemblies were powerful, up to a point, but in practice still depended on the magistrates, who had control over business discussed and election timetables. The other important body was the Senate. Senators were appointed for life, and this simple but all-important fact made the Senate the most continuous element in the structure of the state.

1.2　Punic Wars (264 B.C.–146 B.C.)

Not until Rome had expanded to the toe of Italy just across Sicily did it become aware that it was challenged by another sea power, Carthage. The city was founded about 700 B.C. by the Phoenicians. Carthage spread its influence across North Africa, southern Spain, Sardinia, Corsica, and Sicily. It was the Carthaginians' interest in Sicily that brought them into conflict with the Romans. Thus the Punic Wars erupted (the term *Punic* derives from *Poeni*, the Latin name for the Phoenicians, the settlers of Carthage).

The wars were fought in land and sea, in three rounds. The first Punic War ended with the Carthaginians being driven out of Sicily. In 218 B.C., Carthage's general Hannibal suddenly struck and instigated the second phase of the war. Before the Romans realized what their enemy was doing, Hannibal had brought his army with elephants through Alpine passes into Italy. The army remained there for 13 years until in 207 B.C., the Roman general Scipio Africanus took an army to besiege Carthage. Hannibal was called to defend the city and was finally defeated in 202 B.C. In a final act of vengeance, the Romans leveled the city of Carthage. The former possessions of Carthage in Sicily, Spain, and Africa became the first Roman provinces. However, Rome's conquest of Greece grew out of a special invitation. Around 200 B.C., ambassadors from various Greek city-states appealed to Rome for aid in resisting the King of Macedonia, who had been allied with Carthage. The Romans sent an army. Their professed aim was to secure the liberty of the Greek cities and then they would withdraw troops from Greece. But in the course of endless maneuvering and fighting, the Romans carved one province after another out of the Hellenistic kingdoms. By the early 1st century A.D., from Gibraltar to Jerusalem fell the shadow of mighty Rome.

2. Roman Empire

With the victory of wars and the conquest of lands one after another, it seemed increasingly difficult for the Republic to rule the vast territory. A new form of government must be established to provide peace and security, and command the respect and loyalty of its citizens. This task fell on Octavian in 29 B.C. After a long period of civil wars, first between Julius Caesar and Pompey, and then mainly between Mark Antony and Octavian, Caesar's grandnephew and adopted son, Octavian stood supreme over the Roman world. He was now the sole master and the one who finally managed to turn military dictatorship into legitimate and permanent monarchy.

2.1   Political Settlement Under Octavian

Octavian soon wielded an absolute and autocratic power implied in the title that was conferred to him by the Senate—Augustus ("revered"), which had formerly been reserved for the gods. Augustus retained the Senate as the deliberative body of the Roman state, but the decrees were usually screened first by him. He held the office of a consul, the right to command. When he gave up the consulship in 23 B.C., Augustus was granted *maius imperium*—greater right to command. Later Augustus was given the power of a tribune, which enabled him to propose laws and veto any item of public business. Consequently, the popular assemblies gradually declined in its importance.

Augustus maintained a standing army of 28 legions, with each numbering 5,400 soldiers. The legionaries served 20 years and were recruited only from the citizens. Augustus also maintained a large contingent of auxiliary forces enlisted from the subject peoples. They were recruited only from non-citizens, served for 24 years, and along with their families received citizenship after their terms of service. Augustus was also responsible for establishing the Praetorian Guard. Roughly 9,000 men, they had an important task of guarding the person of the *princeps*. They usually served for 16 years. Eventually, the Praetorian Guard would play an important role in deposing emperors and proclaiming their successors. Augustus also built a permanent fleet to eradicate piracy, making the Mediterranean a peaceful highway of trade and communication and contributing to the unification of the empire.

2.2　Evolution of Roman Law

As we have seen, "customary" laws were recorded in the Twelve Tablets during the 5th century B.C. and remained the basis of Roman law for centuries. After 366 B.C., a praetor was appointed to administer justice to citizens as well as foreigners under Roman jurisdiction. This official had a still wider basis for interpretations, for he could draw on various foreign laws, as well as on Roman law, in arriving at fair decisions and settlements. Thus there grew up, in the days of the Republic, two distinct bodies of law: the law of citizens, or *jus civile*, and the law of nations, or *jus gentium*. By the 1st century A.D., the basic provisions of the two bodies of law had been brought close together; after 212, when all free inhabitants of the empire were declared Roman citizens, the dual system disappeared. From that time on, one system of law prevailed throughout the empire.

2.2.1　*The Idea of "Natural Law"*

According to Cicero's definition, "Law is the just distinction between right and wrong, made conformable to most ancient nature." In the later Republic, the Romans gradually developed an idea that the law of the state should reflect what is right according to universal reason. Most of the jurists were well-educated men and lovers of Stoic philosophy. They observed that the law from different nations had many elements in common. This similarity in legal ideas among the peoples of the empire coincided nicely with the Stoic belief that there was one law in nature, the law of reason. From this the jurists inferred the reality of "natural law" and concluded that human rules could and should conform to this "higher law." Thus, the Roman experience, supported by Hellenistic philosophy, gave rise to the doctrine of natural law.

The doctrine of natural law has deeply influenced legal theories in the West and is also the basis of the idea of law and human rights contained in the United States' Declaration of Independence.

2.2.2　*The Codification of Roman Law*

It was not until the 6th century that a complete codification of the Roman law was achieved under the emperor Justinian. Justinian's *Corpus Juris Civilis* (Body of Civil Law) consists of several parts: the *Digest* is a summary of judicial opinions and commentaries; the *Code* is a collection of statutes from Hadrian to Justinian; the *Novels* includes a collection of statutes enacted after the publication of the *Code*; and the *Institutes* is a brief discussion of legal principles. The *Corpus Juris Civilis* became the basis of imperial law in the Byzantine Empire until its end in 1453. The law, since it was written in Latin (it was, in fact, the last product of Eastern Roman culture to be written in Latin, which was soon replaced by Greek), became the basis of the legal system in Europe.

This imperial edifice begun by Augustus and completed by his successors lasted for the next two centuries. The governing structure that Augustus had built remained remarkably stable for nearly two centuries after his time. The army generally confined itself to defending the frontiers and for the most part loyally upheld. When Octavian died, the matter of succession became a problem which led to revolt and anarchy. However, from 96 to 180 was the age of the Good Emperors when the empire was in the hands of the exceptionally able emperors Nerva, Trajan, Hadrian, Antoninus Pius, and Marcus Aurelius. According to Edward Gibbon, this era was "the period in the history of the human world, during which the condition of the human race was most happy and prosperous."

At its greatest extent during the 2nd century A.D., the Roman Empire measured nearly 3,000 miles from east to west and nearly 2,000 miles from north to south. Beyond the frontiers, there were as yet no enemies capable of making any permanent breaches in Rome's defenses. To the south were the desert tribes of northwestern Africa. To the north, the Germanic barbarian tribes were still not advanced and powerful enough to challenge the empire. The chief antagonist in the east was the empire of Parthia, but it was a mere "regional power" compared with the intercontinental empire of Rome.

3. The Fall of Roman Empire

At the end of the 3rd century and the beginning of the 4th century, the Roman Empire, under Diocletian and Constantine, gained a new momentum. The empire was transformed by a new governmental structure, a rigid economic and social system, and a new state religion—Christianity.

3.1   Reconstruction Under Diocletian and Constantine

When Marcus Aurelius died, the throne was succeeded by his incompetent son Commodus who was assassinated in 192. The violent death triggered the civil war and it didn't end until 284 when Diocletian, a general from Illyria, became the victor in the power struggle. During the period except for some short time of stability, the empire was in constant fighting and confusion. In some 50 years of anarchy, there were 26 emperors, only one of whom died peacefully in bed. It was during the reign of Diocletian (284–305) and of Constantine (310–337) that the imperial disintegration was stemmed and the empire saw a temporary rejuvenation. In order to save the foundering empire, Diocletian took drastic action. He ruled much like an Oriental despot, concentrating all power in his person and basing it upon control of the army. Given that the anarchy before his coming to power was mainly due to the succession problem, he took special measures to provide for orderly imperial succession. He first associated himself with another man to whom he gave the title

Augustus and later added two more sub-associates with the title of Caesar. The empire was divided among the four. To facilitate administration, Diocletian reduced the size of provinces and increased their numbers. Another important move was that he moved the center of the government from Rome to Nicomedia so as to be closer to the eastern provinces. Furthermore, he replaced stationary defenses along the frontiers by mobile defenses that could be swiftly dispatched to threatened places.

Despite his plan for smooth succession, Diocletian failed and retired in 305. Out of the civil war that followed, Constantine triumphed. He abolished the scheme for associate emperors but retained all the other innovations of Diocletian. He even furthered the eastern move by moving his capital from Rome to Byzantium on the Bosporus, renaming it Constantinople. By doing so, Constantine hastened the split between East and West. In the 4th and 5th centuries, it was customary to have two emperors, one ruling the East from Constantinople, another ruling the West from Rome.

Diocletian and Constantine greatly strengthened and enlarged the administrative bureaucracies of the Roman Empire. Most of the public funds went to the two enlarged institutions—the army and the civil service. To deal with these financial burdens, Diocletian and Constantine devised new economic and social policies. Like their political policies, these economic and social policies were all based on coercion and loss of individual freedom. For instance, in order to fight inflation, in 301, Diocletian issued an edict to set maximum wages and prices for the entire empire. But it was largely unenforceable. In the 3rd century, the city councils begun to decline. Since the city councilors were forced to pay expenses out of their own pocket when the taxes they collected were insufficient, the wealthy no longer wanted to serve in these positions. Some fled and resumed their duties only by coercion. So was true for numerous occupations in late Roman Empire. In rural areas, large landowners took advantage of depressed agricultural conditions to enlarge their landed estates. Free tenant farmers became dependent on these large estates and soon discovered that the landlords had obtained government cooperation in attaching farmers to their land. In a word, the economic and social policies of Diocletian and Constantine, though temporarily successful, in the long run stifled the very vitality of the Romans' economic and social life.

3.2　The End of Western Roman Empire

The weakening of the Roman Empire was a lengthy and gradual process. For a long time, the empire had been facing serious problems. One of these problems was the economic weakness of the western portion of the empire. The west had fewer people, cities, and economic resources than the east. To meet the needs of the army and the civil service, the government had to raise tax rates from time to time. This led to gradual impoverishment of the country. Besides the economic problem, the empire began to suffer from an inability to ensure stable and effective leadership. Toward the end of the 2nd century when Commodus was assassinated, the line of emperors by adoption and designation came to an end. The empire was under constant chaos and civil wars. These difficulties, in turn, made it harder for the empire to deal with the third major problem: the still unconquered barbarian peoples who lived to the north of its European frontiers. These were the Germanic peoples, under whose hands the end of the empire was sealed.

During the 1st and 2nd centuries, the Romans had made the Rhine and Danube rivers as the empire's northern boundary. The Romans called all the peoples to the north of the rivers "Germans" and regarded them as uncivilized barbarians. It is widely agreed that the Germanic barbarians began to move in on the empire not because of any deliberate plan of conquest but as a result of a momentous shift in the intercontinental balance of forces that had helped Rome endure for so long. Shortly before the beginning of the Christian era, a nomadic nation known as the Huns living to the north of China began to move westward across the steppes. Finally, in 370, they burst into Europe. For three-quarters of a century, they dominated a region stretching from Europe's eastern borders all the way to the Rhine, and the impact on the barbarian peoples of the region was devastating, destroying some and causing others to flee. Among those who fled were the Visigoths living on the lower Danube River, who in 376 begged to be admitted to Rome's territory. Their plea was granted. After crossing into the Danubian provinces and defeating the Roman emperor Valens at the Battle of Adrianople in 378, the Visigoths remained in the Danubian area until they moved west under their chief, Alaric, into Italy and eventually into Spain and the southwestern part of Gaul. In 410, the Visigoths, led by their leader Alaric, captured and sacked Rome.

By this time, other Germanic tribes were also passing into the Roman Empire and settling down. In the early 5th century, the Burgundians arrived in southern Gaul, while the Franks moved into northern Gaul. Another group, the Vandals, under their leader Gaiseric, moved through Gaul and Spain into North Africa. They toppled Carthage and set up a kingdom in the territory now called Tunis. From this vantage, they attacked Mediterranean shipping and even pillaged Rome in 455. However, the date considered to signal the end of the Roman Empire was in 476 when Odoacer of German origin, a new "master of soldiers," deposed the last Roman emperor.

3.3　Theories on the Decline of the Empire

The German invasion and conquest of the West was long considered to be responsible for the end of the ancient world. This view was developed by Renaissance scholars and historians in the 18th century as well. However, historians in the 19th and 20th centuries, after examining evidence more closely, convinced that the German conquest was not the only contributing factor. Long before the external invasion, the empire had been weakened by its internal disintegration.

Scholars influenced by their own fields of interest, methods, and approaches, have projected different reasons for the decline of the empire. Political historians argued that failure to provide orderly imperial succession caused anarchy and governmental collapse, and that imperial reliance on the military brought despotism which destroyed citizens' initiative and freedom. Military historians claimed that the decline in the size of the empire's army enabled the Germans to pour across the frontier defense. Economic historians attributed the fall of the empire either to the unfavorable economic balance between the east and the west, or to the economic regionalism and self-sufficiency based on an agrarian economy, or to the slave labor-based economy. Some scholars tried to relate the decline to physical phenomena. Soil erosion was suggested as a major cause for the drop in agricultural production; improper rotation of crops and insufficient fertilization were alleged to have impoverished the soil. Geographers even believed that during the 3rd and the 4th centuries, the Mediterranean basin underwent a period of abnormally hot and dry weather which had a devastating effect upon vegetation and human life. For the British historian Edward Gibbon, the Christian church was also to be blamed because it undermined the Romans' civic duty and military courage. Last but not the least, cultural historians noted the general decline in Roman culture. Creativity and originality which had been flourishing in ancient Greece were lacking in Roman times. Instead, summarizing, commenting, and copying were considered as a norm in literature, history, philosophy, science, and other fields.

4. Literature and Historiography

The greatest prose writer of the 1st century B.C. was Cicero. Apart from a distinguished politician in the troubled days of the Republic, he was also known for his speeches in the law court and the Senate. In addition, his philosophical essays on the art of government, justice, and theology, in which he provided digests of the best Hellenistic thought, gave the Romans a literature of philosophy that they had lacked before and made Greek thought available to future generations.

In the field of historical writing, Livy's (59 B.C.–17 A.D.) *The History of Rome* was perhaps the best. However, unlike the Greek historians, Livy's history was hardly an objective inquiry; it was moralistic in character, drawing chiefly from previous histories and well-worn legends about ancient heroes. For him, the purpose of history was "to behold object lessons of every kind of model as though they were displayed on a conspicuous monument." Livy even addressed the reader directly: "From this you should choose for yourself and for your state what to imitate and what to avoid as abominable in its origin or abominable in its outcome." With good reason Kraus and Woodman had remarked, "It is of great importance that readers should be aware that the very nature of Roman historiography has been subjected to severe questioning and that the debate continues." Another historian Tacitus (55–120) also believed that history had a moral purpose: "It seems to me a historian's foremost duty to ensure that merit is recorded, and to confront evil words and deeds with the fear of posterity's denunciations." His two books *Annals* and *Histories* dealing with the period from 14 to 96 are the best sources for early imperial history. He is known for the brevity and compactness of his Latin prose, as well as for his penetrating insights into the psychology of power politics.

The History of Rome

By Livy

6. Numitor is restored to the kingship. Romulus and Remus decide to found a new city but then quarrel. They consult the gods to resolve who should give his name to this city and who should be the king.

At the beginning of the disturbance, Numitor kept insisting that an enemy had invaded the city and attacked the palace. He drew off the Alban fighting men to defend and garrison the citadel. After the killing of Amulius, he saw the young men approaching to congratulate him. He immediately summoned a council and revealed his brother's crimes against him, his grandsons' parentage—how they had been born, reared, and recognized—and lastly the killing of the tyrant, for which he was responsible. Romulus and Remus marched with their men through the midst of the assembly and saluted their grandfather as king. From the entire crowd there arose a unanimous shout of assent, thus ratifying the king's name and his power.

After entrusting the government of Alba to Numitor, Romulus and Remus were seized by a desire to establish a city in the places where they had been exposed and raised. The number of Albans and Latins was more than enough; in addition to this group, there were also the shepherds. All of these men easily created the hope that Alba and Lavinium would be small in comparison with the city that they were founding. But these thoughts were interrupted by the ancestral evil that had beset Numitor and Amulius—desire for kingship. From quite a harmless beginning, an abominable conflict arose. Since Romulus and Remus were twins and distinction could not be made by respect for age, they decided to ask the protecting gods of the area to declare by augury who should give his name to the new city and who should rule over it after its foundation. Romulus took the Palatine and Remus the Aventine, as the respective areas from which to take the auspices.

Three outstanding poets adorned the reign of Augustus: Virgil, Horace, and Ovid. Virgil (70 B.C.–19 B.C.) was the most accomplished poet. His long poem *Aeneid*, modeled upon the Homeric epics, tells the legendary story of Aeneas, a Trojan who traveled to Italy, where he became the ancestor of the Romans. In the book, Virgil raised the Romans' virtues of duty, courage, and patriotism. Horace (65 B.C.–8 B.C.) was the leading Roman lyric poet during the time of Augustus. His love lyrics praising Lydia are models; no other compositions quite achieve their clarity and balance. Ovid (43 B.C.–18 A.D.) was best known for the *Metamorphoses*, a 15-book continuous mythological narrative written in the meter of epic, and for collections of love poetry. He fashioned his love poetry after the Greek elegy. His poetry was much imitated during Late Antiquity and the Middle Ages, and greatly influenced Western art and literature.

Biographical writing was of higher quality and proved popular with the upper class. Plutarch (46–120) wrote *Parallel Lives*, some 50 short biographies of Greek and Roman statesmen and generals. The book is a collection of biographies of great Greeks and Romans arranged to facilitate comparison between the talents of the best Greek and Roman leaders.

5. Science and Medicine

In the age of Roman Empire, Alexandria (in Egypt) continued as the hub of scientific and medical works. The Greek astronomer and geographer Claudius Ptolemy (c. 90 B.C.–c. 168 B.C.) lived in Alexandria. It was here that he compiled his marvelous *Almagest*. The book is a primary work of trigonometry. As seen earlier, toward the middle of the 3rd century B.C., Aristarchus of Samos had proposed putting the Earth in motion about the sun. Ptolemy, among others, discounted this because he thought that if the Earth moved in this way, the "fixed" stars in the heavens should change their positions relative to one another. But they didn't. Ptolemy set forth a model of the universe. This system envisaged a geocentric universe, with other bodies moving in a grand circle around a central point (see Figure 4-1). Ptolemaic System was generally accepted in the West before the Scientific Revolution in the 17th century.

His *Geography* introduced the system of latitudes and longitudes as used today. At the time, there was in fact no satisfactory way to determine longitudes and, as a result, Ptolemy seriously underestimated the size of the Earth, opting for a circumference of 180,000 stadia. One of the major consequences of this error was that subsequent navigators and explorers assumed that a voyage westward to India would not be nearly so far as it was. Had Columbus not been misled in this way, he might never have risked the journey he did make.

Figure 4-1   The Ptolemaic System

In Ptolemy's system, the Earth is in the center, surrounded by nine layers of sky, which are from near to far Lunar, Mercury, Venus, Solar, Mars, Jupiter, Saturn, Stellar, and Prime Mover.

Of equal influence were a series of books written at the same time by a Greek physician, Galen (131–c. 210) of Pergamum (in Asia Minor). Galen stressed the importance of personal hygiene to health, and his views on anatomy and physiology were accepted before the emergence of scientific biology in the 17th century.

6. The Rise and Development of Christianity

The empire, while bettering the lives of its subjects through peace and security, had deprived most of them of any faith in their own ability and worth. As the emperor became puissant and commanding in all aspects, the individual felt himself to be a minute object tossed into a vast ocean by distant forces over which he had no control; he could no longer believe in local institutions or identify himself with them, and yet he desperately needed to believe in something and to be reassured that somebody cared about him. Traditional beliefs often failed to satisfy his spiritual needs and aspirations. A new religion, coming from the East, was to proclaim a faith and a message of hope, which was so sympathetic that ultimately it became the church triumphant in the empire. It was Christianity.

6.1　Origin of Christianity

Much of the spiritual heritage of Christianity came from Judaism. Jesus was born around 4 B.C. in Bethlehem of Judaea and died there around 33 A.D. He came to believe that one day God would give the Jews a savior or messiah to deliver them from their oppressors. Instead of believing in God's kingdom on the earth, Jesus spoke of a heavenly kingdom, which disappointed the radicals. Jesus' message was basically simple. According to Jesus, what was important was not strict adherence to the letter of the law and the attention to rules and prohibitions but the transformation of the inner person: "Do to others what you would have them do to you." In the Sermon on the Mount, Jesus preached the ethical concepts—humility, charity, and brotherly love—that would form the basis for the value system of medieval Western civilization.

6.2　Spread of Christianity

Through the preaching and missionary work of its disciples, particularly Paul who brought Christ's teaching not only to the Jews but also to the Gentile, Christianity became a faith for all people, men and women, rich and poor, powerful and weak. By the end of the 1st century, it had swept around the Mediterranean and taken root in all the cities. The unity of the empire and the ease of communication made it possible for Christians to travel and spread the "good news."

The fact that Christians would only worship God instead of the emperor like other Roman people did marked them as unusual and potentially dangerous. Persecutions of Christians happened, but were not systematic. There was a brief persecution of Christians in Rome by Nero in 64, but the reasons were not clear. Another persecution was during the reign of Marcus Aurelius who seemed to believe that the growing number of Christians might be a disruptive force to imperial unity.

6.3　Triumph of Christianity

In the 4th century, Christianity prospered as never before, and Constantine played a vital role in its new status.

In 312, Constantine was about to engage a crucial battle against his chief rival Maxentius. According to a traditional story, before the battle, he had a vision of a Christian cross with the words, "In this sign you will conquer." He carried the day. Having won the battle, Constantine was convinced of the power of the Christian God. Although he was not baptized until the end of his life, in 313, he issued the famous Edict of Milan, which officially tolerated the existence of Christianity. Under Theodosius the Great (379–395), Christianity was made the official religion of the Roman Empire.

Christianity was to provide the spiritual and intellectual foundation for the Middle Ages, and in doing so to give the West new ideas and a new view of the world.

Key Terms

Roman Republic → the Twelve Tables → Punic Wars → Roman Empire → Augustus → Roman law → natural law → Diocletian and Constantine → split of Roman Empire → invasion from the Germans → fall of Roman Empire → Cicero, Livy, Virgil, Horace, Ovid → Claudius Ptolemy and his *Almagest* → rise of Christianity

Exercises

① Vocabulary Building

✎ Fill in each blank with a synonym to the word or phrase in the brackets.

1) It was during the reign of Diocletian (284–305) and of Constantine (310–337) that the imperial _____ (disintegration) was _____ (stemmed) and the Empire saw a temporary _____ (rejuvenation). In order to save the _____ (foundering) empire, Diocletian took _____ (drastic) action. He ruled much like an Oriental despot, _____ (concentrating) all power in his person and basing it upon control of the army.

2) Improper rotation of crops and _____ (insufficient) fertilization were _____ (alleged) to have _____ (impoverished) the soil.

3) The empire, while _____ (bettering) the lives of its subjects through peace and security, had _____ (deprived) most of them of any faith in their own ability and worth. As the emperor became _____ (puissant) and _____ (commanding) in all aspects, the individual felt himself to be a(n) _____ (minute) object _____ (tossed) into a vast ocean by distant forces over which he had no control; he could no longer believe in local institutions or identify himself with them, and yet he _____ (desperately) needed to believe in something and to be reassured that somebody cared about him.

4) In 312, Constantine was about to _____ (engage) a crucial battle against his

chief rival Maxentius. According to a traditional story, before the battle, he had a(n) _____ (vision) of a Christian cross with the words, "In this sign you will conquer." He _____ (carried the day). Having won the battle, Constantine was _____ (convinced) of the power of the Christian God.

❷ Translation

❧ Translate the following sentences into Chinese.

1) However, from 96 to 180 was the age of the Good Emperors when the empire was in the hands of the exceptionally able emperors Nerva, Trajan, Hadrian, Antoninus Pius, and Marcus Aurelius. According to Edward Gibbon, this era was "the period in the history of the human world, during which the condition of the human race was most happy and prosperous."

2) Ptolemy seriously underestimated the size of the Earth, opting for a circumference of 180,000 stadia. One of the major consequences of this error was that subsequent navigators and explorers assumed that a voyage westward to India would not be nearly so far as it was. Had Columbus not been misled in this way, he might never have risked the journey he did make.

❸ Questions

❧ Answer the following questions.

1) What impact did the geography have on the history of Rome?

2) What was the significance of the Punic Wars in Rome's expansion?

3) In his efforts to solve the problems Rome had faced during the late Republic, what changes did Augustus make in Rome's political, military, and social institutions?

4) What is "natural law"?

5) How do you evaluate Diocletian and Constantine's measures to reconstruct the Roman Empire? Were they successful? Why or why not?

6) What did Constantine do to help Christianity spread in the Roman Empire?

❹ Topics for Discussion

❧ Below are three topics related to this chapter. Read them and finish the discussion.

1) There are a few theories about the fall of Roman Empire. Based on your reading and research, form your own theory and exchange it with your classmates.

2) Make comparisons between Homer's epics and Virgil's *Aeneid*.

3) Based on your reading and research, give an account of Ptolemaic geocentric universe as well as his view about geography. Explain their merits and demerits.

⑤ Writing

❧ Read the following direction and finish the writing.

According to Epicureans, fear feeds on ignorance. You may agree or disagree with him. Write a short essay with the title of "Fear and Ignorance."

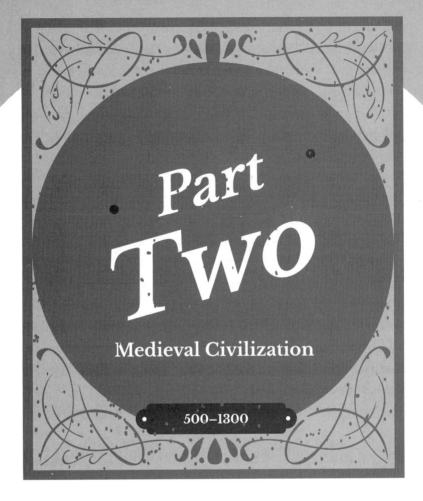

Part
Two

Medieval Civilization

500–1300

In the following thousand years, the inhabitants of Europe were learning about and preserving what was left of Greco-Roman civilization. By adaptation and fusion, they eventually forged a culture in which new ideas and institutions were blended with the classical civilization. These years of transition in Europe, from the end of the Roman Empire to the modern European epoch beginning in the 16th century, comprise what historians label the Middle Ages. In the first five hundred years after the fall of Rome, the civilized lands were raided, conquered, and settled alternatively by Germanic and Slavic barbarian peoples, as well as nomads from Asia. The eastern half of the Roman Empire evolved without a break into the Greek-ruled empire of Byzantium which managed to keep up many traditions of the Eastern Roman Empire—its Greek culture, its bureaucratic government, and its subordination of the Church to the emperor. In the West, however, the effects of the upheaval were more drastic. The cities declined; education, literature, and art found refuge in the monasteries; and there were no more emperors in Rome. Popes took over their place as rulers in Rome and eventually became independent heads of the Church. The growing power of the Pope led inevitably to the Investiture Struggle with the monarchies for the supremacy over the State, highlighted by the conflicts between Gregory VII and Henry IV, Innocent III and King John of England, and Boniface VIII and King Philip of France. In the kingdoms, a new pattern of social life and government arose—feudalism. Meanwhile, the gain of farming wealth, together with closer contacts with the world outside Europe, led to an increase in trade and a revival of urban life. By 1300, western Europe, with its centralized Catholic Church, its powerful feudal kingdoms, and its prosperous towns and cities, had become the heartland of a new civilization, as brilliant as any in the past.

Chapter 5

The Germanic Kingdoms

Apart from the Roman and Christian ingredients, there was now a new element in the medieval civilization, the Germanic. The Germanic barbarians were the last major wave of northern barbarians moving into the south. They built kingdoms, but most of them were short lived. However, the way of life of the Germanic barbarians influenced various features of the emerging civilization of Europe.

1. The Ostrogothic Kingdom in Italy

The Roman emperor Zeno in Constantinople was not pleased with Odoacer's actions and plotted to unseat him. Zeno brought another German tribe, the Ostrogoths, into Italy. The Ostrogoths had recovered from a defeat by the Huns in the 4th century and under their king Theodoric (493–526) had attacked Constantinople. Theodoric was such a dangerous neighbor that Zeno contrived his removal in 488 by inviting him to act as his deputy to defeat Odoacer and bring Italy back into the empire. Theodoric accepted the challenge, marched into Italy, killed Odoacer, and then, contrary to Zeno's wishes, established himself as ruler of Italy in 493. With Ravenna as his capital, Theodoric expanded north, east, and west at the expense of other German tribes. But however rapid the rise of Ostrogothic power was, its decline was equally rapid with the death of Theodoric. By the middle of the 6th century, the Byzantine Empire, under the emperor Justinian (527–565), had reconquered Italy, but managed only to reduce it to political anarchy. Another German tribe, the Lombards, invaded Italy in 568 and conquered much of northern and central Italy. Thereafter, Italy was to remain a geographical expression until its political unification in 1870.

2. The Visigothic Kingdom in Spain

Under their chief Alaric, the Visigoths moved into Italy and eventually into the Roman provinces of Spain and the southwestern part of Gaul where, with varying political vicissitudes, the Visigothic kingdom existed from 415 to 711. Its history was one of weakness and decline. First losing their conquests in the north of the Pyrenees to the Franks, and then seeing savage civil wars breaking out between factions of venal and greedy aristocrats, the Visigoths finally lost Spain in the early 8th century when the Arabs poured across the Strait of Gibraltar from northern Africa.

3. The Vandals' Kingdom in Carthage

Settled in the early 5th century as military allies on Gaulish soil, the Vandals took advantage of the chaos to begin marauding campaigns that turned into conquests. After ravaging Gaul, they passed into Spain, and then later in 429, into Africa. They occupied Carthage and set up a kingdom in the territory now called Tunis. They molested Mediterranean shipping from time to time and even pillaged Rome in 455, an event that led to a somewhat unjust association of their name with brigandage and wanton destruction and inspired a French scholar of the 18th century to coin the word "vandalism." With the death of their king Gaiseric in 477, Vandal power speedily crumbled, and their state was conquered by the forces of the Eastern Roman emperor Justinian in 532.

All the Germanic kingdoms established in the south of Europe have one feature in common, that is none of them proved to be permanent political structures; all were transitory, succumbing before either Moslem, or Byzantine, or other German tribes. But there were two Germanic kingdoms established in the north which were destined to become permanent and to survive during the Early Middle Ages. One of them was the Anglo-Saxon kingdom in England and the other was the kingdom of the Franks in the north of the continental Europe. It was these two nations, together with the non-Germanic Irish, that played the leading role in preserving Roman and Christian civilizations and spreading them beyond the former frontiers of the Western Empire.

4. The Frankish Kingdom

Considered as the real founders of the new Europe, the Salian Franks were located as early as the middle of the late 5th century on the left bank of the Rhine as military allies of the Roman emperors and remained there until the late 5th century when there was no longer any Roman emperor for them to fight for. Free then to shape their own political fortune in the troubled waters of Gaul, the Franks capitalized on their opportunity in a grand manner under their great leader Clovis, who, with Alfred the Great and Charlemagne, fills out the trinity of great political leaders in early medieval Europe.

Due to his military prowess, Clovis became the head of all the Frankish tribes and established the Merovingian dynasty. An event that proved to be decisive for his career was that Clovis married a Burgundian princess, a Christian, and was persuaded to accept Christianity for himself and his people. This endeared him and his people to the papacy and helped them gain papal support for all their conquests on the grounds that their conquests were to protect the true faith against heathens and heretics.

5. Anglo-Saxon England

With the withdrawal of the Roman military force by 430, Britain was open to the Anglos and Saxons, who were Germanic tribes from Denmark and northern Germany. After feud and war, political consolidation began in the 7th century. Britain was comprised of seven Germanic kingdoms, sometimes called the Heptarchy by historians. In the 9th century, political leadership fell to the Wessex kings whose destiny was to unify Britain into a strong English kingdom. The rise of Wessex power coincided with a new wave of Germanic invaders, the Danes from Denmark and northern Scandinavia, who during the 9th century conquered all the regions in the north and east of the Thames River, an area subsequently called the Danelaw. Led under the greatest king Alfred the Great (870–900), Wessex escaped Danish conquest, successfully held the Danes at the Thames, and forced them into concluding a settlement whereby they were to be content with the Danelaw and were to accept the Christian faith. By 950, all the Danelaw had been conquered and the Anglo-Saxon kingdom of England had been forged under the drive of the Wessex kings.

Key Terms

the Ostrogothic kingdom in Italy → the Visigothic kingdom in Spain → the Vandals' kingdom in Carthage → the Frankish kingdom → Clovis → Anglo-Saxon England → Danelaw → Alfred the Great

Exercises

1 Vocabulary Building

❧ Fill in each blank with a synonym to the word in the brackets.

Settled in the early 5th century as military allies on Gaulish soil, the Vandals took advantage of the chaos to begin _____ (marauding) campaigns that turned into conquests. After _____ (ravaging) Gaul, they passed into Spain, and then later in 429, into Africa. They occupied Carthage and set up a kingdom in the territory now called Tunis. They _____ (molested) Mediterranean shipping from time to time and even _____ (pillaged) Rome in 455, an event that led to a somewhat unjust _____ (association) of their name with _____ (brigandage) and _____ (wanton) destruction and inspired a French scholar of the 18th century to _____ (coin) the word "vandalism."

❷ Translation

> ✍ Translate the following sentences into Chinese.

1) Under their chief Alaric, the Visigoths moved into Italy and eventually into the Roman provinces of Spain and the southwestern part of Gaul where, with varying political vicissitudes, the Visigothic kingdom existed from 415 to 711. Its history was one of weakness and decline. First losing their conquests in the north of the Pyrenees to the Franks, and then seeing savage civil wars breaking out between factions of venal and greedy aristocrats, the Visigoths finally lost Spain in the early 8th century when the Arabs poured across the Strait of Gibraltar from northern Africa.

2) Free then to shape their own political fortune in the troubled waters of Gaul, the Franks capitalized on their opportunity in a grand manner under their great leader Clovis, who, with Alfred the Great and Charlemagne, fills out the trinity of great political leaders in early medieval Europe.

❸ Questions

> ✍ Answer the following questions.

1) What kingdoms were established by the Germanic people? Which kingdoms survived and why?

2) What factors do you think can account for Clovis' conquests?

3) What is the "Danelaw"?

Chapter 6

The Byzantine Empire

The history of the Byzantine Empire began when Constantine moved his capital in 330 to Byzantium on the Bosporus. Theodosius the Great (379–395) was the last emperor to rule over a united empire. Upon his death, the empire was divided between his two sons and was never again united. During the 5th century, the emperors spent most of their time defending Constantinople and keeping Germanic tribes from moving westward, but in the 6th century, the Byzantine Empire entered the phase that would transform its institutions and make its culture distinct from that in the West. Also in the 6th century, Latin began to be replaced by Greek, and soon men were to speak of the Latin West and the Greek East.

1. The Reign of Justinian (527-565)

Justinian was the last Byzantine emperor who was Roman in thought and Latin in speech. Imbued with a sense of imperial grandeur, Justinian embarked upon the lofty project of reconquering the West and restoring the Roman Empire. In 533, Justinian defeated the Vandals and restored northern Africa to the empire. The next achievement was the conquest of Ostrogothic Italy in 552. Turning then to Visigothic Spain, he reduced only the southeastern coast. His achievement, however remarkable, was in essence hollow and transitory. Within a short time, most of the conquests were lost and Justinian left behind him an exhausted empire to meet new and deadly threats from the Persians, the Slavs, and the Arabs.

2. From Eastern Roman to Byzantine Empire

After Justinian's death, the Byzantine Empire met threats from all sides. The Persians, pushing into Syria, took Damascus, Antioch, and Jerusalem, and proceeded into Egypt and Asia Minor. Emperor Heraclius (610–641) led a spirited army straight into Persian territory, reached the Tigris at Nineveh, and won a great victory. The Persians sued for peace, agreeing to return Byzantine territory and the Holy Cross which had been taken from Jerusalem.

Threats also arose along the northern frontier, especially in the Balkans, by the Slavs.

During the 2nd century, the Slavs were known to the Romans as a people living somewhere to the east of the Germans. From about the 3rd century onward, the Slavs began their warlike expansion. They moved south, crossed the Danube River, and broke the defenses of Byzantium. They took over most of the empire's provinces in the region known today as the Balkans. Meanwhile, the widely scattered Slavic tribal confederacies were themselves beginning to divide into different groups. There was a western group, the forerunner of such modern nations as the Czechs and the Poles; a southern group, including tribes that already called themselves Croats and Serbs; and an eastern group, out of which the Russians, the Ukrainians, and other nations would in time evolve.

The most serious challenge to the Eastern Empire was the rise of Islam. When the Arabs established a new empire around the Mediterranean, they began to plunder the islands, the European coast, and Asia Minor. The Arabs launched two serious offenses, trying to reduce Constantinople separately in 655 and in 717, but only to fail. Never again would the Arabs threaten Constantinople.

However, the Arabs reduced the territory of the Byzantine Empire to the fringes of the northern Mediterranean coast. Now the heart of the Byzantine Empire became and would remain Asia Minor. By the 8th century, the Eastern Roman Empire had been transformed into what historians call the Byzantine Empire, a civilization with its own unique characters that would last until 1453.

3. Byzantine Culture

Byzantium played a major cultural role in the development of Western civilization. The codification of Roman law, the *Corpus Juris Civilis*, still forms the foundation of legal systems of most Western countries at present. In addition, Byzantium inherited the internationally dominant Greek culture of the eastern Mediterranean and the Middle East. The rich literature of ancient Greece was conserved in archives and libraries, and Byzantine scholars enriched their heritage by adding their own commentaries and summations.

The religion of Byzantium was the Greek Orthodox Church headed by the Patriarch of Constantinople rather than the Roman Church headed by the Pope at Rome. Considered as chosen by God, the emperor played a crucial position in the Byzantine state. Since his power was absolute and sacred, the emperor exercised control over both Church and State.

The importance of the religion to the Byzantines explains why an enormous number of artistic talents were poured into the construction of churches, church ceremonies, and church decoration. They had extremely impressive achievements in architecture. The principal monument was the mighty church of Hagia Sophia (see Figure 6-1). It employs domes and half-domes to create a vast interior space. The most striking feature is the main dome, over 100 feet in diameter and 180 feet in height. It does not rest, like the dome of the Pantheon, upon a cylindrical wall. Instead, it rests on four giant arches, which mark off a central square beneath the dome. The arches carry the downward thrust to four stone corner piers, which are reinforced by massive stone supports on the outside. Arched windows, piercing the base perimeter of the dome, crown the interior with a halo of light. This temple inspires, in its own fashion, the sense of marvel and holy mystery that the cathedrals in Europe were to achieve centuries later, and has served as a model for thousands of churches and mosques in Middle Eastern lands.

Figure 6-1　Cathedral of Hagia Sophia

Justinian's cathedral, later a mosque and now a museum, was the work of two architect-mathematicians, Anthemius of Tralles and Isidorus of Miletus.

(Source: Visual China Group)

Key Terms

Justinian → invasion from the Slavs → Byzantine culture → the *Corpus Juris Civilis* → Greek Orthodox Church → Hagia Sophia

Exercises

① Vocabulary Building

> Fill in each blank with a synonym to the word in the brackets.

The arches carry the downward _____ (thrust) to four stone corner piers, which are _____ (reinforced) by _____ (massive) stone supports on the outside. Arched windows, _____ (piercing) the base perimeter of the dome, _____ (crown) the interior with a halo of light. This temple _____ (inspires), in its own fashion, the sense of marvel and holy mystery that the cathedrals in Europe were to achieve centuries later, and has served as a model for thousands of churches and mosques in Middle Eastern lands.

② Translation

> Translate the following sentences into Chinese.

1) Emperor Heraclius led a spirited army straight into Persian territory, reached the Tigris at Nineveh, and won a great victory. The Persians sued for peace, agreeing to return Byzantine territory and the Holy Cross which had been taken from Jerusalem.

2) However, the Arabs reduced the territory of the Byzantine Empire to the fringes of the northern Mediterranean coast. Now the heart of the Byzantine Empire became and would remain Asia Minor. By the 8th century, the Eastern Roman Empire had been transformed into what historians call the Byzantine Empire, a civilization with its own unique characters that would last until 1453.

③ Questions

> Answer the following questions.

1) What threats did the Byzantine Empire receive? And where were these threats from?

2) Give an account of the rise, expansion, and split of the Slavs.

④ Topic for Discussion

> Below is a topic related to this chapter. Read it and finish the discussion.

Based on your reading and research, explain the difference between the Greek Orthodox Church and Latin Christianity in terms of both theology and rites.

Chapter 7

The Rise and Expansion of Islam

When Rome and Byzantium were producing different versions of European civilization, in the North African and Middle Eastern territories of the old Roman Empire, a new and totally different civilization was to develop due to another great invasion from Arabia. The Arabs brought a militant faith and succeeded in building a brilliant and distinctive culture—both known by the name of Islam which had a profound effect on the development of the West. Its relation with the West was intriguing and confusing, sometimes friendly, sometimes antagonistic, and remains so till today.

1. Mohammed

The life of the Arabic tribes was simple and their religion was primitive. They had long been revering sacred rocks, trees, and wells till Mohammed, whose religion of Islam transformed the Arabs and upset much of the civilized world. In his thirties, he began to experience visions that he believed were inspired by Allah. He concluded that Arab polytheism was wrong, and that there was but one God (Allah), the creator of the world and man. To attain salvation when the final judgment came, man must live righteously and obey various precepts which Mohammed formulated.

However, the Meccans regarded him as an upstart and fraud. Making no headway in Mecca, Mohammed finally accepted the invitation from a group of Judaized Arabs in Yathrib to go there and become their prophet. In 622, he and a small band of followers made the trip to Yathrib which was renamed Medina (the city of the Prophet). This event became the year 1 in the Islamic calendar. His political and military skills enabled him to put together a reliable military force, with which he returned to Mecca in 630, conquering the city and converting the townspeople to the new faith. From Mecca, Mohammed's ideas spread quickly across the Arabian Peninsula and within a relatively short time, had resulted in both the religious and the political unification of the Arab society.

2. Arabic Conquests and the Caliphate

Once the Arabs had become unified under Abu Bakr, Mohammed's father-in-law, they began to move outward. The Byzantines and the Persians were the first to feel the strength of the newly united Arabs. By 640, the Muslims had taken possession of the province of Syria from the Byzantine Empire. To the east, by 650 they had conquered the entire Persian Empire. In the meantime, Egypt and other areas of northern Africa had been added to the new Muslim empire. By the mid-7th century, problems arose again over the succession to the Prophet after Ali, Mohammed's son-in-law, was assassinated and the empire didn't re-establish peace until the general Muawiya, the governor of Syria and one of Ali's chief rivals, became caliph in 661, thus establishing the Umayyad dynasty. This internal dissension over the caliphate created a split in Islam between the Shi'ites, those who accepted only the descendants of Ali as the true rulers, and the Sunnites, who claimed that the descendants of the Umayyads were the true caliphs. This 7th-century split in Islam has lasted until the present day.

The civil war only temporarily halted the Arab expansion. Arab armies, pushing into the north region of Mesopotamia, occupied Armenia and the land up to the Taurus Mountains. By 710, all northern Africa from the Red Sea to the Strait of Gibraltar was under the rule of Umayyad Caliphate. But the thrust of Islam was not yet spent. They crossed the Strait of Gibraltar and by 718, all Visigothic Spain had been conquered and Islamic forces had begun sweeping into southwestern France. By the middle of the 8th century, an empire more vast than any before had been established. Only by the great effort of its fleet did the Byzantine Empire hold on to a small part of the eastern Mediterranean and cling to Constantinople and adjacent territory. The Arabs securely held three sides of the Mediterranean and dominated its waters.

In 750, a revolt broke out in Persia with its core supporters composed of the Abbasid family, descended from Mohammed's uncle Abbas and from Ali, and thus began the Abbasid Caliphate. The new dynasty chose Baghdad as a new capital, which was destined to become celebrated in literature and a legend as one of the richest and most exotic cities in the world. The Abbasid's long rule coincided with exceptionally rich intellectual and artistic achievements that would eventually influence western Europe intellectually.

3. The Faith of Islam

Mohammed set his revelations in the context of Judaism and Christianity, identifying Allah with Yahweh (Jehovah) and accepting the line of Jewish prophets from Abraham through Jesus. That is why Abu Bakr and his army, in prosecuting the Holy War and converting all of Arabia, had slain whoever would not accept Islam except for Jews and Christians, because they were considered people of the Book.

At the heart of Islam, which means "submission to the will of Allah," is its sacred book, the Qur'an (Koran), with its basic message that there is no God but Allah and Mohammed is his Prophet. Islam emphasizes the need to obey the will of Allah. This means following a basic ethical code consisting of the Five Pillars of Islam: belief in Allah and Mohammed as his Prophet; standard prayer five times a day and public prayer on Friday at midday to worship Allah; observance of the holy month of Ramadan (the ninth month on the Muslim calendar) by fasting from dawn to sunset; making a pilgrimage to Mecca in one's lifetime, if possible; and giving alms to the poor and the unfortunate. The faithful who observed the law were guaranteed a place in an eternal paradise.

In its ideals, Islam was a far simpler faith than, say, Christianity. It was egalitarian and there was in theory no clergy, no Church, no rank in which some followers were more privileged, or closer to God, than others. That is one important reason why Islam has appealed to so many people that it has the largest number of believers in the world.

4. The Culture of Islam

What characterized the Arabs after their conquest was their ability to accommodate and adjust to different cultures. Tolerant of those they conquered, the Arabs preserved and assimilated the great Greco-Roman civilization into their own. Eventually, it was the Muslim world that introduced elements of the Greco-Roman civilization that had been largely forgotten for hundreds of years to medieval Europe. Muslim scholars collected all the great Greek classics and translated them into Arabic. By the end of the 9th century, the Muslim world was familiar with the main body of Greek philosophy, science, medicine, and mathematics. The Muslims also became familiar with Persian, Hindu, and Chinese learning.

4.1　Muslim Scholarship

In 641, Alexandria fell to the Muslims, a city that for many years had been the mathematical, medical, and philosophical center of the world, and the Muslims came across countless books and manuscripts on these subjects in Greek. Since the Abbasid rulers moved the capital to Baghdad, the city had grown from nothingness to a world center of prodigious wealth and international significance, standing alone as a rival to Byzantium. It is said that the Caliph al-Ma'mun had a dream in which Aristotle appeared and as a result of this dream, the Caliph decided to send envoys as far afield as Constantinople in search of as many Greek manuscripts as they could find, and to establish a center devoted to translation in Baghdad.

The philosopher Al-Kindi made a thorough study of Aristotle and began the reconciliation of Greek thought and Muslim theology. He is often referred to as the first Arab philosopher. Al-Kindi advocated the Greek way of thought and insisted on the difference between philosophy and theology. In his view, theology should be made subject to the rules of philosophy, such as logic. In doing so, he risked the ire of the orthodox Muslims. He also argued that philosophy was open to all, unlike theology, where there was a hierarchy of access to the truth. Averroës was the greatest philosopher at that time. He developed a rational and naturalistic interpretation of Aristotle that marked a break with a philosophical tradition which attempted to use Aristotle to support Islamic doctrine. Averroës realized that Aristotelian thought contradicted Islamic precepts and made no attempt at reconciliation. His writings, through Latin translation, profoundly affected the interpretation of Aristotle in Europe.

In medicine, the Arab achievements were equally spectacular. Two Islamic doctors from this time must rank among the greatest physicians in all history. Al-Razi wrote on all sorts of medical subjects and contributed a learned discussion of smallpox. He was the first chief physician of the hospital at Baghdad where he established courses in pharmacy, extended medical treatment to the poor, and initiated the licensing of physicians. The finest work in medicine, however, was done by Ibn Sina, more known in the West by a Latinized name Avicenna. His most famous work was *The Canon*, a majestic synthesis of Greek and Arabic medical thought. The range of diseases and disorders considered is vast, from anatomy to purges, tumors to fractures, the spreading of disease by water and by soil, and the book codifies some 760 drugs. In the 12th century, the book was translated into Latin and replaced *Galen* to serve as the basic textbook in European medical schools until at least the 17th century.

In the field of astronomy and mathematics, there was al-Khwarizmi whose name had become a household word throughout the educated world. In his work *Concerning the Hindu Art of Reckoning*, he gave such a complete account of Hindu system that he is probably responsible for the widespread but false impression that our system of numeration is Arabic in origin. It is the Arabs who probably added a tenth symbol, the zero. With this new mathematical knowledge, the Arabs made advances in astronomy. They could more accurately observe and calculate the movements of heavenly bodies.

4.2　Muslim Architecture

The Arabs had been almost wholly ignorant of architecture and building techniques until they saw what the Greeks, Romans, and Persians had constructed. It was also under the Umayyads that the earliest examples of Islamic architecture were created—the Dome of the Rock (691), in Jerusalem and the Great Mosque of Damascus (706). Unfortunately, most of the mosques constructed during the Middle Ages were destroyed by the Mongols when they swept into the Middle East in the 13th century. Only in Spain have most of the medieval mosques survived.

There were some general ideas of aesthetics that had been established as tradition. One was the idea of ornament, or embellishment. Islam concedes that God created the world and ornamented it, and gave man the ability to produce devices of embellishment. There is more to this idea of ornament, in fact. Since God created the world and that is perfect, there is little scope for man to truly create—all he can do is to adorn what God has produced. Another was the idea of arabesque. One theory holds that the Muslims were forbidden by their religion to reproduce man and animals in art forms, so they created other designs to decorate their buildings, for instances, the exquisite patterns of flowers and leaves, beautiful calligraphy, and arabesques by combining geometric figures and arranging them in intricate patterns. However, another theory holds that arabesques were not necessarily rooted in any prohibition on the representation of the human figure. The Qur'an does not prohibit such representation, and paintings and sculptures in early Islamic societies were by no means unknown. Rather, the idea of arabesques arose from geometry. The Arabs took from the Greeks' idea that proportion was the basis of beauty and science as well.

Key Terms

Mohammed → Islam → Mecca → unification of Arab society → Arabic conquests → the Caliphate → the faith of Islam → Allah → the culture of Islam → Muslim scholarship → philosophy → medicine → the system of numeration → Muslim architecture

Exercises

❶ Vocabulary Building

✓ Fill in each blank with a synonym to the word in the brackets.

1) The Arabs brought a(n) _____ (militant) faith and succeeded in building a(n) _____ (brilliant) and _____ (distinctive) culture—both known by the name of Islam which had a(n) _____ (profound) effect on the development of the West. Its relation with the West was _____ (intriguing) and _____ (confusing), sometimes friendly, sometimes _____ (antagonistic), and remains so till today.

2) Islam _____ (concedes) that God created the world and _____ (ornamented) it, and gave man the ability to produce devices of embellishment. There is more to this idea

of ornament, in fact. Since God created the world and that is perfect, therefore, there is little _____ (scope) for man to truly create—all he can do is to adorn what God has _____ (produced).

3) One theory holds that the Muslims were _____ (forbidden) by their religion to reproduce man and animals in art forms, so they created other designs to decorate their buildings, for instances, the _____ (exquisite) patterns of flowers and leaves, beautiful calligraphy, and arabesques by combining geometric figures and arranging them in _____ (intricate) patterns.

❷ Translation

❧ Translate the following sentences into Chinese.

1) His political and military skills enabled him to put together a reliable military force, with which he returned to Mecca in 630, conquering the city and converting the townspeople to the new faith. From Mecca, Mohammed's ideas spread quickly across the Arabian Peninsula and within a relatively short time, had resulted in both the religious and the political unification of the Arab society.

2) Islam emphasizes the need to obey the will of Allah. This means following a basic ethical code consisting of the Five Pillars of Islam: belief in Allah and Mohammed as his Prophet; standard prayer five times a day and public prayer on Friday at midday to worship Allah; observance of the holy month of Ramadan (the ninth month on the Muslim calendar) by fasting from dawn to sunset; making a pilgrimage to Mecca in one's lifetime, if possible; and giving alms to the poor and the unfortunate. The faithful who observed the law were guaranteed a place in an eternal paradise.

3) What characterized the Arabs after their conquest was their ability to accommodate and adjust to different cultures. Tolerant of those they conquered, the Arabs preserved and assimilated the great Greco-Roman civilization into their own. Eventually, it was the Muslim world that introduced elements of the Greco-Roman civilization that had been largely forgotten for hundreds of years to medieval Europe.

❸ Questions

❧ Answer the following questions.

1) According to Mohammed, how does a man attain salvation?

2) What is the basic message of Islam?

3) What are the Five Pillars of Islam?

4) What does Europe owe to the Muslim world in terms of Greco-Roman civilization?

5) Why do we have a false impression that the system of numeration is Arabic in origin?

6) What are the theories on the idea of arabesques in Arabic architecture?

4 Topics for Discussion

❧ Below are three topics related to this chapter. Read them and finish the discussion.

1) Make a comparative study between Islam and Christianity, focusing on their differences as well as similarities.

2) How did the Arabs assimilate other cultures into their own?

3) Based on your reading and research, give an account of the functions of religion.

5 Writing

❧ Read the following direction and finish the writing.

The Arabian proverb says, "A fig tree, looking on a fig tree, becometh fruitful." There is also a saying, "Diligence, above all, is the mother of good luck." Based on what you have learned and experienced in your life, write a short essay with the title of "Diligence and Good Luck," incorporating the two sayings into your essay.

Chapter 8

Remaking of Europe

For more than five hundred years after the fall of Rome, Germanic and Slavic barbarian peoples, as well as nomads from Asia, continually raided, conquered, and settled in the civilized lands that had once belonged to the empire. As with earlier invasions, however, what enabled these less advanced peoples to make such inroads was the fact that they were already growing in organization and skills as a result of contacts with civilization, and they ended by adopting the way of life of the civilized people they attacked. By 1000, civilization had spread throughout Europe, and the three thousand-year-old European barbarian way of life had come to an end. As a result, the renewed European civilization was one of many vigorous ethnic cultures and many powerful competing states.

1. The World of the Carolingians

By the 8th century when Islam was spreading across Africa and Asia, the kingdom of the Franks was falling apart as the Merovingian dynasty was losing its control of the Frankish lands. It was the Carolingians who rebuilt the Frankish kingdom. The family name came from the name of its most famous member, Charles the Great, or Charlemagne (*Carolus* being the Latin for Charles). The Carolingians began the rise of western Europe to become the heartland of Western civilization. Though their power melted away in its turn, their achievements outlasted.

1.1 The Rise of the Carolingian Dynasty

Late in the 7th century, the Carolingian family became the wealthiest and most powerful of all nobles. Charles Martel, the mayor of the palace of Austrasia, became the virtual ruler of these territories. When Charles Martel died in 741, his son, Pepin, deposed the Merovingians and assumed the kingship of the Frankish state for himself and his family. The deposition was approved by the Pope and Pepin was shortly crowned king and anointed by a representative of the Pope. This was the first time in the history of the Frankish kingdom that a king inaugurated his reign with a solemn religious ceremony. It was not long before clerical coronation and anointing became the normal ceremony for inaugurating kings throughout Europe.

Later, it was Pepin's turn to do the Pope a favor. The Lombard kings of northern Italy were pushing southward, depriving the popes of their power in Rome and in nearby territories. The Pope, Stephen Ⅱ, turned to Pepin for protection. Two years later, Pepin fulfilled his obligation by crossing the Alps, defeating the Lombards, and transferring a strip of territory across central Italy to the governing authority of the Pope. Thus, by the so-called Donation of Pepin, the States of the Church came into being as a sovereign political entity. The Donation of Pepin had an immediate result: It sealed the alliance between the Frankish state and the papacy, the two strongest forces in the West. The outcome of this alliance was the empire of Charles the Great.

1.2   Charlemagne's Empire

Charles, Pepin's son and Charles Martel's grandson, was a dynamic and powerful ruler known in history as Charles the Great or Charlemagne (his French name that first appeared more than a century later). He was a fierce warrior, a resolute statesman as well as a wise patron of learning. He greatly expanded the territory of the Carolingian Empire.

Charlemagne was engaged in almost constant wars throughout his reign. He led his army into Italy in 774 at the Pope's request and broke the Lombard power. His hardest campaigns were against the Saxons to the northeast of the Frankish kingdom. Not until 804, after 18 campaigns, was Saxony finally pacified and added to the Carolingian domain as well as the Christianity. He marched farther south and attacked the nomadic nation of the Avars, who had invaded central and eastern Europe in the 6th century. The Avars disappeared from history after their utter devastation by Charlemagne. Now at its height, Charlemagne's empire covered much of western and central Europe. Not until the time of Napoleon in the 19th century would an empire of this size be seen again in Europe.

On Christmas Day of 800, while Charlemagne was attending Mass in Saint Peter's Basilica in Rome, Pope Leo placed a crown on Charlemagne's head and proclaimed him "emperor of the Romans." The imperial coronation has been much debated by historians about its significance. On the one hand, the Pope had his own reasons. First, he needed a strong protector in Italy. Second, by taking the initiative in 800, the Pope succeeded in defining the relationship between the restored empire and the Church. As a donor, the Pope put the emperor under obligation to the papacy. Finally, the action also gave force to the later claim that the papacy had a right to withdraw what it had given, as it would do in the Investiture Struggle for the supremacy over the State. On the other hand, Charlemagne could perceive the usefulness of the imperial title; after all, he was now on an equal level with the Byzantine emperor, a status he did not reject.

In any case, Charlemagne's coronation was a truly historic event. It was not just a restoration of the Roman Empire; more importantly, it symbolized the fusion of Roman, Christian, and Germanic elements. It was this fusion that constituted the foundation of European civilization.

2. The Rise of Western Europe

After Charlemagne died, the promise of order and stability his rule had featured faded in the renewed civil wars and invasions. From this disintegration of the empire, the primary contours of western Europe began to take shape.

2.1　The Dissolution of Charlemagne's Empire

When Charlemagne died, he was succeeded by his only son, Louis the Pious. Though a good man, Louis was unable to exercise a strong rule over his lands, nor over his warring sons. In 843 after his death, the three sons arrived at a settlement by the Treaty of Verdun. According to the Treaty, Lothar was confirmed as emperor and had the middle portion of the former empire which included Italy and the territory in the north of the Alps; Louis received the portion of the former empire east of the Rhine, which would become Germany; Charles, the youngest son, inherited the western part, which would become France.

The Treaty did not prevent the three sons from fighting. Within a short time, the middle kingdom disappeared altogether, and most of its territory was taken over by the ruler of the eastern portion. The disintegration of Charlemagne's empire was speeded up by ferocious attacks from outside, mainly those of the Muslims from the Mediterranean, the Magyars on the eastern frontier, and the Vikings from the north.

With expansion to North Africa, Spain, and southern Gaul, the Arabs began a new series of attacks in the Mediterranean in the 9th century. They raided the southern coasts of Europe, especially Italy, and established themselves in Sicily and Sardinia. They even captured Rome and pillaged the surrounding countryside in 846. On the eastern frontier, there appeared another nation of Asiatic nomads, the Magyars or Hungarians. The Magyars were a people from western Asia, and by the end of the 9th century, they had moved west into eastern and central Europe. They established themselves on the plains of Hungary and from there made raids into western Europe. The Magyars were finally crushed at the Battle of Lechfeld in Germany in 955. At the end of the 10th century, they were converted to Christianity and settled down to establish the kingdom of Hungary.

Perhaps the strongest blow against Europe came from the Norsemen or Vikings of Scandinavia. The Norsemen were the northernmost branch of the Germanic peoples. Known as the most valorous warriors and superb shipbuilders and sailors, the Vikings began their adventures along the coastline of western Europe. Norwegian Vikings moved into Ireland and western England; the Danes attacked eastern England, Frisia, the Rhineland, and western Frankish lands. By 878, the Danes occupied an area known as the Danelaw in northeastern England. Agreeing to accept Christianity, the Danes were eventually assimilated into a larger Anglo-Saxon kingdom. One band of the Frankish lands at the mouth of the Seine River was given to the Vikings, which came to be known as Normandy. Swedish Vikings dominated the Baltic Sea and progressed into the Slavic areas to the east. By the 10th century, the Viking expansion was drawing to a close. Like the Magyars, the Vikings were also assimilated into European civilization. Once again, Christianity proved a decisive civilizing force in Europe.

2.2   The Western Franks, the Eastern Franks, and England in the 10th Century

In the Western Frankish Kingdom, now coming to be known by the modern name of France, by the 9th and 10th century, the Carolingian rulers could not exert strong control over the great lords. Hugh Capet, Count of Paris, was elected as the new king in 987. Though wielding littler power outside his own area and considered as equal by other nobles, he succeeded in making his kingship hereditary.

The same thing happened to the Eastern Frankish Kingdom. When the last Carolingian king died in 911, the powerful dukes elected one of their own members, Conrad of Franconia, to serve as the king of Germany. Later, in order to ward off the attacks from the Magyars, the great lords elected the most powerful family, the dukes of Saxony, to fill the office of king. The best known of the Saxon family was Otto Ⅰ (936–973), who defeated the Magyars at the Battle of Lechfeld in 955 and encouraged an ongoing program of Christianization of both the Slavic and Scandinavian peoples. Otto also intervened in Italian politics and for his efforts, he was crowned emperor of the Romans by Pope John ⅩⅡ in Rome in 962. The empire he founded came to be known as the Holy Roman Empire, though his holdings included only Germany and the northern and central portions of Italy. The rulers of Holy Roman Empire could never enforce the principle of hereditary succession, but they remained powerful down to the Late Middle Ages. The Holy Roman Empire was not finally abolished until 1806.

In 9th-century England, the long struggle of the Anglo-Saxon kingdoms against the Vikings' invasions ultimately produced a unified kingdom. King Alfred the Great of the southern kingdom of Wessex defeated a Danish army in 879 and made peace with the Danes. Even though he had to concede the Danelaw to the invaders, his successors in the 10th century were able to recover the lost territory and build a united English state for the first time. Alfred also believed in the power of education. He invited scholars to his court and encouraged the translation of the works of such Church Fathers as Augustine and Gregory the Great from Latin into Anglo-Saxon (Old English), the vernacular, or the language spoken by the people.

3. Central and Eastern Europe of the Slavs

The Slavs were originally a single people in central Europe who were divided into three major groups: the western, southern, and eastern Slavs.

In the east region of the Germanic kingdom, the western Slavs founded the Polish and Bohemian kingdoms. The Germans assumed responsibility for converting these Slavic peoples. By the end of the 10th century, the Poles, the Czechs, and the Hungarians all accepted Catholic or Western Christianity and became closely tied to the Roman Catholic Church.

The southern Slavic peoples were converted to the Eastern Orthodox Christianity of the Byzantine Empire due to the efforts of two Byzantine missionary brothers, Cyril and Methodius. So eager were the Byzantines to make their message acceptable that they even allowed the Slavs to worship in their own language, rather in Greek, as opposed to the Latin Church, which insisted that no other language than Latin be used in public worship. The brothers even adapted the Greek alphabet to the sounds of the Slav language and thus created a Slavonic (Cyrillic) alphabet, and translated the Bible into Slavonic. The Bulgars were originally an Asiatic people who conquered much of the Balkan Peninsula. They were also assimilated into the native southern Slavs. By the 9th century, they formed a largely Slavic Bulgarian kingdom and embraced the Eastern Orthodoxy.

The eastern Slavic peoples, from whom the modern Russians, White Russians, and Ukrainians are descended, had settled in the territory of present-day Ukraine and European Russia. There, beginning in the late 8th century, they began to contend with Viking invaders. It turned out that the Swedish Vikings eventually dominated the native peoples. The conquerors took up residence in Kiev and created the Russia state, a union of eastern Slavic territories known as the principality of Kiev. In 988, Prince Vladimir of Kiev made a bargain with Byzantium: In return for the marriage to the emperor's sister, he was baptized into the Greek Orthodox Church. Thus, Russia became the easternmost of the states that shared the religious and cultural heritage of Byzantium.

Key Terms

Charles Martel → Donation of Pepin → Charlemagne → imperial coronation → dissolution of Charlemagne's empire → the Treaty of Verdun → attacks from the Arabs, Magyars, and Norsemen → Huge Capet → Otto Ⅰ → Holy Roman Empire → the central and eastern Europe of the Slavs

Exercises

1 Vocabulary Building

❧ Fill in each blank with a synonym to the word in the brackets.

1) In 741, Pepin _____ (deposed) the Merovingians and _____ (assumed) the kingship of the Frankish state for himself and his family. The deposition was approved by the Pope and Pepin was shortly crowned king and _____ (anointed) by a representative of the Pope. This was the first time in the history of the Frankish kingdom that a king _____ (inaugurated) his reign with a solemn religious ceremony.

2) With _____ (expansion) to North Africa, Spain, and southern Gaul, the Arabs began a new series of attacks in the Mediterranean in the 9th century. They _____ (raided) the southern coasts of Europe, especially Italy, and established themselves in Sicily and Sardinia. They even captured Rome and _____ (pillaged) the surrounding countryside in 846.

3) Perhaps the strongest _____ (blow) against Europe came from the Norsemen or Vikings of Scandinavia. The Norsemen were the northernmost branch of the Germanic peoples. Known as the most _____ (valorous) warriors and _____ (superb) shipbuilders and sailors, the Vikings began their adventures along the coastline of western Europe.

2 Translation

❧ Translate the following sentences into Chinese.

1) Later, it was Pepin's turn to do the Pope a favor. The Lombard kings of northern Italy were pushing southward, depriving the popes of their power in Rome and in nearby territories. The Pope, Stephen Ⅱ, turned to Pepin for protection. Two years later, Pepin

fulfilled his obligation by crossing the Alps, defeating the Lombards, and transferring a strip of territory across central Italy to the governing authority of the Pope.

2) Charlemagne marched farther south and attacked the nomadic nation of the Avars, who had invaded central and eastern Europe in the 6th century. The Avars disappeared from history after their utter devastation by Charlemagne. Now at its height, Charlemagne's empire covered much of western and central Europe. Not until the time of Napoleon in the 19th century would an empire of this size be seen again in Europe.

3) So eager were the Byzantines to make their message acceptable that they even allowed the Slavs to worship in their own language, rather in Greek, as opposed to the Latin Church, which insisted that no other language than Latin be used in public worship.

Questions

Answer the following questions.

1) When did western Europe become the heartland of Western civilization?

2) What is the significance of Charlemagne's coronation as emperor?

3) What impact did the Vikings have on the history and culture of medieval Europe?

4) List the achievements of King Alfred the Great.

Topics for Discussion

Below are two topics related to this chapter. Read them and finish the discussion.

1) In this chapter, there are at least two cases in which translation plays an important role in converting the local people to a new religion. Based on your reading and research, give an account of the functions of translation.

2) As the beginning in *Three Kingdoms* goes, division and unification take turns through history ("天下大势，分久必合，合久必分"). Work in groups and have a discussion on your understanding of the division and unification through the history of Europe.

Writing

Read the following direction and finish the writing.

As we learn from the end of this chapter, in return for the marriage to the sister of the emperor of Byzantium, Prince Vladimir of Kiev was baptized into the Greek Orthodox Church, enabling Russia to share the religious and cultural heritage of Byzantium. Based on your knowledge and study, write a short essay with the title of "Marriage and Politics."

Chapter 9

Feudal Europe

Since the beginning of the 10th century, the Carolingian Empire was only an empty title. As a result of internal anarchy and invasions from the Vikings, Hungarians, and Muslims, its central authority had disappeared. Politically, the 10th century saw the reconstruction of Europe into small kingdoms, duchies, and counties organized in accordance with feudal principles. Europe entered into a stage of relative stability and economic growth. In order to understand how this feudal Europe came into being, we must investigate how feudalism became the social and political basis of Europe and how these feudal states employed feudal institutions in their governments until the middle of the 12th century.

1. Feudalism

The disintegration of the Carolingian Empire and constant invasions led to a new type of social and political organization. When governments ceased to be able to defend their subjects, it became important to find some powerful lords who could offer protection in exchange for service. The contract sworn between a lord and his subordinate is the basis of this organization that later generations of historians called "feudalism." Feudalism came into being in northern France during the 10th century and spread outward partly through campaigns of conquest by the French and partly by imitation. By the 12th century, not only France but also England, the Holy Roman Empire, Spain, Sicily, and even Byzantium were governed according to feudal principles.

1.1 Origin and Definition of Feudalism

It is widely believed that feudalism has two origins: Germanic *comitatus* and late Roman *precaria*. By tradition of the Germanic tribes, the celebrated chief and his followers entered into a mutually honorable relationship whereby the chief promised glory and plunder and the followers pledged loyalty and service unto death.

Another origin was a late Roman institution called *precaria*, where a grantee received a land for a specific amount of time without any change of ownership. However, such land could be taken back at any time. Eventually, under the Franks, the tenure was extended to a term of years or for life in return for service. Sometimes the granted land was called *benefice* because it had been obtained as a boon from the grantor. It was under the Carolingians that the honorable relation of the German *comitatus* was fused with *benefice* to form real feudalism.

1.2 Vassalage and Fief-Holding

The essence of real feudalism was the combination of vassalage and fief-holding (see Figure 9-1). A noble man entered into a mutually honorable relation with another noble man who granted him a fief primarily in return for military service. An individual who served a lord in a military capacity was known as a vassal, and the land or some other type of property granted to a vassal in return for military service came to be known as a fief.

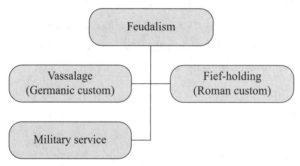

Figure 9-1　Two components of feudalism: vassalage and fief-holding

In the 8th century, when larger breeds of horses and especially the stirrup from Asia were introduced, a military change began to occur. Light cavalry gave way to heavy cavalry. But heavy cavalrymen needed elaborate coats of armor and specially bred horses. Of course, horses, armors, and weapons were expensive to purchase and maintain, and learning to wield these instruments skillfully from horseback took much time and practice. It happened to be that wealth at that time existed mainly in the form of land. Consequently, lords who wanted men to fight for them had to grant each vassal a piece of land that provided the support for the vassal and his family. In return for the land, the vassal provided his lord with military service.

When subinfeudation developed, fief-holding became complicated. The vassals of a king might also have sub-vassals who would owe them military service in return for a grant of land from their estates. Those sub-vassals, in turn, might likewise have vassals, who at such a level would be simple knights. However, the hierarchy was theoretical in that more often than not the king at the top, for instance the Capetian kings, possessed little real power over the great lords who held fiefs throughout France. One thing we have to bear in mind is that the lord-vassal relationship at all levels always constituted an honorable relationship between free men and did not imply any sense of servitude.

1.3   Principles of Feudal Tenure

The fundamental component of feudalism was vassalage. The ceremony through which a man became a vassal was called homage. The men went and knelt before the lord, placed his hands between the lord's, and became his men, swearing fealty and pledging to fight for and protect him. The lord in turn accepted the homage and fealty, raised the vassal to his feet, and kissed him.

When a lord granted his vassal a fief, it was also done through a ceremony called investiture. The lord customarily handed the vassal a stick, a knife, or a piece of turf. The vassal received possession, but not ownership of the fief. Upon his death, his son could receive possession of the fief after becoming the lord's vassal and receiving investiture.

In order to ensure that a fief would not be fragmentized after the death of the father, thus weakening the value of the military and political services, a rule of passing it intact to the eldest son was developed. This was called primogeniture and it proved to be most efficient.

The principal service entailed by the fief was military. Besides, the vassal had other services to offer. Feudal aids were mainly of a pecuniary nature. Whenever a lord had his eldest son knighted, or his eldest daughter married, it was customary for the lord to collect standard contributions from his vassals. If the lord was captured in battle, he had the right to call upon his vassals to ransom him. The vassal was also expected to extend hospitality to his lord when the latter visited him. Another obligation was suit to court. The lord could summon his vassals to court for a variety of reasons.

1.4   Significance of Feudalism

It is true that the rise of feudal system coincided with the break-up of central authority in the Carolingian Empire, but can it be justified to claim that feudalism was a destructive political force? Based on what we learned about feudal principles and institutions, and the role they played in the leading European states between the 10th and 12th centuries (see the next section), it is clear that in order to accomplish what was necessary in military and political services, feudalism was the only solution for a society counting on the land. Feudalism was a most effective system when it comes to small states where the principles of feudal tenure could operate and be enforced. For governing small states and for providing the essential military and political services, the feudal system proved to be an excellent method. Therefore, feudalism was a constructive, not a destructive political force. The small states built upon it became strong and permanent; from them was to come the future political progress of western Europe.

2. Growth of Feudal States

Any feudal monarch might claim to be the supreme ruler, but in fact his actual power was limited by the extent of his hereditary family territories within the kingdom, or royal domain. It was only in these territories that he was entitled to do justice, levy taxes, recruit knights, and exercise government authority. Outside the royal domain, it was the great lords who held these powers. However, in the High Middle Ages, kings did find ways to strengthen their royal power. The revival of commerce, the growth of cities, and the emergence of a money economy eventually enabled monarchs to hire soldiers and officials and to rely less on their vassals. The most important feudal states developed at this time were England, France, and Germany.

2.1   England: Norman Conquest, Magna Carta, and Parliament

By the 10th century, England had repulsed the Danes and established a unified Anglo-Saxon kingdom. At the beginning of the 11th century, Anglo-Saxon England had fallen subject to Scandinavian control after a successful invasion by the Danes in 1016. Danish King Canute (1016–1035) ruled the country till 1042, when the Anglo-Saxon line of kings was restored in the person of Edward the Confessor (1042–1066). After Edward's death, William, duke of Normandy, by virtue of certain relations with the deceased king, laid claim to the English throne. In 1066, in a remarkable expedition, William the Conqueror defeated the Anglo-Saxon forces and was crowned king of England at Christmas, and began the Norman government in the history of England. The outstanding achievement of William the Conqueror (1066–1087) was to subdue England and introduce strong central authority. This was much indebted to feudalism which was introduced into England by William, where its institutions provided the means of establishing an especially strong government. The Norman Conquest of England introduced the legal principle that all land was held from the king, to whom feudal services were due. In 1086, by the Oath of Salisbury Plain, William required all sub-vassals to swear loyalty to him as their king or liege lord. Henceforth, all sub-vassals vowed their primary loyalty to the king rather than to their immediate lords. A strong, centralized monarchy was created. Gradually, a process of fusion between the Normans and the Anglo-Saxons created a new England. Although the Norman ruling class spoke French, the intermarriage of the Norman-French with the Anglo-Saxon nobility gradually merged Anglo-Saxon and French into a new English language.

During the reign of King John (1199–1216), a rebellion broke out on the part of many leading barons who resented the ongoing growth of king's power. In 1215, King John was forced to assent Magna Carta, the "Great Charter." Much of Magna Carta was aimed at limiting government practices that affected the relations between the king and his vassals on the one hand, and between the king and the Church on the other. What the barons wanted from the king was to ensure that it operated within the traditional feudal framework of mutual rights and responsibilities between overlords and vassals. The king promised that in the future, should he need to collect money from his vassals, he would do so only with the consent of a council composed of the vassals themselves. He also promised that he would not deprive any freeman of life, liberty, property, or protection of the law. In this way, out of the collision between the monarch and the traditions of feudalism, England took its first steps toward a constitutional and parliamentary government.

Magna Carta

John, by the Grace of God, king of England, lord of Ireland, duke of Normandy and Aquitaine, count of Anjou, to the archbishops, bishops, abbots, earls, barons, justiciars, foresters, sheriffs, reeves, servants, and all bailiffs and his faithful people greeting.

1. In the first place we have granted to God, and by this our present charter confirmed, for us and our heirs forever, that the English church shall be free, and shall hold its rights entire and its liberties uninjured... We have granted moreover to all free men of our kingdom for us and our heirs forever all the liberties written below, to be had and holden by themselves and their heirs from us and our heirs.

...

12. No scutage or aid shall be imposed in our kingdom except by the common council of our kingdom, except for the ransoming of our body, for the making of our oldest son a knight, and for once marrying our oldest daughter, and for these purposes it shall be only a reasonable aid...

13. And the city of London shall have all its ancient liberties and free customs, as well by land as by water. Moreover, we will and grant that all other cities and boroughs and villages and ports shall have all their liberties and free customs.

It was in the reign of Edward Ⅰ (1272–1307) that the role of the English Parliament, an institution of great importance in the development of representative government, began to be defined. The word "parliament" was originally applied to meetings of the king's Great Council in which greater barons and chief prelates of the Church met with the king's judges and principal advisers to deal with judicial affairs. But in need of money in 1295, Edward Ⅰ invited two knights from every county and two residents (known as burgesses) from each city and town to meet with the Great Council to pass new taxes. This was the first Parliament.

Eventually, Parliament evolved into two chambers: the House of Lords composed of great barons and clerics of the country, and the House of Commons composed of representatives of the shires and certain towns.

2.2　France: Louis Ⅵ, Philip Ⅱ, and Philip Ⅳ

Between 987 and 1108, the history of the royal domain of the Capetian dynasty was one of weakness and steady retreat before such encroaching vassals as the counties of Champagne, Anjou, and Flanders, as well as the duchy of Normandy. However, it was the reign of Louis Ⅵ the Fat (1108–1137) that inaugurated two centuries of constant increase in royal power and laid the foundation for the great state of France. Aided by his chief adviser and minister Suger, abbot of the monastery of Saint Denis, Louis waged an offensive against political anarchy. All vassals guilty of misdemeanours were summoned to court to answer the charges; if they did not heed the summons, Louis waged war on them and destroyed their castles.

It was in the duel with the English kings that a powerful French monarchy was forged. Ever since Duke William of Normandy had conquered England, his descendants had been both fully independent rulers of England yet also vassals of the king of France. In the 12th century, by marriage and inheritance, the English kings added to Normandy a whole series of other fiefs that gave them control of the entire western half of France. Although being vassals, they were overwhelming challengers against their French overlords. Philip Ⅱ played off the jealousy of other French barons against England, and even encouraged the sons of his English rival, Henry Ⅱ, in rebellions against their own father. In 1204, by declaring King John of England a rebellious vassal in his capacity as duke of Normandy, Philip Ⅱ confiscated Normandy together with other French possessions of the English kings.

Philip Ⅳ (1268–1314) was particularly effective in strengthening the French monarchy. One of his remarkable achievements was the introduction of the Estates-General. After being involved in a struggle with the Pope, Philip Ⅳ summoned representatives of the Church, nobility, and towns to meet with him in 1302, thereby inaugurating the Estates-General, the first French parliament. By the end of the 13th century, France was the largest, wealthiest, and best-governed monarchical state in Europe.

2.3　Germany: The Weakening of Monarchy

In the same centuries when the kings of France became truly powerful monarchs, Germany moved in exactly the opposite direction because of the emperors' involvement in grandiose adventures far in Italy. Ever since Otto the Great, his Italy policy proved to be the bane of German politics. His two successors ignored their great inheritance in Germany and frittered away their time in Italy. Otto Ⅱ died while leading an expedition to enforce his claim to southern Italy. Otto Ⅲ never knew Germany because he was reared in Italy under the direction of his Greek mother and educated in the Byzantine tradition. It was the height of folly for them to imitate Charlemagne. They forfeited the opportunity to forge a strong central government and let the duchies remain strong and free of regnal authority; here began the pattern of German particularism and decentralization that kept Germany in chaos until its unification by Bismarck in the 19th century.

With the death of Henry Ⅱ in 1024 came the end of the rule of Saxon kings. Conrad, duke of Franconia, was chosen as king, thus initiating the Franconian rule of Germany. Under his son Henry Ⅲ (1039–1056), Franconian power reached its apogee. By consolidating his father's gains, extending German influence into Hungary, and following the wise policy of maintaining peace while looking to the reform of local and central governments, Henry Ⅲ did remarkably well in maintaining his authority in Germany and Italy. One thing particular about his achievements was that he governed through bishops. By so doing, he prevented the noble family from entering the key offices and making them heritable possessions.

It was due in large part to Henry Ⅲ that the Church was undergoing a striking spiritual revival. Unfortunately, such happy relation between the Church and the State did not last long. Henry Ⅲ wielded ultimate authority in appointing and dismissing popes just as he did to bishops and abbots. An invigorated Church led by militant popes and bishops could not endure this subservience. The result was the Investiture Struggle which plagued the reign of his son Henry Ⅳ.

Key Terms

feudalism → Germanic *comitatus* → Roman *precaria* → vassalage → fief → subinfeudation → feudal Tenure → growth of feudal states → Norman conquest → William the Conqueror → Magna Carta → Louis Ⅵ, Philip Ⅱ, Philip Ⅳ → duel between France and England → weakening Germany → Henry Ⅲ

Exercises

1 Vocabulary Building

✎ Fill in each blank with a synonym to the word in the brackets.

1) By tradition of the Germanic tribes, the _____ (celebrated) chief and his followers

entered into a(n) _____ (mutually) honorable relationship whereby the chief promised glory and _____ (plunder) and the followers promised loyalty and service unto death.

2) In order to _____ (ensure) that a fief would not be _____ (fragmentized) after the death of the father, thus _____ (weakening) the value of the military and political services, a rule of passing it _____ (intact) to the eldest son was developed. This was called _____ (primogeniture) and it proved to be most efficient.

3) In the same centuries when the kings of France became truly powerful _____ (monarchs), Germany moved in exactly the opposite direction because of the emperors' involvement in _____ (grandiose) adventures far in Italy. Ever since Otto the Great, his Italy policy proved to be the _____ (bane) of German politics. His two successors ignored their great inheritance in Germany and _____ (frittered) away their time in Italy.

4) It was the height of _____ (folly) for them to _____ (imitate) Charlemagne. They _____ (forfeited) the opportunity to _____ (forge) a strong central government and let the duchies remain strong and free of _____ (regnal) authority; here began the pattern of German particularism and _____ (decentralization) that kept Germany in chaos until its unification by Bismark in the 19th century.

❷ Translation

❧ Translate the following sentences into Chinese.

1) Since the beginning of the 10th century, the Carolingian Empire was only an empty title. As a result of internal anarchy and invasions from the Vikings, Hungarians, and Muslims, central authority had disappeared. Politically, the 10th century saw the reconstruction of Europe into small kingdoms, duchies, and counties organized in accordance with feudal principles. Europe entered into a stage of relative stability and economic growth.

2) For governing small states and for providing the essential military and political services, the feudal system proved to be an excellent method. Therefore, feudalism was a constructive, not a destructive political force. The small states built upon it became strong and permanent; from them was to come the future political progress of western Europe.

3) In the same centuries when the kings of France became truly powerful monarchs, Germany moved in exactly the opposite direction because of the emperors' involvement in grandiose adventures far in Italy. Ever since Otto the Great, his Italy policy proved to be the bane of German politics. His two successors ignored their great inheritance in Germany and frittered away their time in Italy.

4) Unfortunately, such happy relation between the Church and the State did not last long. Henry Ⅲ wielded ultimate authority in appointing and dismissing popes just as he did to bishops and abbots. An invigorated Church led by militant popes and bishops could not endure this subservience. The result was the Investiture Struggle which plagued the reign of his son Henry Ⅳ.

❸ Questions

❧ Answer the following questions.

1) What is feudalism? What are the principles for feudal tenure?

2) What did William the Conqueror in England and Louis Ⅵ in France do to strengthen the royal power?

3) How did Philip Ⅱ maneuver to take back French possessions of the English kings?

4) Why did Germany fail to become a truly powerful monarch?

❹ Topics for Discussion

❧ Below are two topics related to this chapter. Read them and finish the discussion.

1) How did England take its first steps toward a constitutional and parliamentary government?

2) You may find such expressions as "take French leave" which show that the British and the French are somewhat unpleasant in each other's eyes. Based on your reading and research, explain where the dislike or hostility comes from.

❺ Writing

❧ Read the following direction and finish the writing.

As this chapter mentions, Magna Carta plays an important role in the formation of British constitutional and parliamentary government. You may also know something about such significant papers as Declaration of Independence, Emancipation Proclamation, and Bill of Rights. Try to do a study on one of the momentous papers, and write a short essay with the title of "My Understanding of ×××."

Chapter 10

The Medieval Church

Never before had the Church been so dominant in the affairs of Westerners, nor has it been so since. It has reasons. First of all, in the Early Middle Ages, the Catholic Church had played a leading role in converting and civilizing first the Germanic invaders and later the Vikings and the Magyars. Second, spiritually, because the central role of the Church was to guide souls to everlasting salvation, the Church was regarded as the primary institution in society. In addition to providing spiritual guidance, the medieval Church served society in other numerous ways. Bishops and archbishops functioned as vassals of kings and emperors. The regular clergy preserved and copied manuscripts and provided elementary schooling for youths, thus keeping literacy and learning alive. At the same time, they preserved the useful arts of weaving, pottery-making, and metalworking in their workshops, and developed more efficient tools and techniques of farming in these fields. It is no exaggeration to say the Church was the primary institution in society.

1. Christian Doctrine

By the 5th century, the Church had developed an efficient local and central organization that recognized the authority of one supreme ecclesiastic—the Pope in Rome. In addition, the Church had vigorously disputed over its doctrine and hammered out a sacred tradition which became official throughout the West.

The doctrine rested essentially upon the Christian Bible. At first, there were only the Old and New Testaments, but other writings came to be added to the sacred law. All these sacred writings were called canons (laws). The Old Testament mainly consisted of a Greek translation of the old Hebrew books—Septuagint. The New Testament recorded the custom and doctrine developed in the era after Christ and consisted of the Four Gospels, Paul's Epistles, the Epistles of the other apostles, the Acts of the Apostles, and the Apocalypse, and other minor writings. This authoritative law governed all orthodox Christians of the West.

A group of beliefs developed, which provided the basis of Christian worship and helped to express the fundamental doctrine that Christ had founded the earthly Church to provide a way of salvation for all men. Salvation rested upon the holy sacraments. There was a general theory of the sacraments. God had created the sacraments as a means of providing divine aid for sinful men and women to enable them to be saved. Besides, God had instituted his priests as the principal administrators of these rites. Seven Sacraments were acknowledged, including Baptism, Confirmation, Marriage, Penance, Eucharist, Ordination, and Extreme Unction. It was believed that only a selected group of men, the clergy, had the rights to administer these sacraments, because they, by virtue of the Sacrament of Ordination, had attained this elevated status. According to the theory of Apostolic succession, Christ had laid His hands upon the apostles and conferred upon them divine authority to continue His work of salvation. The apostles in turn commissioned others, and they others, so the succession continued.

However, within the clergy, there was a difference in authority. Only a bishop received all the Apostolic power, and among the bishops of Antioch, Alexandria, and Rome, only the bishop in Rome held a superior rank over others, because it was in Rome that Peter and Paul had suffered martyrdom and that Peter had been the first bishop of the Church. This Petrine theory which supported the supremacy of the bishop of Rome as Pope was based on the Gospel of Matthew (16: 18–19). According to Matthew, Christ had told Peter: "Thou art Peter; and upon this rock I will build my church...And I will give unto thee the keys of the kingdom of heaven."

2. Gregory the Great

Although Western Christians came to accept the bishop of Rome as head of the Church, there was no unanimity on the extent of the power the Pope possessed. It was by Gregory the Great that the centralization of the Church's organization, its missionary zeal, and the phenomenal growth of monasticism reached the climax.

Possessed of the best training and endowed with extraordinary common sense and wisdom, Gregory made Petrine supremacy a reality and transformed the papacy into a world power. Through his efforts, the papacy attained a universal authority that went beyond all political boundaries and gave the West a bond of union.

The greatest accomplishment of Gregory was the conversion of the Anglo-Saxons. In the last quarter of the 6th century, the holy St. Columba of Irish Christianity began to convert the Celts, the Picts, and the Anglo-Saxons. Desiring to win the Anglo-Saxons to the Roman brand of faith, Gregory launched a missionary project and sent preachers to Britain. In 597, the Benedictine monk Augustine arrived at Canterbury, the capital of Kent. The King and his people were soon converted, and from Kent the faith was spread to the other Anglo-Saxon kingdoms. As the Roman faith spread northward in Britain, it had to compete with Irish missionaries, and it was doubtful for some time which brand of Christianity would triumph. A council was held in 664 to determine which type of Christianity should be accepted. The council decided that Britain should be organized in the orthodox fashion under papal government. The conversion was not limited to the Anglo-Saxons, however. With the support of the papacy and the Carolingian House, St. Boniface carried the Christian faith into eastern Germany.

3. Early Church Fathers

A number of intellectuals in the early Church profoundly influenced the development of Christian thought in the West. Among them, the most renowned were St. Ambrose (340–397), St. Jerome (347–420), and St. Augustine (354–430), known as the great trio of Church Fathers.

Ambrose, as governor and bishop of Milan, never produced any great scholarly works but concentrated his writing on the practical side of religion. He was best known for his zeal in converting the pagans and for his eloquent and passionate sermons. A strong defender of spiritual supremacy over temporal affairs, he even forced the emperor Theodosius to beg forgiveness for permitting the cruel massacre of the people in Thessalonica in 390.

Unlike Ambrose, Jerome was a scholar. Throughout his life, he was engaged in scholarly work and his great achievement was a Latin translation of the Bible, known as the Vulgate. Before him, there had been various Latin translations of the Bible, but with a lot of errors. The Pope commissioned Jerome to do a new one. For the New Testament, he employed the best Greek texts, but for the Old Testament, he ignored the Greek Septuagint and translated directly from Hebrew texts. In this way, he produced a new and accurate Latin translation that was declared the official Bible of the Church.

The last yet the greatest of the trio was Augustine. Born in North Africa to a pagan father and a Christian mother, Augustine received a very good Latin education. Driven by intense intellectual curiosity to seek answers to the fundamental questions of human existence, he studied broadly pagan philosophy and religion, including Neoplatonism and Manichaeism, but he was not satisfied. At this time, he listened to the sermons of Ambrose who suggested that the Old Testament could be understood only through symbolic interpretation and that there could be an agreement between the New Testament and Platonic philosophy. Augustine immersed himself in the Scriptures since and after some amazing religious experiences, he understood that what he must do was to believe in Christ and His message. He immediately received baptism and began working for the Christian Church. He went back to North Africa, where he served as bishop of Hippo until his death.

Augustine's ideas on theology dominated Christian thought down to Thomas Aquinas in the 13th century. For centuries, the core of Augustinian thought, that reason should be subordinated to faith, was the foundation of all medieval theologies. He adapted Platonic philosophy to Christian doctrine so that the former became theology's principal handmaiden till the introduction of Aristotelianism in the 12th and 13th centuries. His most influential work *The City of God*, which was written in response to the sack of Rome by the Visigoths in 410, at least in part countered the charge that the plundering of Rome resulted from the desertion of the pagan gods for Christianity. In the argument, he developed a teleological interpretation of history—that is, history was determined by God for His own ends. Augustine was one of those who repudiated the ancient idea of time as cyclical; instead, he said, time was linear and, moreover, it was the property of God who could do with it as He liked. In this way, the Creation, the covenant with the Old Testament patriarchs, the Incarnation, and the institution of the Church may all be seen as the unfolding of God's will. He said that the Last Judgment would be the last event in history. The fall of Rome, he insisted, took place because Rome had fulfilled its purpose: the Christianization of the empire. The real purpose of history, he said, was to pit self love against the love of God— "Self love leads to the City of Man, love of God to the City of God. These two cities will remain at odds and conflicted throughout time, until the City of God is eternalized as heaven and the City of Man as hell." This interpretation of history prevailed throughout the Middle Ages. With Augustine centuries of pagan thought ended, and with him began centuries of new thought imbedded in the concept that only by subordinating human reason to Christian faith can man perceive truth and attain salvation. In this sense, Augustine is considered as the first medieval man and the last classical man.

The City of God

By Saint Augustine

I have already said, in previous Books, that God had two purposes in deriving all men from one man. His first purpose was to give unity to the human race by the likeness of nature. His second purpose was to bind mankind by the bond of peace, through blood relationship, into one harmonious whole. I have said further that no member of this race would ever have died had not the first two—one created from nothing and the second from the first—merited this death by disobedience. The sin which they committed was so great that it impaired all human nature—in this sense, that the nature has been transmitted to posterity with a propensity to sin and a necessity to die...

When a man lives "according to man" and not "according to God," he is like the Devil...

When man lives according to himself, that is to say, according to human ways and not according to God's will, then surely he lives according to falsehood. Man himself, of course, is not a lie, since God who is his Author and Creator could not be the Author and Creator of a lie. Rather, man has been so constituted in truth that he was meant to live not according to himself but to Him who made him—that is, he was meant to do the will of God rather than his own. It is a lie not to live as a man created to live...

Moreover, our first parents only fell openly into the sin of disobedience because, secretly, they had begun to be guilty. Actually, their bad deed could not have been done had not bad will preceded it; what is more, the root of their bad will was nothing else than pride. For, "pride is the beginning of all sin."

This life of ours—if a life so full of such great ills can properly be called a life—bears witness to the fact that, from its very start, the race of mortal men has been a race condemned. Think, first, of that dreadful abyss of ignorance from which all error flows and so engulfs the sons of Adam in a darksome pool that no one can escape without the toll of toils and tears and fears. Then take our very love for all those things that prove so vain and poisonous and breed so many heartaches, troubles, griefs, and fears; such insane joys in discord, strife, and war; such wrath and plots of enemies, deceivers, sycophants...all the shameless passions of the impure—fornication and adultery, incest and unnatural sins, rape and countless other uncleannesses too nasty to be mentioned; the sins against religion—sacrilege and heresy, blasphemy and perjury...

Yet, for all this blight of ignorance and folly, fallen man has not been left without some ministries of Providence, nor has God, in His anger, shut up His mercies. There are still within the reach of man himself, if only he will pay the price of toil and trouble, the twin resources of law and education. With the one, he can make war on human passion; with the other, he can keep the light of learning lit even in the darkness of our native ignorance...

What we see, then, is the two societies that have issued from two kinds of love. Worldly society has flowered from a selfish love which dared to despise even God, whereas the communion of saints is rooted in a love of God that is ready to trample on self. In a word, this latter relies on the Lord, whereas the other boasts that it can get along by itself. The city of man seeks the praise of men, whereas the height of glory for the other is to hear God in the witness of conscience. The one lifts up its head in its own boasting; the other says to God "thou art my glory, thou liftest up my head."

4. Monastic Reform Movements

However, many problems arose within the Church. The popes exercised control over the territories in central Italy known as the Papal States; this kept the popes involved in political matters, often at the expense of their spiritual obligations. The Church became large landholders. With this growing wealth, the monastic establishments were more and more involved in the worldly affairs and the monastic ideal had also suffered. A number of people believed that it was time to reform the Church.

The first effort was made in the Burgundian monastery of Cluny. The first abbot, Berno, set out to revive the strictness of the Benedictine Rule. His efforts were carried on by a series of extraordinary abbots, whose reputation for holiness brought generous support and gifts from wealthy nobles throughout western and central Europe. The Cluniac Reform was a striking success. Monastic life was restored to something like its original rigor, simony (the selling of Church services or offices) was exposed and reduced, and the rule of priestly celibacy was more strictly enforced.

But in the end, Cluny's very success brought about its decline. A new order appeared. This order arose in a barren area of Burgundy with the founding of an abbey at Citeaux in 1098. Under the leadership of the saintly and charismatic Bernard of Clairvaux, the order expanded in a large scale. They wore white robes to distinguish themselves from the black of the Benedictines. But they too became soiled by economic success and worldly power.

A third reform followed a similar course. Early in the 13th century, a young Italian called Francis of Assisi gave up his home to travel in voluntary poverty, supported by begging along. Instead of living in remote cloisters, he and his fellows chose to work among the needy of the towns, serving the poor and stressing the ideal of Christian love and brotherhood.

Francis was a mystic—one who sought God's truth through inner inspiration and revelation. He and his fellows were doubtful of book learning and human reason. Of a contrary view was the Spaniard Dominic. Dominic saw God's truth as a reasoned ideology and the order of friars he founded was devoted chiefly to scholarship, teaching, and preaching.

5. Investiture Struggle

The most significant reform of the medieval Church was associated with the papacy itself. One of the reformers' primary goals was to free the Church from the interference of lords and emperors in the election of Church officials. The Italian Hildebrand, later elected as Pope Gregory Ⅶ (1073–1085) took up the issue. Thanks largely to his efforts, a new system was brought into being for the election of popes—the College of Cardinals. It was under his efforts that the papacy was made a monarchy in fact as well as in theory. The administration of the papacy came to be like that of a state.

Gregory held the view that as successor of St. Peter and designated representative of God on this Earth, the Pope was not only to wield the spiritual leadership of God's Church, but to supervise the secular institutions and their rulers. It was only natural for him to claim that he should be supreme over emperors and kings. The independency and supremacy of the papacy was evidenced by its strong position under Gregory the Great and by the fact that emperors were crowned by the popes. This inevitably brought him into collision with the other main authority in Christian society, the State.

5.1 The Struggle of Gregory Ⅶ and Henry Ⅳ

For many years, German kings had appointed high-ranking clerics as their vassals in order to use them as administrators. In 1075, Pope Gregory Ⅶ issued a decree forbidding important clerics from receiving investiture from lay leaders.

The immediate cause of the Investiture Struggle was a disputed election to the bishopric of Milan in northern Italy, an important position because the bishop was also the ruler of the city. Gregory Ⅶ and Emperor Henry Ⅳ backed their own candidates for the position. Gregory employed every means to bring Henry down. He plotted with the Emperor's enemies in Germany, subjected him to excommunication and deposition, and turned to the Normans in southern Italy for military assistance. Excommunication is a censure by which a person is deprived of receiving the sacraments of the Church. Henry gave in. He begged the Pope to forgive him for his offenses and restore him to communion with the Church. The investiture argument was settled later by compromise: Henry's successor agreed in 1122 to give the Pope the investiture of religious symbols, but he retained the emperor's traditional influence over the selection of German bishops.

5.2 The Struggle of Innocent Ⅲ and King John

During the reign of Innocent Ⅲ, the papacy reached its height of prestige and power. Its strength was shown by the humbling of King John of England, who, after a bitter dispute with Innocent over the election of the archbishop of Canterbury, was forced to submit. John was deposed; afterward, in 1213, he was granted the realm of England as a fief from Rome, but only after pledging homage to the Pope.

5.3 The Conflict Between Boniface Ⅷ and King Philip Ⅳ

Papal claims were carried even further by the aggressive Boniface Ⅷ. He met his match, however, King Philip (the Fair) of France. Philip, who was waging war against England, levied a tax on church properties in 1296. Boniface answered this bold move with angry denunciations. A few years later, Boniface issued a papal bull titled "Unam Sanctam", in which he declared that all secular rulers were subject to the Pope and that the Pope could be judged by God alone. Philip, much more determined and tougher than his English counterpart, sent a military force across the Alps and kidnapped the aged pontiff. Though rescued by the Italian nobles, Boniface died of shock soon afterward in 1303. Philip's strong-arm tactics had produced a clear victory for the national monarchy over the papacy, and no later Pope has dared renew the extravagant claims of Boniface Ⅷ.

To ensure his position and avoid any future papal threat, Philip exerted high pressure on the College of Cardinals to elect a French man as Pope. Using the excuse of turbulence in Rome, the new Pope took up his residence in Avignon. He and his successors remained in Avignon for the next 72 years, creating new crises for the Church. These events set the stage for a rapid decline of the papacy. The popes had overreached themselves in their pursuit of worldly power, and the 14th and 15th centuries would see the unhappy consequences of papal extremism.

6. The Crusades

The greatest testimony to the revival of the Church in the High Middle Ages was the series of Crusades mounted against the Muslims for the purpose of recapturing the birthplace of Christianity. Lasting for two centuries, the Crusades in the Holy Land failed to achieve their aim, but they provided a dramatic expression of the confidence and zeal in reviving the West.

6.1　Invasion of the Seljuk Turks

The Seljuk Turks were a nomadic people from Central Asia who had been converted to Islam. By the 11th century, they had reduced the Arabian caliphate in Persia and Mesopotamia, and captured Baghdad, posing a great threat to the Byzantine Empire. In 1071, the Turks crushed a Byzantine army at the Battle of Manzikert and then moved toward the imperial capital itself. The eastern emperor, despite his distrust of the West and the schism, decided to mend his relations with the Christian West and sent an urgent appeal for help to Pope Urban Ⅱ.

6.2　The First, Second, Third, and Fourth Crusades

Urban Ⅱ accepted the plea for help more than readily. He looked upon the plea as an opportunity for the papacy to muster and lead the first great offensive against the East since the Roman Empire. In the autumn of 1095, Urban went to Clermont in the south of central France where he convened the great ecclesiastics and nobles of Europe. In an inspiring address, he called upon the nobles to bury their differences and unite to rescue the Holy Land from infidel hands. He promised rich lands and glory as well as assurance of all sorts of spiritual rewards to those who would make the great sacrifice. Soon, thousands enrolled in the sacred army, signifying their action by sewing a cross upon their tunics. That was why the volunteer was called a crusader and the expedition a Crusade.

The main crusading armies began their trip in the autumn of 1096 and in the summer of 1098 reached Jerusalem. Thanks to Italian supplies, Jerusalem was taken after a six-week siege. As for the tangible gains of the crusaders, they carved out themselves a group of states along the eastern shores of the Mediterranean. Running north to south, there were the Latin States of the County of Edessa, the Principality of Antioch, the County of Tripolis, and the Kingdom of Jerusalem.

The first Crusade was a success because of the immense fervor generated by an inspired papacy, and because the Turks failed to unite themselves. During the 12th century, the situation was reversed. In less than 50 years after the capture of Jerusalem, the Turks had united in Syria and retaken the County of Edessa. A second Crusade was launched by Louis Ⅶ of France and Conrad Ⅱ of Germany. Without cooperation, the mission was a dismal failure. In 1187, Jerusalem fell under the reassumed attacks of the Turks. The fall of Jerusalem aroused the foremost kings of Europe to embark on a new offensive. But again disunity robbed the third Crusade of success.

The last serious military expedition launched against the Muslims was inspired by the great Pope Innocent Ⅲ. However, this Crusade was most peculiar since few warriors knew where they were going or what they hoped to achieve. The army led by the counts of Flanders and Champagne marched to Venice which was to supply boats for the trip to Syria. Unfortunately, they did not have enough money to pay the Venetians. Venice proposed that if the crusaders would first go to the port Zara, the Venetians' commercial rival, and capture it, the Venetians would provide transportation to Syria. Zara was attacked and captured in 1202. Soon afterwards, the son of the Byzantine emperor who had just been deposed at Constantinople, came to the crusaders with another proposal. If they would first sail to Constantinople, capture it, and restore his father to the throne, he would then provide the money, supplies, and men to assure the conquest of Syria and Egypt. In the summer of 1203, defying the order of Innocent Ⅲ to fight no more Christians, the crusaders captured Constantinople and restored the deposed emperor to power. However, an immediate insurrection, which resulted in the death of the restored emperor and his son, rendered the efforts of the crusaders fruitless. The crusaders stormed the city, and the booty was equally divided between them and the Venetians. The infidels in Syria and Egypt had long ago been forgotten. Even the great Innocent Ⅲ could not control the Crusade he proclaimed.

Although a number of other Crusades were conducted in the 13th century, they all ended with failure. With the capture of Acre in 1291, all the Holy Land had been reconquered by the Muslims.

6.3　Effects of the Crusades

Some scholars may say that the Crusades accelerated the cultural exchange between

Christian Europe and the Muslim world, but others believe that this interaction was more intense and more meaningful in Spain and Sicily than in the Holy Land. There is no doubt that the Crusades did contribute to the economic growth of the Italian port cities, especially Genoa, Pisa, and Venice. But it is important to remember that the growing wealth and population of 12th-century Europe had made the Crusades possible in the first place.

There were side effects too. The first widespread attack on the Jews began with the Crusades. As some Christians argued, to undertake holy wars against infidel Muslims while the "murderers of Christ" ran free at home was unthinkable. The massacre of Jews became a regular feature of medieval European life.

Key Terms

Christian Doctrine → the holy sacraments → theory of the sacraments → Petrine theory → Gregory the Great → early Church Fathers, Sr. Ambrose, St. Jerome, Sr. Augustine → monastic reform movements → Investiture Struggle → Gregory Ⅶ and Henry Ⅳ → Innocent Ⅲ and King John → Boniface Ⅷ and King Philip Ⅳ → the Crusades

Exercises

1 Vocabulary Building

➣ Fill in each blank with a synonym to the word in the brackets.

1) He was best known for his _____ (zeal) in _____ (converting) the pagans and for his eloquent and passionate sermons. A strong defender of spiritual supremacy over _____ (temporal) affairs, he even forced the emperor Theodosius to beg forgiveness for permitting the cruel _____ (massacre) of the people in Thessalonica in 339.

2) This interpretation of history _____ (prevailed) throughout the Middle Ages. With Augustine centuries of _____ (pagan) thought ended, and with him began centuries of new thought _____ (imbedded) in the concept that only by _____ (subordinating) human reason to Christian faith can man _____ (perceive) truth and attain salvation.

3) Philip, who was _____ (waging) war against England, _____ (levied) a tax on

church properties in 1296. Boniface answered this bold move with angry _____ (denunciations). A few years later, Boniface issued a papal _____ (bull) titled "Unam Sanctam", in which he declared that all secular rulers were subject to the Pope and that the Pope could be judged by God alone.

❷ Translation

✎ Translate the following sentences into Chinese.

1) Salvation rested upon the holy sacraments. Seven Sacraments were acknowledged, including Baptism, Confirmation, Marriage, Penance, Eucharist, Ordination, and Extreme Unction. It was believed that only a selected group of men, the clergy, had the rights to administer these sacraments, because they, by virtue of the Sacrament of Ordination, had attained this elevated status.

2) His most influential work *The City of God*, which was written in response to the sack of Rome by the Visigoths in 410, at least in part countered the charge that the plundering of Rome resulted from the desertion of the pagan gods for Christianity. In the argument, he developed a teleological interpretation of history—that is, history was determined by God for His own ends. Augustine was one of those who repudiated the ancient idea of time as cyclical; instead, he said, time was linear and, moreover, it was the property of God who could do with it as He liked.

3) Yet, for all this blight of ignorance and folly, fallen man has not been left without some ministries of Providence, nor has God, in His anger, shut up His mercies.

❸ Questions

✎ Answer the following questions.

1) What is the basic difference between the Old Testament and the New Testament?

2) What are sacraments? What is the general theory of the sacraments?

3) What contribution did Gregory the Great make?

4) What were the major reasons for a cycle of monastic reforms?

5) What were the reasons for launching the Crusades? What effects did the Crusades produce?

❹ Term Explanation

✎ Explain the meaning of the following term in your own words.

Investiture Struggle

5 Topics for Discussion

 Below are four topics related to this chapter. Read them and finish the discussion.

1) Make a comparative study between superstition and religion, focusing on their differences as well as similarities.

2) Please do some research and give a brief account of the differences between Roman Catholic and Protestantism.

3) There are various interpretations of "sin." Based on your knowledge and study, form your own understanding of the word, and exchange it with your classmates.

4) How much do you know about the translation history of the Bible? Based on what you have learned from this course, give a brief outline of it.

6 Research and Presentation

 In groups, do research and make a presentation based on the following direction.

In his book *Confessions*, St. Augustine gave a semi-biographical account of his conversion to Christianity. According to him, after some amazing religious experiences, he began to believe in God. Read the book, find out the amazing experience, and present the story to the class.

7 Writing

 Read the following direction and finish the writing.

Based on what you have learned from this chapter, analyze the reasons that caused the failure of the second and the third Crusades. You may find that cooperation and unity mean a lot for a team to succeed in an undertaking. Write a short essay with the title of "My Understanding of Team Spirit."

Chapter 11

Medieval Culture

People who know little about the Middle Ages commonly associate it with ignorance, superstition, extreme devotion to the Church, and intellectual bankruptcy. This supposed uniformity could not be further from the truth. There was a Dark Age in the Early Middle Ages, but with the coming of the 11th century there began a lively cultural renaissance that stimulated solid achievements in the following centuries. Medieval Europe witnessed the growth of a new culture, not at all dark, retrograde, and uniform, but bright, progressive, and diverse. Noticeable achievements were made especially in learning, writing, and the arts. By the end of the 13th century, medieval culture had not only attained but surpassed the level of Greco-Roman civilization.

1. The Rise of Universities

One aspect that signified the intellectual revival was the emergence of universities in their modern sense. The university, as we know it with faculty, students, and degrees, was a product of the High Middle Ages. The word "university" is derived from the Latin word *universitas*, meaning a corporation or guild, and referred to either teachers or students.

The first steps toward higher education were taken in southern Europe, where access to Muslim and Byzantine learning was easiest. As early as the 9th century, Salerno began to offer medical training, and late in the 11th century, legal training began in the northern Italian town of Bologna. These universities were professional in nature. It was in Paris in the 13th century that Europe's foremost institution of learning was established. Whereas Salerno and Bologna limited themselves to professional training in medicine and law, Paris had the first university to offer the four major curricula that have become identified in the West with the idea of a university: medicine, law, theology, and liberal arts. From Paris, the movement spread to England, Germany, and the rest of western Europe. By 1300, 18 universities had been founded, and by 1500 the total number exceeded 80.

The liberal arts curriculum of the university consisted of seven subjects: grammar, rhetoric, and logic (the *trivium*); arithmetic, geometry, astronomy, and music (the *quadrivium*). Today, we refer to the *trivium* as humanistic studies and to the *quadrivium* (except music) as mathematical studies.

Students in medieval universities earned their degrees on the basis of oral examinations. After attending lectures and reading in the subjects of the *trivium* for several years, a student would ask to be examined orally. If he performed well, he was granted the preliminary degree of Bachelor of Arts, a prerequisite for going on to the *quadrivium*. After another several years of study, he would take the oral examination once again. If he passed, he was awarded the degree of Master of Arts. The higher degrees were teaching degrees. The Latin word *doctor* (teacher) was used for the degrees in theology, law, and medicine. The doctor of philosophy degree came later.

Student life was quite different from what it is today. Professors lectured at their homes or in hired halls, and students lived independently. This unregulated life sometimes led to ill health and immoral conduct. About 1250, Louis IX's chaplain, Robert de Sorbon, founded a "college" with a dormitory for the theology students at the University of Paris to live in. Later, faculty members were assigned to the college. This pattern gradually spread to universities beyond France.

2. Thirteenth-Century Learning

Another aspect of the intellectual revival in the High Middle Ages was a resurgence of interest in the works of the Greeks and Romans. In the 12th century, through the Muslim world and through Latin translations of Arabic works, western Europe was introduced to a large number of Greek scientific and philosophical works, including those of Galen and Hippocrates on medicine, Ptolemy on geography and astronomy, and Euclid on mathematics. Among them, the complete works of Aristotle were special. This great influx of Aristotle's works had an overwhelming impact on the intellectual life in the West.

2.1　Development of Scholasticism

Whether in monastic or cathedral schools or the new universities, theology, the formal study of religion, reigned as "queen of the sciences." The word "scholasticism" is used to refer to the philosophical and theological system of the medieval schools. In essence, this method consisted of posing a question, presenting contradictory authorities on that question, and then arriving at conclusions. In the 12th century, the Church had been fearful of Aristotelianism because it seemed to contradict so much of what had been accepted for about 800 years. The Church became disturbed as numerous scholars, under the influence of the Arabic philosopher Averroës, accepted a naturalistic interpretation of Aristotle's premises and conclusions. Sensing that Aristotle could not be banned from Western Christendom, the popes encouraged the Dominicans and the Franciscans to attempt the reconciliation of Aristotelianism with the Christian faith and theology. Therefore, a primary preoccupation of scholasticism was the attempt to reconcile faith with reason, and demonstrate that what was accepted on faith was in harmony with what could be learned by reason.

The most renowned scholastic scholar of the High Middle Ages was Thomas Aquinas. As a theologian of high excellence, Aquinas devoted most of his learning to reconciling Aristotelianism with Christian dogma. His task was to harmonize the truth of reason with the truth of revelation. He was certain that the two truths could not be in conflict with each other. As he stated, "For although the natural light of the human mind (reason) is insufficient to show us these things made manifest by faith, it is nevertheless impossible that these things which the divine principle gives us by faith are contrary to these implanted in us by nature (reason)." In Aquinas' view, there were only three truths that could not be proved by natural reason and therefore must be accepted. These were the creation of the universe, the nature of the Trinity, and Jesus' role in salvation. Beyond this, Aquinas took Aristotle's side against Augustine more controversially and more influentially. In his *Summary of Theology*, he dealt with Christian salvation and ethics. His method consisted of asking 631 questions and attempting to supply satisfactory answers by using canon law and syllogistic reasoning.

The intellectual achievement of Thomas Aquinas is one of the towering accomplishments of all ages. Through his labor, Aristotelian philosophy was placed in the service of Christian theology and the two harmonized in favor of the latter. Henceforth, the Thomist philosophical position supplanted the Augustinian-Platonic authority and still dominates the thought of the Catholic Church.

2.2 The Problem of Universals

In the field of Christian theology, the prime concern of the 11th and 12th centuries was the fundamental nature of universals and particulars. Principally because of Augustine who had inherited much of Plato's thought and passed it on to later ages, medieval theologians believed that particulars could not be understood nor have any reality unless they were associated with and partaking in the nature of their general ideas or universals. They adhered to the Platonic principle that only general ideas or universals are real and truth could be discovered only by contemplating the universals. These scholars were called realists. The nominalists, on the contrary, were adherents of Aristotle's ideas and believed that only individual objects are real. In their view, universal ideas and concepts were simply names. Truth could be discovered only by examining individual objects.

3. Christian Architecture

Throughout the Middle Ages, the Church was a powerful creative force. Nowhere is this force displayed more clearly than in the arts—above all, in Christian architecture. Christian churches, though borrowing some features from the temples of the late Roman Empire, were different from pagan temples in many ways. A pagan temple was considered the "home" of a god or goddess, which ordinary people might never enter, whereas the Christian God dwelt "in a house not made with hands." Therefore, it was not God but His worshipers who needed a building to bring themselves close to Him. The churches were intended to convey something of the nature of God and the universe He ruled to the believers. Paintings and sculptures were used to teach these lessons and stories to the mass of believers. It was this theory that was responsible for the overwhelming impression that great churches in the Middle Ages created: an impression of orderly and logical perfection as well as mystical and inexpressible holiness.

3.1   The Romanesque Style

Romanesque churches were based on the pattern of the Roman basilica, such as its rectangular shape, round arch, and vault. However, development in worship services led to a shift to the cruciform structure. A transept, or cross arm, was added at right angles to the nave, with entrances at either end (see Figure 11-1). This new plan provided more space for the clergy participating in the Mass, and it became the favored plan for large churches all over the West.

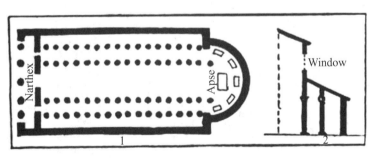

Figure 11-1   The Roman basilica

Apart from its functional merits, the cruciform plan had symbolic meanings. The cross plan was so located that the nave ran from west to east, with the altar at the eastern end. Thus, the worshipers faced more or less in the direction of Jerusalem. The façade of the building usually had three main portals, symbolizing the Trinity.

Romanesque churches replaced the flat wooden ceiling of Roman churches with a long, round stone arch called barrel vault (see Figure 11-2), or cross vault (two barrel vaults intersected) (see Figure 11-3). Because stone vaults were extremely heavy, Romanesque churches required massive pillars and walls to hold them up. This left little space for windows, making Romanesque churches notoriously dark inside (see Figure 11-4).

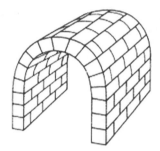
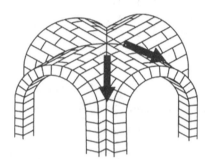

Figure 11-2　A tunnel vault　　　　　Figure 11-3　Cross vaults

Figure 11-4　The Romanesque style: Saint Agata in Agone Church

(Source: Visual China Group)

3.2　The Gothic Style

Romanesque churches had their own shortcomings. Their thick walls gave a feeling of confinement, their massive arches seemed ill-proportioned, and their small windows did not provide a rich illumination. During the 12th to 13th centuries, Romanesque churches gave way to a new expression, Gothic cathedrals, which were one of the greatest artistic triumphs of the High Middle Ages. The Gothic cathedral, pointing to heaven, stood high above the houses in the town. It symbolized the commanding position of the Church in the lives of medieval men and women. (see Figure 11-5)

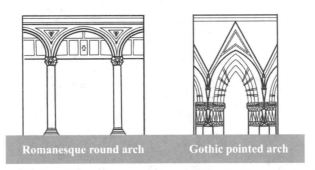

Romanesque round arch　　　Gothic pointed arch

Figure 11-5　A Romanesque round arch and a Gothic pointed arch

It was the new religious belief that made the Gothic style a reality. The educated clergy believed that the church should reflect a true image of the universe: a vast structure, designed by its creator to be perfectly harmonious in every detail and glowing with light that flowed from God. Two innovations were fundamental to Gothic cathedrals. The combination of ribbed vaults and pointed arches replaced barrel vaults of Romanesque churches. The use of this innovation created an impression of upward movement, a sense of weightless upward thrust that implied the energy of God (see Figure 11-6). Another innovation was the flying buttress (see Figure 11-7), which made it possible to distribute the weight of the church's vaulted ceilings outward and downward and thereby to eliminate the heavy walls used in Romanesque churches to hold the weight of the massive barrel vaults.

Figure 11-6   Pointed arches

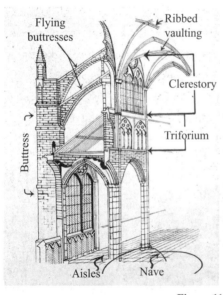

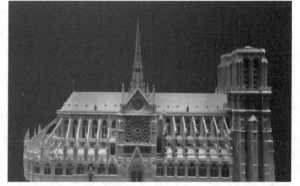

Figure 11-7   The flying buttress

Stained glass is the special glory of the Gothic church. The use of stained glass was based on the belief that natural light was a symbol of the divine light of God; light is invisible but enables people to see; so too is God invisible, but the existence of God allows the world of matter to be. The windows, of varied shapes and sizes, consist of mosaics of colored glass. The glass pieces are held together by lead strips and bars creating geometrical designs. The function of these windows is to illustrate biblical stories. Thus in its immensity, its harmonious beauty, and its glowing illumination, the building conveys something of the image of the universe and its creator.

Key Terms

the rise of universities → *universitas* → Salerno → Bologna → Paris liberal arts → development of scholasticism → Thomas Aquinas → *Summary of Theology* → the problems of universals → realists → nominalists → Christian architecture → the Romanesque style → the Gothic style

Exercises

1 Vocabulary Building

🔊 Fill in each blank with a synonym to the word in the brackets.

1) Medieval Europe witnessed the growth of a new culture, not at all dark, _____ (retrograde), and _____ (uniform), but bright, _____ (progressive), and diverse. Noticeable achievements were made especially in learning, writing, and the arts. By the end of the 13th century, medieval culture had not only _____ (attained) but surpassed the level of Greco-Roman civilization.

2) The most _____ (renowned) scholastic scholar of the High Middle Ages was Thomas Aquinas. As a theologian of high _____ (excellence), Aquinas devoted most of his learning to _____ (reconciling) Aristotelianism with Christian dogma. His task was to _____ (harmonize) the truth of reason with the truth of _____ (revelation).

❷ Translation

❧ Translate the following sentences into Chinese.

1) People who know little about the Middle Ages commonly associate it with ignorance, superstition, extreme devotion to the Church, and intellectual bankruptcy. This supposed uniformity could not be farther from the truth. There was a Dark Age in the Early Middle Ages, but with the 11th century began a lively cultural renaissance that stimulated solid achievements in the following centuries.

2) They adhered to the Platonic principle that only general ideas or universals are real and truth could be discovered only by contemplating the universals. These scholars were called realists. The nominalists, on the contrary, were adherents of Aristotle's ideas and believed that only individual objects are real.

3) Stained glass is the special glory of the Gothic church. The use of stained glass was based on the belief that natural light was a symbol of the divine light of God; light is invisible but enables people to see; so too is God invisible, but the existence of God allows the world of matter to be.

❸ Questions

❧ Answer the following questions.

1) When did the first university arise in southern Europe?

2) What is liberal arts?

3) How did the universities come into being?

4) What were the major concerns of the scholasticism?

❹ Term Explanation

❧ Explain the meaning of the following terms in your own words.

1) Romanesque church

2) Gothic architecture

❺ Topic for Discussion

❧ Below is a topic related to this chapter. Read it and finish the discussion.

Compare the early rising universities and the contemporary higher institutions, focusing on their differences as well as similarities.

⑥ Writing

✎ Read the following direction and finish the writing.

A famous British scholar John Ruskin once said, "No person who is not a great sculptor or painter can be an architect. If he is not a sculptor or painter, he can only be a builder." How do you understand it? Based on your knowledge and study, write a short essay with the title of "Beauty in Architecture."

Part Three

Early Modern Europe

1300–1650

In the Christian Europe of the Middle Ages, medieval civilization seemed to reach a turning point— a "critical mass"—and gradual development turned into spectacular change.

Two of the most famous events connected with this change were Christopher Columbus's voyage of 1492 and the beginning of the Protestant Reformation in 1517. It is for this reason that the year 1500 has become the benchmark date of the "end" of the Middle Ages and the "beginning" of the modern period. In fact, medieval civilization began to change as early as 1300, and it took 350 years for a recognizably more modern pattern of civilization to appear. In the three and a half centuries of the first series of modern shifts in civilization, Europe's social and political structures, as well as its place in the world, were all transformed.

From the booming agriculture and bustling cities of the Middle Ages came the freeing of the serfs in western Europe and the rise of international banking and capitalism. The powerful feudal states began to rely more on royal bureaucrats, mercenary armies, and national taxation than the services of warriors and landowners. Meanwhile, closer links with other civilizations of the East brought from distant lands technical ideas that Europe turned into revolutionary advances— firearms, printing, and clocks. The discovery and exploration of new lands made Christian Europe the world's farthest-flung intercontinental civilization.

The changes in culture and religion were equally drastic, and their roots in the past were equally deep. Medieval scholars and thinkers had always felt themselves to be the heirs of Greece and Rome, and this finally led them into a determined effort to revive the ancient traditions—the Renaissance. Out of this encounter with the Greco-Roman past came new ideals of human personality and behavior, new philosophical ideas, new questions about Christian belief and practice, and new forms of art and literature that challenged the cultural traditions of the Middle Ages.

Chapter 12

An Age of Discovery and Expansion

Europeans had long been attracted to lands outside Europe. However, for almost a millennium, Catholic Europe had been confined to one geographical area. Its one major attempt to expand beyond those frontiers, the Crusades, had largely failed. The motives for European expansion are multifold. However, three primary motives can be pinned down: God, glory, and gold. As Peter Watson pointed out, "To begin with, interest in the New World was confined to the gold that might be found there and the availability of vast numbers of new souls for conversion to the Christian faith." An economic motive is obvious. The Italian merchants who carried the Crusaders to the Near East built up trade with the Levant and helped to produce a flourishing Mediterranean commercial activity. The jealousy on the part of the Western or seaboard European powers of the Italian monopoly of the trade with the East led to attempts to discover another route to the Indies. Furthermore, with the closing of the overland routes, a number of people in Europe became interested in the possibility of reaching Asia by sea to gain access to spices, precious metals, and new areas of trade. The spices desperately needed in Europe continued to come to Europe via Arab intermediaries but were outrageously expensive. This resulted in that great era of exploration which brought about the commercial revolution and the beginning of modern world trade. Another major reason for overseas voyages is religious zeal. Was the New World perhaps the Garden of Eden, or Paradise? Early accounts all dwelt on the innocence, simplicity, fertility, and abundance of the natives, who went around naked without any apparent feelings of shame. This was a view especially seductive to religious figures and to humanists. Angry and despairing at the state of the European Church, members of the religious orders saw a chance in the New World to found afresh the primitive Church of the Apostles in a continent uncorrupted by the vices of European civilization. Of course, spiritual and secular affairs were closely intertwined in the 16th century. Grandeur and glory as well as plain intellectual curiosity and spirit of adventure also played some role in European expansion. These influences may be described vaguely, but on the whole accurately, as psychological. The opportunity for adventure and the possibility of achieving wealth and glory were present.

Once the voyages of exploration started, they brought many surprises. Africa turned out to be a huge continent, stretching much farther into the Southern Hemisphere than geographers and sailors had suspected. The Atlantic route from Europe to the Indies was far greater than even the most pessimistic estimates had allowed, and that vast stretch of ocean contained an unsuspected "New World."

1. Portugal and the African Route

The little kingdom of Portugal took the lead in sponsoring exploration. It had only a short history of independence, having emerged when the Muslims were being expelled from the Iberian Peninsula. The Portuguese favored the relatively conservative plan of looking for a route southward around Africa and then eastward to India. This would enable ships to hold close to land so as to fill their holds with food and fresh water whenever they ran short. It also held the promise of making direct and profitable contact with the wealthy peoples of West Africa. Exploration started early in the 15th century, but proceeded slowly, partly because the African coastline proved far longer than expected, and partly because the Portuguese rulers had many other concerns besides sponsoring exploration. At last, in 1488, Bartolomeu Dias (c.1450–1500) took advantage of westerly winds in the South Atlantic to round the Cape of Good Hope, but he feared a mutiny from his crew and returned home. Ten years later, Vasco da Gama (c.1460–1524) followed the same route, rounded the cape, and stopped at several ports controlled by Muslim merchants along the coast of East Africa. Then, da Gama's fleet crossed the Arabian Sea and reached the port of Calicut, on the southwestern coast of India, on May 18, 1498, thereby linking Europe with the Orient.

For the next several years, Portuguese fleets returned annually to the area, seeking to destroy Arabic shipping and establish a monopoly in the spice trade. In 1509, a Portuguese armada defeated a combined fleet of Turkish and Indian ships off the coast of India and began to impose a blockage on the entrance to the Red Sea to cut off the flow of spices to Muslim rulers in Egypt and the Ottoman Empire. In 1510, Admiral Alfonso de Albuquerque (c.1462–1515) set up port facilities at Goa, and Goa became the headquarters for Portuguese operations throughout the entire region. In 1511, Albuquerque sailed into Malacca, a Muslim harbor and a major stopping point for the spice trade. For the Portuguese, control of Malacca would help them destroy the Arab spice trade and also provide them with a way station on the route to the Moluccas, then known as the Spice Islands. After a short but bloody battle, the Portuguese seized the city and massacred the local Arab population. From Malacca, the Portuguese launched expeditions further east to China and the Spice Islands. The Portuguese trading empire was now complete.

2. Spain and the Atlantic Route

An important figure in the history of Spanish exploration was an Italian known as Christopher Columbus (1451–1506). Since contacts with the Muslims had brought renewed knowledge of Greek philosophy and science, the educated people in Europe at that time all knew that the Earth was round. The question was: On the surface of the round Earth, how far away was Asia from Europe, going westward? Columbus convinced that the circumference of the Earth was smaller and that Asia was larger than his contemporaries believed. He also thought that Asia could be reached by sailing due west instead of eastward around Africa. Columbus believed China to be about 3,000 nautical miles west of Lisbon—just near enough for a ship to arrive without resupplying with food and water. His critics put the figure at about 6,000 miles, much too far for a ship to sail without resupplying (the actual distance is more than 12,000 miles). After being rejected by the Portuguese, he persuaded Queen Isabella of Spain to finance his expedition.

With three ships manned by 90 men, Columbus set sail on August 3, 1492. On October 12, he reached the Bahamas and then went on to explore the coastline of Cuba and the northern shores of Hispaniola (present-day Haiti and the Dominican Republic). Still seeking Japan or China, Columbus spent several months exploring the Caribbean, and he mistook the islands for the "Indies." He died in 1506 still believing he had opened a westerly route to Asia. After Columbus, state-sponsored explorers joined the race to the New World. The first two decades of the 16th century witnessed numerous overseas voyages that explored the eastern coasts of both North and South America. Perhaps the most dramatic of all these expeditions was the journey of Ferdinand Magellan (1480–1521) in 1519. After passing through the straits named after him at the southern tip of South America, he sailed across the Pacific Ocean and reached the Philippines (named after King Philip of Spain) where he met his death at the hands of the natives. Although only one of his original fleet of five ships survived and returned to Spain, Magellan's name is still associated with the first known circumnavigation of the Earth.

Competition and rivalry for the newly discovered land existed between Portugal and Spain. In 1494, a treaty was signed in Tordesillas in Spain which divided the newly discovered world into separate Portuguese and Spanish spheres of influence. Hereafter, the route east around the Cape of Good Hope was to be reserved for the Portuguese while the route across the Atlantic was assigned to Spain.

In 1519, a Spanish expedition under the command of Hernan Cortes (1485–1547) made for Mexico, where the Aztecs had created a well-organized civilization, boasting rich cities, splendid temples and palaces, and superb artistic creations. Cortes' conquest of the Aztecs was cruel. When he arrived at Tenochtitlan, he received a friendly welcome from the Aztec monarch

Moctezuma. At first, Moctezuma believed that his visitors were a representative of Quetzalcoatl, the god who had departed from his homeland centuries before and had promised that he would return. Filled with fears, Moctezuma offered gifts of gold to the foreigners and gave them a palace to use while they were in the city. But conflict eventually erupted between the Spaniards and the Aztecs. Lack of advanced iron weapons and horses and resistance to the deadly germs that the invaders brought with them, the Aztecs were finally destroyed. The pyramids, temples, and palaces were leveled. The mighty Aztec Empire in Mexico disappeared.

The Inca Empire high in the Peruvian Andes suffered the same destruction. In December 1530, Francisco Pizarro (c.1475–1541) landed on the Pacific coast of South America with only a small band of 180 men. Pizarro was lucky because the Inca Empire had already succumbed to an epidemic of smallpox. Like the Aztecs, the Incas had no immunities to European diseases, and very soon, smallpox was devastating entire villages, and even the emperor fell victim. In the civil war when the emperor's two sons fought for the throne, Pizarro took advantage of the situation and eventually captured Incan capital, Cuzco, thus establishing a new colony of the Spanish Empire. Jared Diamond recorded this destruction in his *Guns, Germs and Steel*.

Guns, Germs and Steel

By Jared Diamond

On the next morning a messenger from Atahuallpa arrived, and the Governor said to him, "Tell your lord to come when and how he pleases, and that, in what way soever he may come I will receive him as a friend and brother. I pray that he may come quickly, for I desire to see him. No harm or insult will befall him."

The Governor concealed his troops around the square at Cajamarca, dividing the cavalry into two portions of which he gave the command of one to his brother Hernando Pizarro and the command of the other to Hernando de Soto. In like manner he divided the infantry, he himself taking one part and giving the other to his brother Juan Pizarro...

At noon, Atahuallpa began to draw up his men and to approach. Soon we saw the entire plain full of Indians, halting periodically to wait for more Indians who kept filing out of the camp behind them. They kept filling out in separate detachments into the afternoon. The front detachments were now close to our camp, and still more troops kept issuing from the camp of the Indians. In front of Atahuallpa went 2,000 Indians who swept the road ahead of him, and these were followed by the warriors, half of whom were marching in the fields on one side of him and half on the other side.

Governor Pizarro now sent Friar Vicente de Valverde to go speak to Atahuallpa...Atahuallpa asked for the Book, that he might look at, and the Friar gave it to him closed. Atahuallpa did not know how to open the Book, and the Friar was extending his arm to do so, when Atahuallpa, in great anger, gave him a blow on the arm, not wishing that it should be opened. Then he opened it himself, and, without any astonishment at the letters and paper he threw it away from him five or six paces, his face a deep crimson.

The Friar returned to Pizarro, shouting, "Come out! Come out, Christians! Come at these enemy dogs who reject the things of God. That tyrant has thrown my Book of holy law to the ground! Did you not see what happened? Why remain polite and servile toward this over-proud dog when the plains are full of Indians? March out against him, for I absolve you!"

The governor then gave the signal to Candia, who began to fire off the guns. At the same time the trumpets were sounded, and the armored Spanish troops, both cavalry and infantry, sallied forth out of their hiding places straight into the mass of unarmed Indians crowding the square, giving the Spanish battle cry, "Santiago!" We had placed rattles on the horses to terrify the Indians. The booming of the guns, the blowing of the trumpets, and the rattles on the horses threw the Indians into panicked confusion. The Spaniards fell upon them and began to cut them to pieces. The Indians were so filled with fear that they climbed on top of one another, formed mounds, and suffocated each other. Since they were unarmed, they were attacked without danger to any Christian. The cavalry rode them down, killing and wounding, and following in pursuit. The infantry made so good an assault on those that remained that in a short time most of them were put to the sword.

3. The Spanish Administration in the New World

The Spanish policy in the New World was a combination of confusion, misguided paternalism, and cruel exploitation. Queen Isabella, by declaring the natives to be subjects of Castile, instituted the Spanish encomienda, a system that permitted the conquering Spaniards to collect tribute from the natives and use them as laborers, and at the same time the holders of an encomienda were supposed to protect the Indians, pay them wages, and supervise their spiritual needs. However, in practice, Spanish conquistadores implemented the system as freely as they pleased. Indians as a result were put to work on plantations and in the lucrative gold and silver mines. Forced labor, starvation, and especially diseases took a fearful toll on Indian lives. A reasonable guess is that 30%–40% of the natives died. On Hispaniola alone, when Columbus arrived in 1493, there were 100,000 natives, but by 1570 only 300 Indians survived. The population of central Mexico, estimated at roughly 11 million in 1519, declined to 6.5 million in

1540 and 2.5 million by the end of the 16th century. Protests against the harsh treatment of the Indians, especially by Dominican friars were heard from time to time. Bartolome de Las Casas (1474–1566), the most famous of them, participated in the conquest of Cuba and received land and Indians in return for his efforts. But in 1514, he underwent a radical transformation and came to believe that the Indians had been cruelly mistreated by his fellow Spaniards. He became a Dominican friar and spent the remaining years of his life fighting for the Indians. It is largely due to the publication of his work *The Tears of the Indians* that the government abolished the encomienda system and provided more protection for the natives in 1542.

The Tears of the Indians

By Bartolome de Las Casas

The fifth Kingdom was called Hiquey, where an ancient Queen, by name Hiquanama, governed, who was afterward crucified by the Spaniards: There was an infinite number of those whom I here saw partly burnt alive, partly torne to pieces, partly put to other tortures, or redeemed from death, to a worse misery and captivity. Now there is so much to be said concerning the slaughters and devastations made by the Spaniards, so many stories to be reckoned up, as would be hardly contained in writing, it being impossible to set down one thing of a hundred: For a conclusion of what I have said before, I will only add one thing more, affirming upon my conscience, that for all the fore rehearsed enormities and villainies committed by the Spaniards, yet the Indians gave them no more occasion to perpetrate so many detestable cruelties upon them, then the most religious persons living in the most reformed Monasteries give to the Nations where they dwell, to extirpate them; and they had as little reason to condemn to a perpetual slavery that poor remnant that escaped alive. And this I shall further add, that I do verily believe, that at that time when the Spaniards began this horrid persecution, they had not committed the least crime against the Spaniards that could merit any revenge. And this I also dare affirm, that the Indians had always just reason to raise war against the Spaniards, and that the Spaniards on the contrary, had never any legal cause of quarrel against them, but only always an intention to exercise a fury on them greater than the most consuming and prodigal rage, that ever made the world of tyrants infamous.

The wars being now at an end, and the inhabitants all killed up, the women and the children being only reserved, they divided them among themselves, giving to one thirty, to another forty, to one a hundred, to another two hundred, and those that had the most, received them on this condition that they should instruct them in the Catholic Faith, though commonly their masters were a company of stupid ignorant, and covetous fellows, and defiled with all manner of vices.

4. Impact of Expansion

Europe's expansion had a two-way impact. It was above all felt in the Western Hemisphere. The European conquest of the Americas was in fact more devastating than any other invasions of recorded history. It is necessary to examine the causes for the Europeans' startling victory over the Native Americans. In fact, the confrontation between the Europeans and the Americans was really a clash between the Old World and the New World, in which the advantage was overwhelmingly on the side of the former. Europe, being one among many Old World civilizations, had a longer and broader history than those of the New World: The European horses that amazed the Indians had first been domesticated in central Asia; the invaders' armor was made of iron, a metal first worked in the Middle East; and the gunpowder for their terrifying firearms had been invented in China. Thus, the Europeans had behind them the collective achievements of all the Old World civilizations. Furthermore, the diseases that the Europeans brought with them were common throughout the Old World but unknown in the New World. It is believed that, having no resistance to these diseases, the native population of the Americas was reduced by as much as 90% in the first 100 years of European rule—a staggering blow to their ability to resist.

What effects did the overseas expansion have on Europe itself? The most immediate motive for the explorations had been economic, and their first effect was economic: Expansion nourished the roots of capitalism. The flow of gold and silver from the New World stimulated general business activity. By 1600, the volume of money in existence in Europe had risen to nearly $1 billion (in today's terms). The overseas trade brought an abrupt shift in the geographical distribution of prosperity and power. Venice, Florence, Genoa, and the smaller Italian cities, which had long enjoyed a strategic position between the Middle East and northern Europe now dwindled in importance; for the countries of western Europe facing upon the Atlantic now had the advantage of geographical position. Later, as Britain, France, and Holland became the main trading gateways between Europe and the rest of the world, the center of prosperity and power shifted to northwestern Europe.

Just as important as the economic results of the expansion of Europe were its religious and cultural ones. For many centuries, Christianity had been almost entirely confined within the narrow limits of Europe; now between 1500 and 1600, it replaced Islam as the world's farthest-flung intercontinental religion. In addition, the growth of Europe's worldwide power had the effect of strengthening the non-religious elements in Western culture. Europe's newfound success had a profound effect on the outlook and psychology of Western men and women. By confirming the usefulness of curiosity, daring, and ruthlessness, it raised the value they placed on these traits. The success also strengthened materialism by making more widespread the enjoyment of wealth and the chance of acquiring it. It broadened the intellectual horizons of Europeans to some degree, but contributed little to their respect for non-Western ideas and institutions. On the contrary, the startling victories of the Europeans fortified their optimism and strengthened their faith in their own superiority. In both its religious and its non-religious aspects, Western civilization now became a worldwide civilization. For the first time in history, a civilization was to leap every barrier of race and geography and to spread its influence around the globe. Some areas, of course, would be touched only superficially, but European values and ideas would become familiar almost everywhere.

Key Terms

God, glory and gold → spice trade → Bartolomeu Dias → Cape of Good Hope → Vasco da Gama → Goa → Christopher Columbus → the New World → Ferdinand Magellan → circumnavigation of the Earth → Treaty of Tordesillas → the Aztec Empire and Hernan Cortes → the Inca Empire and Francisco Pizarro → *The Tears of the Indians* → the encomienda system → impact of European expansion

Exercises

1 Vocabulary Building

✎ Fill in each blank with a synonym to the word or phrase in the brackets.

1) The spices _____ (desperately) needed in Europe continued to come to Europe via Arab _____ (intermediaries) but were _____ (outrageously) expensive. This _____ (resulted in) that great era of exploration which brought about the commercial revolution and the beginning of modern world trade. Another major reason for overseas voyages is religious _____ (zeal).

2) At first, Moctezuma believed that his visitors were a representative of Quetzalcoatl, the god who had _____ (departed) from his homeland centuries before and had promised that he would return. _____ (Filled with) fears, Moctezuma offered gifts of gold to the foreigners and gave them a palace to use while they were in the city. But conflict eventually _____ (erupted) between the Spaniards and the Aztecs. Lack of advanced iron weapons and horses and resistance to the deadly germs that the invaders brought with them, the Aztecs were finally destroyed. The pyramids, temples, and palaces were _____ (leveled).

❷ Translation

❧ Translate the following sentences into Chinese.

1) Angry and despairing at the state of the European Church, members of the religious orders saw a chance in the New World to found afresh the primitive Church of the Apostles in a continent uncorrupted by the vices of European civilization.

2) Indians as a result were put to work on plantations and in the lucrative gold and silver mines. Forced labor, starvation, and especially diseases took a fearful toll of Indian lives.

3) The overseas trade brought an abrupt shift in the geographical distribution of prosperity and power. Venice, Florence, Genoa, and the smaller Italian cities, which had long enjoyed a strategic position between the Middle East and northern Europe now dwindled in importance; for the countries of western Europe facing upon the Atlantic now had the advantage of geographical position.

❸ Questions

❧ Answer the following questions.

1) What caused the Europeans to undertake dangerous voyages to the New World and establish colonies?

2) What were Christopher Columbus' beliefs on Asia at the time of his voyages?

3) What was the fate of the Aztec Empire and the Inca Empire? How were they destroyed?

4) What is the encomienda system?

5) What is the impact of European expansion?

❹ Topic for Discussion

❧ Below is a topic related to this chapter. Read it and finish the discussion.

Based on what you have learned from this chapter, do research on the possible reasons why the American Indians were all conquered by European invaders, even though the former outnumbered the latter by a wide margin.

❺ Presentation

❧ In groups, make a presentation on the following topics.

1) different routes of European expansion

2) spice trade

Chapter 13

The Renaissance

By the 14th century, the medieval civilization began to wane in Europe. Instead, over the next five centuries, a distinctively modern civilization emerged in Europe. It has become customary to call the first of these stages of the early modern era the Renaissance. Literally meaning "rebirth of the classical past," the Renaissance, however, should not be understood as rejecting the fervent Christianity of the Middle Ages and as a return to the pagan past. However much the scholars and artists of this age loved the classics, none saw classicism as superseding Christianity. Historians tend to regard the Renaissance as an age when the spiritual life, on the one hand, was vigorous and rich, but on the other hand, when economic, political, and religious activities had their own patterns of growth.

Talking about the Renaissance is a way of talking about some significant changes in education and outlook that transformed the culture of Italy from the late 14th century to the early 16th century, and that eventually influenced the rest of Europe in important ways. Some scholars summed up these changes with such terms as individualism, rationalism, and secularism, while some others tended not to define this age with any "ism." Whatever said about this age, the Renaissance can still be viewed as a distinct period of human history characteristic of the blending of medieval and modern cultures.

1. Renaissance Italy

The Renaissance developed first and most distinctively in Italy. Figuring out why this happened is important not only to explain its origins, but also to understand its essential characteristics.

Reasons are not hard to find. One is that the intellectuals of the warring city-states of Italy desperately sought for new models of governance in the older civilizations of Greece and Rome. Another reason is that Italy was the first to receive the intellectuals of Constantinople after the conquests of the Ottoman Turks spurred a diaspora of Greek-speaking refugees. However, there are three other fundamental reasons.

The most fundamental reason is that after the Black Death, northern Italy became the most urbanized region of Europe. Unlike the countries in the north of the Alps, most Italian aristocrats lived in urban centers rather than in rural castles. This prosperous urban life led to new humanist education. Not only was there a great demand for the skills of reading and accounting necessary to become a successful merchant, but the richest families sought to find excellent teachers for their kids. Consequently, Italy produced a large number of lay educators, who were not only good teachers, but thinkers.

A second important reason has to do with the political situation in Italy. Unlike those unified monarchies of France, England, and Spain, Italy had no unifying political institutions, and its particularism had made it the object of political contention. Italians therefore looked to the classical past for their time of glory. They were particularly intent on establishing an independent identity that could help them oppose the intellectual and political supremacy of France. In addition, Italy's geography—one-fifth mountainous and three-fifths hilly, a long, thin peninsula with a very long coastline—discouraged agriculture and encouraged commerce, seafaring, trade, and industry. Together, this political and geographical set-up promoted the growth of towns: By 1300, Italy had 23 cities with a population of 20,000 or more.

Ever since the end of the Roman Empire, Italy had been the scene of continual struggles for power among barbarians, Muslim and Norman invaders, Byzantine emperors, Holy Roman emperors, and last but not least, the popes, who remained constant foes of Italian unity down to the 19th century. As a result, Italy had become a permanently divided country.

There were five great powers in Italy: Milan, Florence, Venice, the Papal States, and Naples. Venice was a merchant republic. Its primary concern was to defend Venice's seagoing trade routes to the East and the trade routes in Europe by bringing the adjacent land region of Italy under Venetian jurisdiction. The Duchy of Milan was the leading power of northernmost Italy. Thanks to its military prowess and diplomatic leadership, Milan came very close to achieving total domination of the northern part of Italy in the early 15th century, but for the resistance of Florence. Florence was governed by a small merchant oligarchy that manipulated the apparently republican government. During the 15th century, the leadership of Florence came into the hands of the Medici banking family and Florence replaced Milan as the leader in northern Italy. The kingdom of Naples in the south of Italy was fought over by the French and the Aragonese until the latter established their domination in the mid-15th century. Central Italy was ruled by the Pope. The absence of the pontiffs during their residence at Avignon had resulted in a period of virtual anarchy in the Papal States. The Renaissance popes of the 15th century directed much of their energy toward reestablishing their control over the Papal States. In order to pursue their interests in the Papal States and Italian politics, the Renaissance popes were involved in war and bloodshed. One of them, Julius II even personally led armies against enemies, much to the disgust of the pious. Unlike the hereditary monarchs, the popes came to rely on the practice of nepotism. Pope Sixtus IV (1471–1484), for example, made five of his nephews cardinals and gave them an abundance of Church offices to build up their finances (the word "nepotism" is in fact derived from the Greek *nepos*, meaning "nephew").

In 1494, the French invaded Italy. Within a year, the French had swept down the peninsula and conquered Naples. Spain, who also claimed the territory of Sicily, would not stand by. An alliance among Spain, the Papal States, the Holy Roman Empire, Milan, and Venice finally forced French army to withdraw from Italy. However, the French launched a second invasion, and from 1499 to 1529 warfare in Italy was virtually uninterrupted. Alliances and counter-alliances followed each other in bewildering succession. In 1529, the Holy Roman Emperor Charles Ⅴ managed to control most of Italy.

2. The Hundred Years' War

Europe in the 14th century was faced not only with famine, plague, economic turmoil, social upheaval, and violence, but also with war and political instability. Of all the struggles the Hundred Years' War (1337–1453) was the most violent and the most devastating.

The great stake in the war was the rich wine-producing region of southwestern France, the Duchy of Gascony. The English king had previously relinquished all the French territories except Gascony, which he held as a fief under the French crown. The French officials endeavored to bring it under the effective domination of Paris, while the local inhabitants preferred a distant lord in England. Meanwhile, a dispute over the right of succession to the French throne also complicated the struggle between France and England. The French King Philip Ⅵ was the nearest relative of the late Charles Ⅳ only in the male line, while Edward Ⅲ of England was his nephew by way of his mother. So, Edward had also a claim to the French throne.

For most of the war, England held the advantage, but in a burst of patriotism and royalism, France finally emerged triumphant from the ordeal. The embodiment of the new spirit was Joan of Arc, a peasant girl who came out of Lorraine. With religious fervor and loyalism, she spurred renewed vigor in the armies. The French began to taste victory and continued to win even after Joan was captured by the English and burned as a witch. The English effort to become a first-rate continental power had failed, but the long war had sharpened the sense of nationhood in England as well as in France.

3. New Monarchies

In the first half of the 15th century, European states continued to disintegrate. In the second half of the century, however, recovery set in and attempts were made to re-establish the centralized power of monarchical governments. These monarchies were labeled as

"Renaissance states" or the "new monarchies," especially the monarchies in Spain, France, and England.

3.1 Machiavelli and Absolutism

Ironically, it was in one of Europe's most politically fragmented regions that the new politics began. Many Italians, tired of the continuing disheartening division and instability, deemed that their nation would benefit from a unified and absolute government.

The first spokesman who challenged medieval Western political thought and argued for Italian unification and political absolutism was Niccolò Machiavelli (1469–1527), a Florentine, a onetime diplomat, and a close observer of Italian affairs. Instead of seeing government as one aspect of God's administration of human affairs as medieval philosophers had claimed, Machiavelli met the doctrine head on. He stated the "modern" view of politics and the state. The state, in his view, does not rest on any supernatural authority; instead, it provides its own justification, and operates according to rules that have grown out of the "facts" of human nature. He thereby removed politics from Christian ideology and placed it on a purely secular (worldly) level.

Means, as well as ends, were a matter of concern to Machiavelli. He may be the first to put forward the idea of conscription, for he advised the prince to build an army of citizens drawn from a reserve of qualified men under a system of compulsory military training. Military strength is not enough in itself, however. The prince must be both "a lion and a fox." The lion, Machiavelli explained, cannot protect himself from traps, and the fox cannot defend himself from wolves. A ruler, in other words, must have both strength and cunning. Machiavelli noted that the most successful princes of his time were masters of deception. They made agreements to their advantage, and broke them when the advantage disappeared. He did not think that the normal rules of conduct, Christian or otherwise, should hold good for a ruler, and the only proper measure for judging the behavior of a prince is his power. Whatever strengthens the state is right, and whatever weakens it is wrong; for power is the end, and the end justifies the means.

Though speaking for Italian unification and political absolutism, Machiavelli's view of government was influential in his own time and prophetic of the evolution of the state in future times. It was largely through his influence that the word "state" came into use to mean "a sovereign political unit." The European states from the 16th century onward moved in the direction outlined by Machiavelli.

The Prince

By Machiavelli

Chapter XVIII Concerning the Way in Which Princes Should Keep Faith

EVERY one admits how praiseworthy it is in a prince to keep faith, and to live with integrity and not with craft. Nevertheless, our experience has been that those princes who have done great things have held good faith of little account, and have known how to circumvent the intellect of men by craft, and in the end have overcome those who have relied on their word. You must know there are two ways of contesting, the one by the law, the other by force; the first method is proper to men, the second to beasts; but because the first is frequently not sufficient, it is necessary to have recourse to the second. Therefore, it is necessary for a prince to understand how to avail himself of the beast and the man...A prince, therefore, being compelled knowingly to adopt the beast, ought to choose the fox and the lion; because the lion cannot defend himself against snares and the fox cannot defend himself against wolves. Therefore, it is necessary to be a fox to discover the snares and a lion to terrify the wolves. Those who rely simply on the lion do not understand what they are about. Therefore, a wise lord cannot, nor ought he to, keep faith when such observance may be turned against him, and when the reasons that caused him to pledge it exist no longer. If men were entirely good, this precept would not hold, but because they are bad, and will not keep faith with you, you too are not bound to observe it with them. Nor will there ever be wanting to a prince legitimate reasons to excuse this nonobservance. Of this endless modern examples could be given, showing how many treaties and engagements have been made void and of no effect through the faithlessness of princes; and he who has known best how to employ the fox as succeeded best.

3.2 Unification of Spain

One widely accepted element in the process of state building is patriotism, a shared national feeling and identification. In Spain, the spirit of patriotism had been ignited during the fierce struggle to expel the Muslims. When the kingdoms of Castile and Aragon, which had led the fight, were linked through the marriage of Queen Isabella of Castile and King Ferdinand of Aragon in 1469, the way was open for a unified Spain. They worked together to strip the royal council of aristocrats and fill it primarily with middle-class lawyers. They reorganized the military forces, replacing the undisciplined feudal troops with a more professional royal army. The development of strong infantry force as the heart of the new Spanish army made it the best in Europe by the 16th century. They also reformed the Spanish Church, gaining the right to name its bishops. They asked the Pope to introduce the Inquisition into Spain in 1478, which worked with cruel efficiency to guarantee the orthodoxy of Catholic belief. Through converting or expelling the Jews and the Muslims, Isabella and Ferdinand succeeded in making Spain the Catholic fortress. To a very large degree, they achieved their goal of absolute religious orthodoxy as a basic ingredient of the Spanish state. To be Spanish was to be Catholic, a policy of uniformity enforced by the Inquisition.

3.3   The Growth of French Monarch

The Hundred Years' War had developed a strong degree of national feeling in France toward a common enemy, England, that the kings could use to re-establish the monarchical power. It was Charles Ⅶ and his son, Louis Ⅺ who completed the building of a strong national state.

In preparing his final charge against the English, Charles summoned the Estates-General of France to raise the money he needed. The Estates-General had the sole power to authorize new taxes. In a burst of patriotic fervor, the Estates-General approved and voted a permanent tax for its support. Unlike the parliament in England who held tight to its control of purse, the Estates-General never developed into a strong parliamentary body.

Louis Ⅺ greatly advanced the French territory through his wily and devious ways. One of his victories was to win back the Duchy of Burgundy, which had long been independent even though it was legally subject to the French crown. Its last Duke Charles the Bold attempted to create a middle kingdom between France and Germany, but his plan had miscarried, and when he was killed in fighting the Swiss without a male heir, Louis took over the Duchy. Three years later, the provinces of Anjou, Maine, Bar, and Provence were brought under royal control. Many historians believed that Louis created a base for the later development of a strong French monarchy.

3.4   England: The King and Parliament

The origins of Parliament in England can go back to the 13th century. Already in 1215, the Magna Carta had expressed the idea that the king needed the advice and consent of his barons before taking measures, such as the levying of unaccustomed taxes. Later in the century, as both the king and barons sought to enlarge their bases of support in the country, the custom grew up of inviting representatives of the shires (counties) and boroughs (towns) to such meetings. These representatives formed the predecessor of Parliament. In 1295, Edward Ⅰ held the precedent-setting "Model Parliament," and during the next century, Edward's successors called Parliament frequently in their need for additional funds to carry on the war in France. Parliament evolved into two chambers: the House of Lords and the House of Commons. Its control over lawmaking and general administration came only slowly, however.

At the close of the Hundred Years' War, England suffered a series of calamities. Confidence in the crown was shattered by the defeat in France, and the nobles were involved in civil warfare led by the House of York against the House of Lancaster (known as the Wars of the Roses). Henry Tudor (1457–1509), who would become Henry Ⅶ, was a relative of the Lancasters. When he at last emerged victorious from these wars in 1485, the strength of the nobles had been broken, and the nation was yearning for peace and unity. Henry restored law and order, and put an end to private warfare, and the 16th century, the century of Henry Ⅷ and Elizabeth Ⅰ, was an era of despotic power in England.

3.5   The Holy Roman Empire: The Habsburgs

Strong central governments did not come to other parts of Europe for centuries. Neither Germany nor Italy became a unified state until 1870s. The main reason is the failure of the Holy Roman emperors to turn their territories into an effectively governed feudal state during the Middle Ages. As a consequence, Germany lingered on as a patchwork of hundreds of fiefs. When one emperor died, noble electors would meet to choose his successor, and this was often the occasion for lengthy bargaining and even bribing. As a result, dynastic consideration instead of national concern guided the politics of central Europe. In 1273, Rudolf of Habsburg, a south German prince, was elected Holy Roman emperor, thus beginning the rule of Habsburg dynasty. Having gradually acquired a number of possessions along the Danube, known collectively as Austria, the House of Habsburg had become one of the wealthiest landholders in the empire.

Much of the Habsburg success in the 15th century was due to a well-executed policy of dynastic marriage instead of military victory. Emperor Frederick Ⅲ (1440–1493) gained Franche-Comté in east-central Europe, Luxembourg, and a large part of the Low Countries by marrying his son Maximilian to Mary, the daughter of Duke Charles the Bold of Burgundy. When Maximilian became emperor, through the marriage of his son Philip the Handsome to the future queen Joanna of Castile in 1498, he helped to establish the Habsburg dynasty in Spain. Since his father Philip died in 1506, Charles succeeded Maximilian as Holy Roman emperor in 1519, and thus ruled both the Holy Roman Empire and the Spanish Empire simultaneously.

4. Humanism

The core of Renaissance intellectual ideals is summarized in the term "humanism." The humanist way of thinking can be most broadly defined as any view that puts the human person at the center of things and stresses the individual's creative, reasoning, and aesthetic power. Renaissance scholars identified the study of classical literary works of Greece and Rome with humanism. This was a study that aimed to replace the scholastic emphasis on logic and metaphysics with the study of liberal arts: language, literature, rhetoric, history, and ethics.

4.1   Humanism in Italy

Petrarch (1304–1374) was dubbed the "father of humanism" because of his devotion to Greek and Roman scrolls. He strongly felt that a Christian writer must cultivate literary eloquence and the best models of eloquence were to be found in the classical texts of Latin literature. Therefore, he hunted eagerly through the libraries of monasteries where the works of ancient authors had remained intact for many centuries. He preferred to write in classical Latin instead of the corrupted Latin of the Middle Ages. Many of his writings were in the form of epics, dialogues, and letters patterned after the style of Cicero and Virgil. However, he was more remembered for his love poems (sonnets) written in Italian.

Petrarch was followed by many others who discovered almost all the works of the writers of Latin antiquity. One of them was Giovanni Boccaccio (1313–1375), one of the first Westerners of modern times to study the Greek language. He instructed his tutor to translate *Homer* into Latin, and thus introduced his contemporaries to their first reading of *Iliad* and *Odyssey*. His most famous work, *The Decameron*, was full of pagan spirit, though he himself was a Christian. The tales in the book feature sensual escapades, deceits, and clever revenges.

Petrarch's ultimate ideal for human life was solitary contemplation and asceticism. However, in Florence the humanist movement took a new direction when it became closely tied to Florentine civic spirit and pride, giving rise to what one modern scholar has labeled "civic humanism." Humanists such as Leonardo Bruni and Leon Battista Alberti agreed that man's nature equipped him for action, for usefulness to his family and society, and for serving the state. In their view, ambition and the quest for glory were bold impulses that ought to be encouraged and channeled toward these ends. It is no accident that humanists served the state as chancellors, councillors, and advisers.

In the second half of the 15th century, a dramatic upsurge of interest in the works of Plato occurred, and the Florentine Platonic Academy was founded under the patronage of Cosimo de' Medici, the de facto ruler of Florence. Marsilio Ficino, one of the Academy's leaders dedicated his life to the translation of Plato's works and the exposition of the Platonic philosophy known as Neoplatonism. Under Neoplatonism, human mind is the image and likeness of God; the whole world is permeated by divinity, everything is touched by a "numinous" quality, nature is in effect enchanted, and God's purpose can be deciphered through number, geometry, form—above all, through beauty; beauty is an essential component in the search of the ultimate reality, and imagination and vision are more significant in that quest than logic and dogma. Marsilio Ficino wrote a book entitled *Platonic Theology* in which he argued that man was of "almost the same genius as the Author of the heavens." He sought to demonstrate that Platonic teachings were in agreement with Christianity. Ficino's disciple Pico della Mirandola went beyond his master and attempted a synthesis of all learning, Eastern and Western. Admiring human freedom and capacity, Pico refused to ignore any source of truth merely because it was not labeled "Christian." Like Ficino, Pico embraced the Platonic view of creation and existence, which holds that humans have become separated from their divine home of pure spirit by some accident of prehistory. Though each soul (spirit) has fallen prisoner to matter (the body), it struggles for liberation and a return to God. This view corresponds to the Christian Doctrine of the Fall and the human longing for salvation.

It is not difficult to find that humanism in Italy was less concerned with the rediscovery of the sciences of the ancients than with the establishment of a pagan set of values, in effect the secular outlook of the Greeks and the Romans, in which man was the measure of all things. This attitude, as Petrarch was the first to realize, had been lost for about a thousand years. Leon Battista Alberti, for instance, elaborated on virture and fortune in great details.

On Virtù and Fortune

By Leon Battista Alberti

And I perceive many who, fallen on evil days through their own stupidity, blame fortune and complain of being tossed about by those stormy waves into which the fools have actually cast themselves!...If any one wishes to investigate carefully what it is that exalts and increases families and also maintains them at a high peak of honor and felicity, he will clearly see that men are themselves the sources of their own fortune and misfortune; nor indeed will he ever conclude that the power of gaining praise, wealth, and reputation should be attributed to fortune rather than to ability.

And if one considers republics and passes in mind all past principalities, he will find that in acquiring and increasing, in maintaining and conserving majesty and glory already achieved, in none did fortune ever avail more than good and sound discipline in living...

I believe the wise man will judge that what is true of principalities is also true of families, and will agree that families have rarely fallen into a state of misery through anything else than their own lace of prudence and diligence. I recognize this happens either because in prosperity they do not know how to control and restrain themselves, or because in adversity they are not wise enough to sustain and support themselves; and hence fortune engulfs and submerges families in those cruel waves into which they actually abandon themselves.

4.2 Humanism in the North of the Alps

The intensive intellectual and artistic activity that characterized the Renaissance in Italy began to wane toward the end of the 15th century. The French invasion of 1494 and the incessant warfare that ensued were the major cause. To these political disasters was added a waning of Italian prosperity. With the discovery of the new Atlantic routes, trade routes were shifting from the Mediterranean to the Atlantic region, a shift that slowly cost Italy its supremacy as the center of European trade. As Italian wealth diminished, there was less and less of a surplus to support artistic endeavors.

However, in the 16th century, Renaissance ideas were spreading from Italy to the rest of Europe. The most prominent northern Renaissance intellectual movement was Christian humanism. Unlike Italian humanists, the northern Christian humanists sought ethical guidance from biblical and religious precepts rather than from Cicero and Virgil. For them, to be a humanist did not mean that one had to adopt a new philosophy, distinct from and hostile to Christianity. The great majority of humanists remained believing Christians probably had the same range of piety as other men; but they looked upon the writings of the ancients with the admiration, love, and respect that had been traditionally reserved for specifically Christian writings. Thus, Renaissance humanism not only multiplied the number of subjects on which they wrote, but, by taking man more and more as the measure of things and gradually displacing the central emphasis upon God of medieval thought, began a momentous change in the character of thought which has continued through all modern times.

Any discussion of the northern Renaissance humanism must begin with the career of Desiderius Erasmus (c.1469–1536). As a wide traveler, Erasmus was a virtual citizen of northern Europe. Erasmus's many-sided intellectual activity may be assessed from two aspects: the literary and the doctrinal. As a Latin prose stylist, he was unequaled since the days of Cicero. However, he was most renowned for what he called the "philosophy of Christ." He believed that the society of his day was sunken in corruption and immorality because people had abandoned the simple teachings of the Gospels. Accordingly, his publications were of three kinds: clever satires meant to show people the error of their ways, such as *The Praise of Folly* (1509), serious moral treatises meant to offer guidance toward proper Christian behavior, such as *Handbook of Christian Knight* (1503), and scholarly editions of basic Christian texts. Among the three, Erasmus considered textual scholarship his greatest achievement. Through scrupulous reading and research, he brought out reliable editions of early Church Fathers. He spent 10 years studying and comparing all the early Greek biblical manuscripts he could find in order to establish an authoritative text. His Greek New Testament, published together with explanatory notes and his own new Latin translation, became one of the most important landmarks of biblical scholarship of all time.

On Free Will

By Desiderius Erasmus

So far we have confined ourselves to comparing the passages of the Scripture which support free will and those which, on the contrary, seem to suppress it entirely. But since the Holy Spirit, who is the author of the whole of Scripture, cannot contradict Himself, we are then constrained, whether we will or not, to seek some moderate conclusion...

Doubtless to Luther and his followers it seems absolutely necessary, for the simple obedience of the Christian soul, that man should depend wholly on the will of God, that he should place all his hopes and his confidence in His promises, and recognizing his own wretchedness, should admire and adore the boundless mercy of Him who freely grants us so many blessings, that he should submit wholly to the will of God, whether He wishes to save him or damn him; that man should take no credit for his own good works but render all glory to the divine grace, remembering that man is only the living organ of the Holy Spirit, purified and consecrated by His free goodness, guided and ruled by His inscrutable wisdom...

I applaud all this gladly, until it becomes extravagant. For when I hear it said that human merit is so null that all works of men, however pious, are sinful; that our will has no more power than the clay in the hand of the potter; that everything we do or will derives from an absolute necessity, my spirit is assailed by many scruples. First, how shall we understand all the texts in which we read that the saints, who were full of good works, observed justice, that they walked justly before God, that they turned neither to the right nor to the left, if all the actions of even the most pious men are sinful, and so sinful that without the divine mercy he for who Christ died would be plunged into hell? On what grounds would one dare to praise the obedience of those who submit to divine commands, and condemn the disobedience of those who do not submit? Why does the Scripture so often mention judgment, if no account is taken of our merits? Or why are we obliged to present ourselves before the sovereign judge if everything is done in us by pure necessity and nothing according to our free will?

5. Renaissance Art

As mentioned above in this chapter, Neoplatonism taught an aesthetic understanding of the world. An interesting offshoot of this idea had a profound effect on the arts. According to Neoplatonism, the feeling for natural beauty came from the soul's remembrance of the divine beauty of Heaven. Hence, aesthetic expression and enjoyment took on a religious connection, which helped explain both the efflorescence of art in the Renaissance and the improved status of artists, especially in Italy. Almost every artist of the later Renaissance was influenced by

Platonism, and some, like Botticelli and Michelangelo, became deeply absorbed in it.

Undoubtedly, the most enduring legacy of the Italian Renaissance has been the contributions of its artists, particularly those who embraced new techniques and approaches to painting. The use of oil paints and the mastery of vanishing perspective are the two most important ingredients that affect the Renaissance artists' achievements. Furthermore, they also experimented with effects of light and shade, and studied intently the anatomy and proportions of the human body.

Living in the early 14th century, Giotto di Bondone (c. 1267–1337) was considered as the pioneer of naturalism. He wanted to recreate an actual scene to give the viewer the feeling of being an eyewitness. In order to accomplish this, he sought to produce the illusion of depth (perspective) on a flat surface and to make the figures look solid and real. He did this by skillful use of light and shadow and by foreshortening the hands and feet (painting the parts supposed to be nearer to the viewer larger than those farther away). In his *Lamentation* (see Figure 13–1), the followers of the dead Christ surround him in dramatic attitudes of grief, while the sky above is full of mourning angels. The painter has used revolutionary techniques of arranging figures in groups and producing a three-dimensional appearance so as to create an image of overwhelming sorrow.

Figure 13-1 Giotto's *Lamentation*

(Source: Visual China Group)

Giotto left a technical challenge to his successors: How could painting be made more naturalistic? A century later, a significant advance was made in this direction by Filippo Brunelleschi (1377–1446), also a Florentine. Brunelleschi made a unique contribution to drawing and painting through his study of perspective. Perspective was important not just for the added realism it gave to paintings, but also for the fact that it involved an understanding of mathematics, which at that time was included in the liberal arts. If painters could demonstrate that their art depended on mathematics, it would further their claim that painting was a liberal art, and not a mechanical one. The essential point about linear perspective is that parallel lines never meet, but they appear to do so, with all parallel lines converging at a vanishing point on the horizon.

One of the first painters to make use of the laws of perspective was Masaccio (1401–1428). His fresco of the *Trinity with the Virgin, St. John the Evangelist, and Donors* for the church Santa Maria Novella in Florence was a startling innovation. What was striking about it was that it presented the illusion of a Roman tunnel vault reaching back through the church wall. As viewers stand back from the wall, they must have gasped at what seems to be a group of sculptured figures placed within a classical, three-dimensioned chapel. No Greek or Roman painter had created such a convincing illusion of height and distance.

Oil paints were pioneered in Flanders (in the Low Countries) and the technique of oil painting is traditionally credited to Jan van Eyck (c.1385–1441), and Hubert van Eyck (1379–1426). Before this time, painters had mixed powdered pigments with plain water, which dried so quickly that painters had to work very fast and their chances of changing what they had done were minimal. The important point about oil painting is that it dries slowly, meaning that alterations can be made, and painters can improve weak patches, or change their minds completely if a new idea occurs to them. This made painters at that time more thoughtful and more reflective, and also enabled them to take their time over mixing colors, to achieve more subtle effects.

Sandro Botticelli (c. 1445–1510), a 15th-century Florentine, was very much influenced by Platonism. He wanted to combine the liveliness and realism of the Renaissance pioneers with elements of mystery. He was one of the first painters to use figures from classical mythology. In his work *Birth of Venus* (see Figure 13–2), the detached and unearthly beauty of Venus fascinated the Florentine intellectuals, who associated love of beauty with man's desire for reunion with the divine. In this way, Botticelli revived the classical tradition of depicting the naked female body as beautiful, noble, and divine.

Figure 13-2   Botticelli's *The Birth of Venus*

(Source: Visual China Group)

The leading experimenter in both art and nature, however, was Leonardo da Vinci (1452–1519), who fulfilled the humanist ideal of the "universal genius": He was a painter, architect, musician, mathematician, engineer, and inventor. He was successful in combining realism with artistic form and elements of mystery by a clever use of light and shadow. By blurring his contours, especially at the corners of the mouth and eyes, he left something to the imagination of the viewer. Each time we look at his *Mona Lisa*, her expression seems to change. Leonardo's most famous painting is *The Last Supper* (see Figure 13–3), completed in 1497. Most earlier paintings had dealt with this subject with Christ and his disciples quietly seated around the supper table in varying settings and kinds of dress. Leonardo chose the precise moment of drama and excitement after Jesus had said, "One of you will betray me." The artist succeeded in portraying the mingled emotions of surprise, horror, and guilt on the faces. Guess who is Juda?

Figure 13-3   Da Vinci's *The Last Supper*

(Source: Visual China Group)

Key Terms

rebirth of the classical past → Italian politics → the Hundred Years' War → Machiavelli and absolutism → patriotism and nationalism in Spain and France → English Parliament and the Wars of the Roses → the Habsburg success → Petrarch, father of humanism → civic humanism → Neoplatonism → Erasmus and Christian humanism → perspective → oil paints → Giotto → Brunelleschi → Masaccio → Botticelli → da Vinci

Exercises

❶ Vocabulary Building

❧ Fill in each blank with a synonym to the word in the brackets.

1) In order to _____ (pursue) their interests in the Papal States and Italian politics, the Renaissance popes were involved in war and _____ (bloodshed). One of them, Julius Ⅱ even personally led armies against enemies, much to the disgust of the _____ (pious). Unlike the _____ (hereditary) monarchs, the popes came to rely on the practice of _____ (nepotism).

2) The whole world is _____ (permeated) by divinity, everything is touched by a "numinous" quality, nature is in effect _____ (enchanted), and God's purpose can be _____ (deciphered) through number, geometry, form—above all, through beauty; beauty is an essential _____ (component) in the search of the _____ (ultimate) reality, and imagination and vision are more significant in that _____ (quest) than logic and _____ (dogma).

3) The _____ (intensive) intellectual and artistic activity that characterized the Renaissance in Italy began to _____ (wane) toward the end of the 15th century. The French invasion of 1494 and the _____ (incessant) warfare that _____ (ensued) were the major cause...As Italian wealth _____ (diminished), there was less and less of a(n) _____ (surplus) to support artistic _____ (endeavors).

❷ Translation

❧ Translate the following sentences into Chinese.

1) Thanks to its military prowess and diplomatic leadership, Milan came very close to

achieving total domination of the northern part of Italy in the early 15th century, but for the resistance of Florence.

2) The great stake in the war was the rich wine-producing region of southwestern France, the Duchy of Gascony. The English king had previously relinquished all the French territories except Gascony, which he held as a fief under the French crown.

3) The prince must be both "a lion and a fox." The lion, Machiavelli explained, cannot protect himself from traps, and the fox cannot defend himself from wolves. A ruler, in other words, must have both strength and cunning.

Questions

🙠 Answer the following questions.

1) Why did the Renaissance begin in Italy?

2) What are the causes for the Hundred Years' War?

3) What is the theory of absolutism?

4) How did nationalism and patriotism help build the new monarchies in Spain and France?

5) What accounts for Germany and Italy's failure to become a unified state?

6) What is the spirit of Renaissance humanism?

7) What is the relationship between Platonism and the efflorescence of art in Renaissance?

8) What achievements did the Renaissance artists make? Who are those revolutionary artists?

Topics for Discussion

🙠 Below are two topics related to this chapter. Read them and finish the discussion.

1) As we have learned from this chapter, Machiavelli put forward a revolutionary view on politics. He did not think that the moral conduct of Christians should hold good for a ruler, and the only proper measure for judging the behavior of a prince is his power. He cautioned the prince about never revealing his true motives and methods, for it is useful to appear to be what one is not. Though the prince must stand ready, when necessary, to act against faith, charity, humanity, and religion, he must always seem to possess those qualities.

Form your views about "The end justifies the means" and support your views with substantial evidence and sound argumentation.

2) Do research on absolutism and despotism, and exchange your findings with your classmates.

5 Presentation

In groups, make a presentation on the following topics.

1) English Parliament

2) Wars of the Roses

3) civic humanism

4) Neoplatonism

5) Christian humanism

Chapter 14

The Reformation

The breakup of medieval civilization was completed in the 16th and 17th centuries by the explosive force of religious revolt and reform. Christianity had been divided into two by the schism of the Latin (Catholic) and the Greek (Orthodox) Churches (see earlier chapters). About 1520, the Reformation broke out within the Latin Church and by the time the conflict died down in about 1650, a third branch of Christianity had arisen: Protestantism. However, instead of being a united movement of reform intended by Martin Luther, Protestantism was split into many different Churches, each with its own ideology and beliefs. In response to the Protestant challenge, the Roman Catholic Church launched a reform to give the Church new strength. The revival of Roman Catholicism is often called the Catholic Reformation, or Counter-Reformation, and it was how those elements that were directly aimed at stopping the spread of Protestantism are termed by some scholars.

Reformation is the religious revolution that took place in the Western Church in the 16th century. Its greatest leaders undoubtedly were Martin Luther and John Calvin. Having far-reaching political, economic, and social effects, the Reformation became the basis for the founding of Protestantism, one of the three major branches of Christianity. In the Middle Ages, the Christian Church had come to be divided between the Catholic West and the Orthodox East. For many centuries, to preserve Western unity, the popes and bishops had exercised continuous watchfulness and strong discipline. During the Middle Ages, thousands of heretics had been burned at the stake in the name of Christian purity and unity. How did the Protestant heretics survive where their predecessors had perished? One reason was that the late medieval Church had suffered a fateful decline.

1. Decay of the Church

During the 13th century, the medieval Church had reached the height of its power. But the 14th and 15th centuries saw a steady fall in the condition of the Church, and by 1500, the organization had reached its low point.

The fortunes of the Church as a whole were closely tied to those of the papacy. Medieval popes like Gregory Ⅶ and Innocent Ⅲ had done much to strengthen the Church's structure. But the popes of later centuries had been less successful in their undertakings, and their failures affected the entire institution. Boniface Ⅷ, for example, was defeated in his struggle with the French King Philip the Fair. After Boniface's death in 1303, Philip moved quickly to avoid future trouble with Rome by forcing the election of a French bishop as Pope Clement Ⅴ. The new relationship was demonstrated shortly thereafter when Pope Clement Ⅴ transferred his court from Rome to Avignon, a papal holding on the lower Rhone River, just east of the border of the French kingdom. Clement secured a French majority in the College of Cardinals, and for some 70 years, a succession of French popes reigned at Avignon. More serious embarrassments to the Church were yet to come. In 1377, the Roman populace selected an Italian Pope, while the French cardinals fled Rome, pronounced the election invalid, and moved to Avignon with the Pope of their own. Each declared the other to be a false Pope and excommunicated him and his followers. The Great Schism lasted about 40 years. Europe now endured the spectacle of a Church divided into opposing camps, with two popes and two Colleges of Cardinals. Conscientious Christians were distressed, for they had no way of being certain who was the Pope and who was the "antipope." Civil rulers supported whichever side seemed more useful politically. Thus, France and its allies recognized Avignon, while England and the German princes recognized Rome. To settle this Schism, a third Pope was elected. But by this time, the papacy had suffered serious damage. The foundation of papal power had previously been its immense moral authority. That position was now gravely weakened, opening the way to contempt and defiance.

2. The Awakening Reform Spirit

Sickened by the pompous formalism of the established rituals of the Church, many devout Christians began to turn inward in their devotions. In northern Europe, the 15th century saw a revival of mysticism and pietism. People joined together in semi-religious communities stressing Christlike simplicity, purity of heart, and direct communion with God. Other Christians were moving, at the same time, toward a new idea of what the Church should be. Their model was "primitive" Christianity which was practiced during the 1st century after Christ. In England, the followers of John Wycliffe became a widespread movement for a time, and the Bohemian supporters of the Czech reformer Jan Hus were able to take and hold an entire country.

2.1 John Wycliffe

A leading Oxford scholar and teacher, Wycliffe was among the first to question openly the need for priesthood. After a lifetime of study, Wycliffe concluded that the Church was suffering from more than just the misbehavior of some of its clergy. He challenged the established role and power of the clergy itself—arguing that God and Scripture (the Bible) are the sole sources of spiritual authority. And to enable ordinary English people to read Scripture for themselves, he made an English translation of the Vulgate Bible. For challenging the accepted doctrines of authority and salvation, he was condemned and forced to retire from teaching.

2.2　Jan Hus

Hus was a priest and a professor at Charles University in Prague, in the kingdom of Bohemia. Already active in efforts to reform the clergy, he was inspired by the writings of Wycliffe to launch stronger, more radical attacks. Bohemia was part of the Holy Roman Empire, and Emperor Sigismund had grown disturbed by the mounting agitation among the Bohemians. When Hus was summoned by the Council of Constance in 1414 to stand trial on the charge of heresy, the Emperor promised him safe-conduct to and from the trial. After a long and cruel imprisonment in Constance, Hus was tried and found guilty. The Emperor did not keep his promise of protection, and Hus, refusing to recant his beliefs, went to his death at the stake. The reaction in Bohemia was instantaneous. Anti-German and anti-papal sentiments were inflamed. A bloody uprising erupted, which lastly took over the country, fought off Catholic campaigns against it, and eventually merged into the Reformation. This was but the beginning of a long series of political-religious wars in Europe.

3. Political and Social Influence

By 1500, ideas for religious reform were in broad circulation, and a century after Hus, the political and social conditions in Europe were also shifting. The new situation would permit the rise of religious founders instead of religious martyrs. National sentiment and political absolutism were working against the principle and practice of the universal Church. As distinctively national cultures took shape, people grew increasingly conscious of belonging to a particular nation—a nation independent of all others.

This popular feeling supported the desire of kings and princes to gain control over the Church in their own territories and to build state Churches, especially in Germany and England, where the kings and princes expected to enlarge their powers in the event of a religious break with Rome. The higher social classes also began to sense that they might benefit from a break with Rome. In Germany, the Church was immensely wealthy, holding from one-fifth to one-third of the total real estate. The landed aristocrats looked on those holdings with covetous eyes, and members of the middle class disliked the fact that Church properties were exempt from taxes. And all classes of German society deplored the flow of

Church revenues to Rome; the feeling that the "foreign" papacy was draining the homeland of wealth thus created another source of support for a religious revolt. These economic, social, and political factors must be kept in mind if we are to understand the nature and success of the Protestant reform movements. The success of the Protestant leaders was due primarily to the new political and social forces. The time was ripe for religious revolt in northern Europe; the division of the Roman Church was at hand.

4. The Revolt of Luther: "Justification by Faith"

Martin Luther (1483–1546), like the other Protestant reformers, did not intend, at the outset, to divide the Church or to start a new Church. He believed that he had the correct vision of the one true Church, and he set out to convert all Christians to his point of view. But because Luther could not, in fact, convert all Christians, and because other reformers then arose whom he could not dominate either, the end result was the division (and subdivision) of the Church.

Luther's beliefs were mainly the product of a long spiritual pilgrimage marked by doubt, agony, and finally conviction. One thing is sure that by the time he completed his liberal arts course at the University of Erfurt in Saxony, he had decided to abandon secular life and enter a monastery. His decision was sealed, as he later explained, when he was caught in a violent thunderstorm, terrified, and interpreted the thunder as a call from God. He finished his doctor's degree in Wittenberg in 1512 and stayed there as a professor of theology. It was when preparing lectures on the Bible that he was struck by certain passages in Paul's Epistle to the Romans, for instance, "The just shall live by faith." (1: 17) After days and nights of pondering, he concluded, "By grace and sheer mercy God justifies (saves) us through faith." Although personally relieved, he began to be troubled. If people received faith according to God's secret judgment, of what use was the ordained priesthood? If every Christian was, in effect, a priest, were not the claims of the clergy absurd and hateful? And what good were the special vows and way of life undertaken by monks and nuns? If works were no help to salvation, what was the benefit of sacraments, pilgrimages, and papal indulgences?

It was in fact the issue of indulgences that set religious passions aflame. In Catholic teaching, indulgences may reduce or eliminate penalties due for sins, both on the earth and in the purgatory. It happened that a Dominican friar Tetzel, who was selling indulgences in Germany, came to Wittenberg. Tetzel, however, made extravagant claims for indulgences, implying that they would automatically remove a sinner's guilt as well as the penalty. For Luther, the idea that a believer could purge himself of guilt in the eyes of God in return for the "good work" of paying money to an indulgence seller was a flagrant distortion of religious teachings. He reportedly nailed the "Ninety-Five Theses" on the door of Wittenberg Castle Church, charging that the money from Tetzel's sale of indulgences was going to Rome for the building of a new Saint Peter's church. He also challenged indulgences in general, implying that they were of doubtful value. His charges struck a sympathetic chord with the laity. Copies of the "Ninety-Five Theses" were distributed throughout Germany. With the challenge against Rome expanding and escalating, it was only natural that Pope Leo X excommunicated Luther who responded by burning the bull (the papal document of excommunication) before the city gates of Wittenberg, thus demonstrating his defiance of Rome. Thanks to the elector Frederick who had his soldiers kidnap Luther and take him to Frederick's castle, Luther remained in the castle for about a year, working on a German translation of the Bible. His "people's" version of Scripture was printed in many thousands of copies, and helped shape the modern German language as well as Protestant doctrine.

Lutheranism was legally acknowledged in the Holy Roman Empire by the Peace of Augsburg in 1555. However, by that time, it had lost much of its momentum. A new Protestant form of Calvinism replaced Lutheranism with a clarity of doctrine and a fervor that made it attractive to a whole new generation of Europeans.

Ninety-Five Theses

By Martin Luther

Out of love and concern for the truth, and with the object of eliciting it, the following heads will be the subject of a public discussion at Wittenberg under the presidency of the reverend father, Martin Luther, Augustinian, Master of Arts and Sacred Theology, and duly appointed lecturer on these subjects in that place. He requests that whoever cannot be present personally to debate the matter orally will do so in absence in writing.

1. When our Lord and Master, Jesus Christ, said "Repent," He called for the entire life of believers to be one of repentance.

2. The word cannot be properly understood as referring to the sacrament of penance, i.e. confession and satisfaction, as administered by the clergy.

3. Yet its meaning is not restricted to repentance in one's heart; for such repentance is null unless it produces outward signs in various mortifications of the flesh.

4. As long as hatred of self abides (i.e. true inward repentance) the penalty of sin abides, viz., until we enter the kingdom of heaven.

5. The Pope has neither the will nor the power to remit any penalties beyond those imposed either at his own discretion or by canon law.

6. The Pope himself cannot remit guilt, but only declare and confirm that it has been remitted by God; or, at most, he can remit it in cases reserved to his discretion. Except

for these cases, the guilt remains untouched.

7. God never remits guilt to anyone without, at the same time, making him humbly submissive to the priest, His representative.

8. The penitential canons apply only to men who are still alive, and, according to the canons themselves, none applies to the dead.

9. Accordingly, the Holy Spirit, acting in the person of the Pope, manifests grace to us, by the fact that the papal regulations always cease to apply at death, or in any hard case.

It is a wrongful act, due to ignorance, when priests retain the canonical penalties on the dead in purgatory.

...

5. Calvin and the Elect: "Predestination"

Luther was by no means the only religious rebel at work during the 1520s. And although he tried to impose his doctrine on the others, he failed to do so outside northern Germany and Scandinavia. The logic of his own thought, in fact, worked against a unified reform movement. He had taught that each individual, guided by the Holy Spirit, must see the truth of Scripture according to his or her own conscience. Once papal authority had been overthrown, there was no logical limit to the number of creeds and denominations. Of the countless separations that followed Luther's revolt, two deserve our special attention because of their far-reaching historical impact. One is the Church of England, the most conservative of the major splits from Rome; the other, initiated by John Calvin, departed most radically from the Catholic tradition—in doctrine, spirit, organization, and ritual.

Born and raised as a Frenchman, Calvin (1509–1564) prepared for the priesthood in Paris when he was a young man. In 1533, Calvin had a sudden idea of religious reform. When he was only 26 years old, he finished the *Institutes of the Christian Religion*, which stood as the principal statement of Protestant theology for some 300 years and as such is comparable to Thomas Aquinas's *Summa Theologia*. By that time, fear of persecution by the Catholic King had forced him to flee France, and he eventually settled down in the Swiss city of Geneva in 1536, and within a short time, his version of reformed Christianity achieved dominance in the community. For some 20 years, until his death in 1564, he guided the Church, the State, and the Academy of Geneva. However, Calvin's influence was not confined to his city. He corresponded with rulers as well as theologians, so many reformers came to him and returned to their homelands with Calvinism. Calvinism thus became the leading Protestant force in France, the Netherlands, Scotland, and England.

The best known and the most controversial of Calvin's doctrine is predestination and election. God, as Calvin declared, foreknows and determines everything that happens in the universe—even events ordinarily credited to chance. It follows that He determines who shall be saved and who shall be forever lost. To the charge that God could not be so unfair as to condemn most of humankind to damnation, Calvin answered that no one deserves salvation and that it is only through God's gracious mercy that some are saved. Further, it is wrong to question the plans and judgment of God. But many would not accept so harsh a doctrine because it is very gloomy and it denies free will. Man has only a worm's eye view of Creation. Whatever God has willed is right, because he has willed it.

In reply to the charge that his doctrine would destroy all incentives to follow a worthy Christian life and cause some people to throw themselves into reckless indulgence, Calvin declared that nothing in the doctrine of predestination excuses any person from striving to obey God's commandments. On the contrary, Calvin argued, no one knows for certain who is of the "elect" and who is "reprobate." All individuals, therefore, should act as if they enjoy God's favor. If they do enjoy that favor, they should want their lives to be shining examples to others; if they do not enjoy it, they should obey God anyway.

Calvin applied this line of reasoning with strict logic to the entire field of Christian morals to direct and keep people's behavior under control. Puritanism as a social discipline was thus developed by Calvin. He criticized any form of decoration and recreation lest they lead to vanity and pride. Card playing, theater, drinking, and dancing are forbidden, since they seduce the heart from chastity and purity. Interestingly but not without logic, Calvin accepted business as a normal Christian vocation. He was the first theologian to praise the capitalist virtues: hard work, thrift, and the accumulation of money, as long as that wealth was not used for self-indulgence and the businessmen, like every other Christian, were sober and disciplined, dedicated to the "service of the Lord." Calvin's faith suited the economic realities of the day and was attractive not only to solid businessmen but also to colonial pioneers. Carried to New England in the 17th century, Calvinism (Puritanism) contributed significantly to the shaping of American life.

6. Henry VIII and the Church of England

The Church of England, or the Anglican Church, represented a sort of compromise between extreme Protestantism and Roman Catholicism. Unlike the reforms in other parts of Europe initiated by individuals, the religious reform in England was mainly carried through by its monarchs. From the time of Henry VIII, who initiated the reform, to the time of Elizabeth I, who completed the reform, changes were prompted primarily by the wishes of the crown.

6.1   Henry's Break from Rome

Henry Ⅷ, intended by his father Henry Ⅶ for a career in the Church, came to the throne when his elder brother Arthur died. After his coronation, Henry formally defended the Catholic view of the sacraments against Luther's public attack. As a reward, Pope Leo Ⅹ gave Henry the title "Defender of the Faith."

But Henry came to resent the Roman interference in the affairs of his kingdom. His break from Rome started with a personal matter. In order to preserve the alliance between England and Spain, Henry had married Catherine of Aragon, the widow of his elder brother. Now he wanted to divorce her because she had failed to produce a male heir, and wanted to marry Anne Boleyn, a lady-in-waiting to Queen Catherine. Henry relied on Cardinal Wolsey, the highest-ranking English Church official and lord chancellor to the king to obtain from Pope Clement Ⅶ an annulment of the king's marriage. The Pope might have been willing to oblige but for the sack of Rome in 1527, which made the Pope dependent on the Holy Roman Emperor Charles Ⅴ, who happened to be Catherine's nephew. Clement decided to do nothing, hoping that something would happen to spare him from making the choice. After nearly six years of waiting, Henry's patience ran out. He married Anne Boleyn in 1533, after his newly appointed archbishop, Thomas Cranmer, had declared his marriage to Catherine annulled. Anne gave birth to a girl, Elizabeth. Clement promptly excommunicated the king and released Henry's subjects from their obligation of obedience to the crown.

Yet, Henry did not wish to become a Protestant or have England turn Lutheran. He sought instead to confirm the Anglican Church—no longer the Roman Catholic Church in England but the Church of England—as a king of rejection of papal supremacy. In 1534, Parliament completed the break of the Church of England with Rome by passing the Act of Supremacy, which declared that the king was "taken, accepted, and reputed the only supreme head on earth of the Church of England," and approved his power to "repress, redress, and reform" all errors, heresies, and abuses in religion. Henry's taking control of the Church of England did not mean that he wished to reform its doctrine. On the contrary, he disliked the Protestant tendencies in the country and had Parliament pass the notorious Six Articles, which required all the king's subjects to accept such Catholic beliefs as transubstantiation, celibacy of the clergy, and the necessity of oral confession in the Sacrament of Penance.

6.2   Reaction Under Mary

Three years after marrying Anne, Henry accused her of adultery and treason, had her beheaded, and then went on to take four more wives in succession. His third wife Jane Seymour gave him a son at last. But the boy, coming to the throne as Edward Ⅵ when only 10 years old (1547), died before coming of age, and the crown passed, after all, to his elder sister Mary, the daughter of Catherine of Aragon.

Mary (1553–1558) was a Catholic who fully intended to restore England to the Roman Catholic fold. But her restoration of Catholicism aroused opposition. One reason was her marriage to Philip Ⅱ, son of Charles Ⅴ and the future king of Spain. Philip was strongly disliked in England. Another reason was that her foreign policy of alliance with Spain aroused further hostility, especially when her forces lost Calais, the last English possession from the Hundred Years' War. Finally, the burning of more than 300 Protestant heretics further stimulated people's hatred against "bloody Mary." As a result, England was more Protestant by the end of her reign than it had been in the beginning.

6.3   The Elizabethan Compromise

Elizabeth (1533–1603), the daughter of Anne Boleyn, inherited the crown upon Mary's death in 1558. She had been raised a Protestant but, unlike her half-sister, was neither devout nor fanatical. As queen, she stood firmly for a Protestant Church and independence from Rome. But her first concern was for the security of the crown and the unity of her subjects. She established the Elizabethan Compromise (or Settlement), which remains to this day the foundation of the Anglican Church. She approved the Parliament to enact a revised summary of official doctrine known as the "Thirty-Nine Articles," which was designed to satisfy all but extremists. The Thirty-Nine Articles were Lutheran or Calvinist on certain matters, including the exclusive authority of Scripture, salvation by faith alone, the number of sacraments, and the freedom of the clergy to marry. The Elizabethan Settlement brought stability because most of the English (who by this time were weary of religious quarreling) were prepared to conform. Elizabeth, who cared little about the private views and doubts of her subjects, was content with outward obedience.

7. The Roman Catholic Response

Catholic reforms were inspired, in part, by the same ideas and ideals that had motivated Luther and other religious rebels. Though some aims were common to both the Catholic and the Protestant reform movements, there were important differences between them. The Protestant leaders wanted a reconstruction of the Church, in accordance with unorthodox theories of authority, priesthood, and salvation. The Catholic reformers, on the other hand, accepted the central doctrine, tradition, and organization of the Church. What they desired was a purer Christian life within the existing Church, in keeping with its historic tradition of self-reformation.

7.1   Society of Jesus

Of all the new religious orders, the most important was the Society of Jesus, known as the Jesuits, which became the chief instrument of the Catholic Reformation. The Society of Jesus was founded by a Spanish nobleman, Igantius of Loyola (1491–1556). The new order was grounded on the principles of absolute obedience to the papacy, a strict hierarchical order for the society, the use of education to achieve its goals, and a dedication to engage in "conflict for God."

The Jesuits pursued two major activities. They established highly disciplined schools, for they believed the thorough education of young people was crucial to combating the advance of Protestantism. In the course of the 16th century, the Jesuits took over the premier academic posts in Catholic universities, and by 1600, they were the most famous educators in Europe. Another prominent activity was the spread of the Catholic faith among non-Christians. Francis Xavier (1506–1552), one of the original members of the Jesuits, carried the message of Catholic Christianity to the East. He was successful in converting tens of thousands in India, Malacca, Moluccas, and Japan. In 1552, Xavier set out for China but died of a fever before he reached the mainland. Jesuit activity in China was taken up by other missionaries, especially an Italian Matteo Ricci (1552–1610). He was the first to lay down the so-called "adaptation" strategy for his succeeding missionaries, i.e. dressing like a Confucian scholar, drawing parallels between Christian and Confucian concepts, and showing the similarities between Christian morality and Confucian ethics. To his credit, Ricci was successful in converting a number of famous Chinese gentry scholars and was even permitted into the imperial court. The Jesuit reports of missionaries' experiences heightened European curiosity about this great society on the other side of the world.

7.2   A Revived Papacy

A severe criticism of the Protestants on Roman Catholicism was the corruption which had been given rise to the involvement of the Renaissance papacy in dubious finances and Italian political and military affairs. The pontificate of Pope Paul Ⅲ (1534–1549) proved to be a turning point in the reform of the papacy. In 1535, Paul took the audacious step of appointing a reform commission to study the condition of the Church. A decisive turning point in the direction of the Catholic Reformation and the nature of papal reforms came in the 1540s. Some Catholic moderates, in the hope of restoring Christian unity, made a final attempt to reach a compromise with the Protestant moderates on a number of doctrinal issues on a colloquy held at Regensburg. However, their efforts were regarded as heresy by Catholic conservatives, who persuaded Paul Ⅲ to establish the Roman Inquisition in 1542 to ferret out doctrinal errors. There was to be no compromise with Protestantism. Any hope of restoring

Christian unity by compromise was fast fading and the activities of the Council of Trent made any compromise virtually impossible. The Council of Trent met intermittently between 1545 and 1563. Moderate Catholic reformers hoped that compromises would be made in formulating doctrinal definitions that would encourage Protestants to return to the Church. Conservatives, however, favored an uncompromising restatement of Catholic doctrine in strict opposition to Protestant positions. After a struggle, the latter group won.

Reformation, if viewed from the perspective of the 20th century, was odd and bloody, but it had historical significance. Obviously, Luther's cause in Germany was indebted to the growing sense of nationality at the time and also stimulated that sense. The turning away from Rome helped the power-seeking princes of northern Europe put the Church under state control. Also, Protestantism and capitalism tended to be mutually reinforced. Calvinism, for instance, gave his blessing to businessmen and by praising hard work and thrift, he supported bourgeois morale and encouraged the accumulation of capital.

Another heritage Reformation left for humans was its contribution to individualism. The Protestantism, by stressing the right and power of all believers to read the Bible for themselves and to communicate directly with God, and thus questioning the authority of Rome, made the first step toward religious individualism and gave new force to the tendency of individualism prevalent in art, literature, and society from the close of the Middle Ages onward.

Key Terms

decay of the Church → John Wycliffe and his English translation of the Bible → the Ninety-Five Theses → Justification by Faith → John Calvin and predestination → Henry VII's break from Rome → bloody Mary → the Elizabethan Compromise → the Roman Catholic reforms → Matteo Ricci and his adaptation strategy → the Council of Trent

Exercises

1 Vocabulary Building

✎ Fill in each blank with a synonym to the word or phrase in the brackets.

1) The Emperor did not keep his promise of protection, and Hus, refusing to _____ (recant) his beliefs, went to his death at the stake. The reaction in Bohemia was

_____ (instantaneous). Anti-German and anti-papal sentiments were _____ (inflamed). A bloody _____ (uprising) erupted, which lastly _____ (took over) the country, _____ (fought off) Catholic campaigns against it, and eventually merged into the Reformation.

2) The landed aristocrats looked on those holdings with _____ (covetous) eyes, and members of the middle class disliked the fact that Church properties were _____ (exempt) from taxes. And all classes of German society _____ (deplored) the flow of Church _____ (revenues) to Rome; the feeling that the "foreign" papacy was draining the homeland of wealth thus created another source of support for a religious revolt.

3) For Luther, the idea that a believer could _____ (purge) himself of guilt in the eyes of God _____ (in return for) the "good work" of paying money to an indulgence seller was a(n) _____ (flagrant) _____ (distortion) of religious teachings.

❷ Translation

☙ Translate the following sentences into Chinese.

1) In reply to the charge that his doctrine would destroy all incentives to follow a worthy Christian life and cause some people to throw themselves into reckless indulgence, Calvin declared that nothing in the doctrine of predestination excuses any person from striving to obey God's commandments.

2) The Pope might have been willing to oblige but for the sack of Rome in 1527, which made the Pope dependent on the Holy Roman Emperor Charles V, who happened to be Catherine's nephew. Clement decided to do nothing, hoping that something would happen to spare him from making the choice.

3) In 1534, Parliament completed the break of the Church of England with Rome by passing the Act of Supremacy, which declared that the king was "taken, accepted, and reputed the only supreme head on earth of the Church of England," and approved his power to "repress, redress, and reform" all errors, heresies, and abuses in religion.

❸ Questions

☙ Answer the following questions.

1) What were the possible causes of the Reformation?

2) What was the essential doctrine of Lutheranism? What did Luther revolt against?

3) Why do we say the logic of Luther's doctrine works against a unified reform movement?

4) What is predestination theory?

5) What was the charge against Calvin's predestination? And how did he defend?

6) Calvin criticized any form of decoration and recreation lest they lead to vanity and pride, but he accepted business as a normal Christian vocation. On what grounds?

7) What is Ricci's adaptation strategy?

8) What is the significance of the Reformation?

④ Topic for Discussion

❧ Below is a topic related to this chapter. Read it and finish the discussion.

Matteo Ricci elaborated on the similarities between Catholicism and Confucianism in his Chinese book *The True Meaning of the Lord of Heaven* (《天主实义》). Read the book and have a discussion on Ricci's findings and arguments.

⑤ Research and Writing

❧ Read the following direction and finish the research and writing.

German sociologist Max Weber created a lively controversy in his book *The Protestant Ethic and the Spirit of Capitalism*, in which he argued that it was only after the emergence of Protestantism, with its concept of "the calling" and "worldly asceticism," that a "rational economic ethic" emerged. R. H. Tawney, in *Religion and the Rise of Capitalism*, stressed Calvinism as even more sympathetic to capitalism than Lutheranism was.

Do research on Protestantism and capitalism, try to find if there is any logic relation between them, and write a report on "Protestantism and Capitalism."

Chapter 15

Politics and Religious Wars

By the middle of the 16th century, after the Reformation and the Counter-Reformation on the part of Catholicism, both Protestantism and Catholicism had become highly militant to spread the word of God as they interpreted it. Although religious beliefs were at the heart of the conflicts, economic, social, and political forces also played an important role in these confrontations.

1. The French Wars of Religion (1562–1598)

The French Valois rulers Francis I (1515–1547) and Henry II (1547–1559) had been strong rulers. But when Henry II was killed accidentally in a tournament, he was succeeded by a series of weak, feeble, and neurotic sons. The strong monarchy broke loose and a series of intermittent civil wars broke out. Religious, political, and social forces all contributed to these wars.

The Huguenots (as the French Calvinists were called) came from all levels of society, and possibly 40%~50% of the French nobility became Huguenots, including the House of Bourbon, which stood next to the Valois in the royal line of succession and ruled the southern French kingdom of Navarre. The spread of French Calvinism forced the French ruler Catherine de Médicis to show more tolerance for the Huguenots which angered the powerful Roman Catholic Guise family. Its partisans massacred a Huguenot congregation at Vassy (1562), causing an uprising in the provinces. Many inconclusive skirmishes followed, and compromises were reached in 1563, 1568, and 1570. In 1572, the Catholic and Calvinist parties had apparently been reconciled through the marriage of the sister of the reigning Valois King Charles IV and Henry of Navarre, the Bourbon ruler of Navarre. Henry was also the acknowledged political leader of the Huguenots, and many Huguenots traveled to Paris to celebrate the wedding. The Guise family managed to persuade the king and his mother to eliminate the Huguenot leaders with one swift blow. The massacre soon began and in three days, 3,000 Huguenots were killed in Paris alone and thousands more were killed in provincial towns. Henry was spared by promising to turn Catholic. The civil war resumed and the turning point came in the War of the Three Henries in 1588–1589. Henry, Duke of Guise, in the pay of Philip Ⅱ of Spain, seized Paris and forced the ruling king Henry Ⅲ to make him as his chief minister. To rid himself of the Guise manipulation, Henry Ⅲ assassinated the Duke of Guise and then joined with Henry of Navarre (now returned to Calvinism) to retake the city of Paris. However, Henry Ⅲ in turn was assassinated by a monk. Henry of Navarre now claimed the throne and converted once again to Catholicism. With his coronation in 1594, the French wars of religion finally came to an end and the religious toleration of the Huguenots was guaranteed by the Edict of Nantes (1598). The French wars of religion demonstrated once again to many French people the necessity for a strong government, laying a foundation for the growth of monarchy in the 17th century.

2. Philip Ⅱ's Spain and the Revolt of the Netherlands

King Philip Ⅱ of Spain (1556–1598) was the greatest advocate of militant Catholicism and the most important political figure in the second half of the 16th century. It was in his reign that Spain reached its greatness, both politically and culturally.

Philip was a good example of the early paternal absolute monarchy. He would expect no opposition to the royal will and he insisted upon personal supervision of most administrative activities, even down to the smallest details. Unwilling to distinguish between important and trivial matters, Philip's meticulousness was tragic for both him and Spain.

Carrying on the work of Ferdinand and Isabella, Philip was a true Spanish nationalist, and his nationalism was not confined to Spain. His national unity included the Spanish possessions in the Netherlands which he had inherited from Charles Ⅴ. The Netherlands came under the rule of the Spanish Habsburgs following the division of the territories of Charles Ⅴ. It consisted of 17 provinces (modern Netherlands, Belgium, and Luxembourg), amongst which seven in the north were largely Germanic in culture and Dutch-speaking, while the rest in the south were French- and Flemish-speaking, and thus closely tied to France. Protestantism first spread there from Germany and then grew rapidly under the Calvinist leadership. In 1567, Philip Ⅱ responded to the spread of Calvinism with cruel repression. In reaction to this challenge to their self-government, both Catholics and Calvinists rebelled in 1566 under the leadership of a local aristocrat and Habsburg official, William the Silent, Prince of Orange-Nassau. There followed nearly half a century of wars, in which the Netherlands gradually became divided. Spain recovered the southern Netherlands for the old rulers and the old religion. In the north, however, the defiant Calvinists, with English help, fought the Habsburg forces on land and sea. In 1581, they declared independence, but it took nearly 30 years before a truce gave them de facto Spanish recognition in 1609. A new country had appeared, the United Provinces of the Netherlands—often known as Holland, the name of its largest province.

The turning point and also the point of Spain's decline was the ill-fated expedition of Spanish Armada. Philip's rivalry with England, born partially of nationalistic motives and partially of fanatical devotion to Catholicism, was a disaster, which resulted in its defeat by England, the destruction of Spanish primacy in sea power, and the rise of British maritime strength.

3. The England of Elizabeth

After the death of Queen Mary in 1558, her half-sister Elizabeth ascended the throne of England. During Elizabeth's reign, England rose to prominence. It became the leader of the Protestant nations of Europe, laid the foundation for a world empire, and experienced a cultural renaissance.

As seen in Chapter 14, Elizabeth's religious policy was based on moderation and compromise. The daughter of Henry VIII and Anne Boleyn who was beheaded by her husband, Elizabeth had a difficult early life and was even imprisoned during Mary's reign. The fluctuation she experienced taught her caution and tolerance. As a ruler, all she wanted for England was to prevent it from being torn apart, whether over matters of religion or politics. She did not care much what her subjects believed actually as long as they did not threaten the state's power.

Caution, moderation, and expediency also dictated Elizabeth's foreign policy. Realizing that war could be disastrous for her island kingdom and her own rule, she tried to avoid entering any war directly. Nevertheless, she found herself leading not only a Protestant nation but also the Protestant cause in Europe. She had to support the Calvinists led by John Know and the nobles in their rebellion against the militant Catholic queen, Mary Stuart, who was Elizabeth's cousin. When Mary fled to England after her forced abdication in 1568, Elizabeth put her in genteel confinement for almost two decades, but not to kill her. Mary was beheaded in 1587 when she became the center of conspiracies to overthrow Elizabeth.

The age of Elizabeth also brought England to the threshold of world power. Mary's husband Philip, who had become King Philip II of Spain in 1556, sought the hand of Elizabeth after the death of his wife. Elizabeth rejected, so Philip finally decided to take her kingdom by force. The execution of Mary exacerbated the cold war with Spain which had resulted from English support of the Dutch rebels and from the Queen's encouragement to English seamen who had been raiding Spanish ships and colonies. In 1588, Philip sent a mighty fleet, the Spanish Armada, against England, only to be routed in the Channel by the English navy and smashed by storms on its return home. With Spain, the leading power of the Continent, thus humbled, the English became conscious of their strength on the sea. Elizabeth's reign marked a turning point in the nation's history. Thereafter, English sea power, commerce, and diplomacy were to exercise a mounting influence over European and world affairs.

Queen Elizabeth I ruled England from 1558 to 1603 with a consummate skill that contemporaries considered unusual in a woman. Queen Elizabeth I was the greatest master of public relations ever to occupy the English throne. The Queen was a highly accomplished speaker. This selection is taken from her speech to Parliament in 1601 when she had been forced to retreat on the issue of monopolies after vehement protests by members of Parliament. The speech was known at once, and ever afterwards, as Queen Elizabeth I's Golden Speech.

The Golden Speech

By Queen Elizabeth I

We perceive your coming is to present thanks unto us; Know I accept them with no less joy than your loves can have desire to offer such a Present, and do more esteem it than any Treasure of Riches, for those We know how to prize, but Loyalty, Love, and Thanks, I account them invaluable, and though God hath raised Me high, yet this I account the glory of my Crown, that I have reigned with your Loves. This makes that I do not so much rejoice that God hath made Me to be a Queen, as to be a Queen over so thankful a People, and to be the mean under God to conserve you in safety, and preserve you from danger, yea to be the Instrument to deliver you from dishonor, from shame, and from infamy; to keep you from servitude, and from slavery under our Enemies; and cruel tyranny, and vile oppression intended against us: for the better withstanding whereof, We take very acceptably your intended helps, and chiefly in that it manifests your loves and largeness of heart to your Sovereign. Of My self I must say this, I never was any greedy scraping grasper, nor a strict fast-holding Prince, nor yet a waster. My heart was never set upon any worldly goods, but only for my Subjects good. What you do bestow on Me, I will not hoard up, but receive it to bestow on you again; yea Mine own Properties I account yours to be expended for your good, and your eyes shall see the bestowing of it for your welfare.

...

To be a King, and wear a Crown, is a thing more glorious to them that see it, than it is pleasant to them that bear it: for my self, I never was so much enticed with the glorious name of a King, or the royal authority of a Queen, as delighted that god hath made me His Instrument to maintain His Truth and Glory, and to defend this Kingdome from dishonor, damage, tyranny, and oppression; But should I ascribe any of these things unto my self, or my sexly weakness, I were not worthy to live, and of all most unworthy of the mercies

I have received at Gods hands but to God only and wholly all is given and ascribed. The cares and trouble of a Crown I cannot more fitly resemble than to the Drugs of a learned Physician, perfumed with some Aromatical savor, or to bitter Pills gilded over, by which they are made more acceptable or less offensive, which indeed are bitter and unpleasant to take; and for my own part, were it not for Conscience sake to discharge the duty that God hath laid upon me, and to maintain his glory, and keep you in safety; in mine own disposition I should be willing to resign the place I hold to any other, and glad to be freed of the Glory with the Labors, for it is not my desire to live nor to reign longer than my life and reign shall be for your good. And though you have had and may have many mightier and wiser Princes sitting in this Seat, yet you never had nor shall have any that will love you better.

4. Thirty Years' War (1618–1648)

The Thirty Years' War, also called "the last of the religious wars," was fought mainly in the Germanic lands of the Holy Roman Empire, but it soon became a European-wide struggle. A brief look at the motives of the European states and the situation in the Holy Roman Empire provides the background necessary to understand the war.

Since the beginning of the 16th century, France had worked to break out of what was perceived as its encirclement by the House of Habsburg. In 1556, the Holy Roman Emperor Charles Ⅴ abdicated and divided his empire into two: Spain, Netherlands, Italy, and the New World were left to Philip, while Ferdinand inherited the Holy Roman Emperor and received the Habsburg possessions in Austria and eastern Europe. France felt threatened by the Spanish Habsburgs and feared the consolidation of the Holy Roman Empire by the Habsburg emperor. The second major party involved in the war was Spain. After the truce negotiation with the Dutch in 1609, Spain determined to retake control of the Netherlands, specifically the northern Dutch provinces. English and Dutch control of the seas forced the Spanish to find another route by way of Italy and western Germany. Finally, the Austrian Habsburg wished to consolidate their holdings in Austria and Bohemia by eliminating Protestantism and establishing stronger central authority. At the same time, they felt frustrated by their lack of real authority over the hundreds of German states. It was among the German states that the Thirty Years' War had its immediate beginning.

By 1609, Germany was dividing into two army camps in anticipation of religious war. One camp was the Protestant Union led by Frederick Ⅳ, a Calvinist ruler of the Palatinate; the other was the Catholic League led by Duke Maximilian of the south German state of Bavaria. The religious tension was exacerbated by conflict between Holy Roman emperors and German princes. The Habsburg emperors looked to Spain for assistance, while the princes turned to France. The war was conventionally held to have begun in 1618, when the future Holy Roman Emperor Ferdinand II, in his role as King of Bohemia, attempted to impose Roman Catholic absolutism on his domains, and the Protestant nobles of both Bohemia and Austria rose up in rebellion. Ferdinand won after a five-year struggle. In the second phase of the war, King Christian IV of Denmark, a Lutheran, saw an opportunity to gain valuable territories in Germany to balance his earlier loss of Baltic provinces to Sweden, and intervened in 1625. His campaign turned out to be a complete fiasco which ended Danish involvement in the Thirty Years' War and finished Denmark as a European power. The third phase came when Gustavus Adolphus, King of Sweden (1611–1635) entered into the war. Gustavus Adolphus was responsible for reviving Sweden and making it into a great Baltic power. Having no desire to see the Habsburgs in northern Germany and being a devout Lutheran, he felt compelled to aid his coreligionists in Germany. Furthermore, he was financed by the French. Adolphus' army swept the imperial forces out of the north and moved into the heart of Germany. At the Battle of Lützen (1632), the Swedish army prevailed but paid a high price for the victory when the king was killed in the battle. In 1634, the imperial army decisively defeated the Swedes at the Battle of Nordlingen at the end of 1634 and drove them out of southern Germany.

When the Swedes wished to continue, the French entered the war directly, beginning the fourth and the final phase of the war. By this time, the religious issues were giving way to dynastic power of politics. The Catholic French were now supporting the Protestant Swedes against the Catholic Habsburgs of Germany and Spain. This phase of war was fought by Sweden in northern Germany, and by France in the Netherlands and along the Rhine in western Germany. In the decisive Battle of Rocroi in 1643, the French beat the Spanish and brought an end to Spanish military greatness. After five years of negotiation, the war in Germany was officially ended by the Peace of Westphalia in 1648. Since the war, Spain had become a second-class power, and France had emerged as the dominant nation in Europe.

The Peace of Westphalia is a landmark in European history. Each prince retained the right to choose from Calvinism, Lutheranism, and Catholicism for his subjects without going to war. And conditions throughout the country were so wretched that none of them used forces to compel conformity. A kind of religious coexistence thus came into being. The Peace of Westphalia also marked a shift in the balance of dynastic power and the emergence of the modern European state system. At the Peace of Westphalia, the German princes won recognition as independent sovereigns, and the Holy Roman Empire was reduced to a shell. Switzerland and the Netherlands, which had once been subject to the Habsburgs, were also recognized as independent states. The biggest winner was the Bourbon dynasty of France, which, with the decline of Germany and of Habsburg Spain, took the lead in Europe, and a century of French dominance was at hand.

Key Terms

the French wars of religion → the Huguenots → King Philip Ⅱ of Spain → Spanish Armada → the England of Elizabeth → Thirty Years' War → the Peace of Westphalia

Exercises

❶ Vocabulary Building

❧ Complete the sentences with the words and phrases in the box, using their proper forms.

mount	ill-fated	fiasco	break loose	in the pay of
raid	with one swift blow	exacerbate	look to	abdicate

1) The strong monarchy _____ and a series of intermittent civil wars broke out.

2) The Guise family managed to persuade the king and his mother to eliminate the Huguenot leaders _____.

3) Henry, Duke of Guise, _____ Philip Ⅱ of Spain, seized Paris and forced the ruling king Henry Ⅲ to make him as his chief minister.

4) The turning point and also the point of Spain's decline was the _____ expedition of Spanish Armada.

5) When Mary fled to England after her forced _____ in 1568, Elizabeth put her in genteel confinement for almost two decades, but not to kill her.

6) Elizabeth's rejection of King Philip Ⅱ of Spain _____ the cold war with Spain which had resulted from English support of the Dutch rebels and from the Queen's encouragement to English seamen who had been _____ Spanish ships and colonies.

7) Thereafter, English sea power, commerce, and diplomacy were to exercise a(n) _____ influence over European and world affairs.

8) The Habsburg emperors _____ Spain for assistance, while the princes turned to France.

9) His campaign turned out to be a complete _____ which ended Danish involvement in the Thirty Years' War.

❷ Translation

❧ Translate the following sentences into Chinese.

1) In the north, however, the defiant Calvinists, with English help, fought the Habsburg forces on land and sea. In 1581, they declared independence, but it took nearly 30 years before a truce gave them de facto Spanish recognition in 1609.

2) Philip's rivalry with England, born partially of nationalistic motives and partially of fanatical devotion to Catholicism, was a disaster, which resulted in its defeat by England, the destruction of Spanish primacy in sea power, and the rise of British maritime strength.

3) As a ruler, all she wanted for England was to prevent it from being torn apart, whether over matters of religion or politics. She did not care much what her subjects believed actually as long as they did not threaten the state's power.

❸ Questions

❧ Answer the following questions.

1) What were the causes of the French wars of religion?

2) What was the fate of Spanish Armada? And what impact did the expedition have on Spain and England respectively?

3) How did Elizabeth I rule England?

4) What were the political motives of the Thirty Years' War?

❹ Term Explanation

❧ Explain the meaning of the following term in your own words.

the Peace of Westphalia

❺ Topic for Discussion

❧ Below is a topic related to this chapter. Read it and finish the discussion.

The following is a quote (Chinese version) from the book *Tolerance* by Hendrik Willem van Loon:

"大凡为宽容而战的人，不论彼此有什么不同，都有一点是一致的：他们的信仰总是伴随着怀疑；他们可以诚实地相信自己正确，却又从不能使自己的怀疑转化为坚固绝对的信念。"

1) Read the book and try to back translate the quote into English.

2) Based on what you have learned from this course, build your argument on religious tolerance, and exchange your views with your classmates.

Chapter 16

Two Systems of State: Absolutism and Constitutional Monarchy

The 17th century is regarded by some historians as a turning point in the evolution of a modern state system in Europe. After the religious disputes and wars, the credibility of Christianity had been irrevocably weakened and the idea of a united Christian Europe gave way to the practical realities of a system of secular states since now state took precedence over the salvation of souls. In the 17th-century state building, absolute and limited monarchy evolved, represented respectively by France and England.

During most of the Middle Ages, kings depended mainly upon the feudal lords for their royal revenue, for their soldiers, and to a very large extent, for their administration of justice. There was no feudal lord who would make any contribution to a cause that would reduce his own power and prestige. The feudal system had become a huge obstacle to centralized government. Another element that hampered the origins of nationalism was the power of the international ecclesiastical state—the Roman Catholic Church. The struggle for the supremacy of power between popes and secular kings, culminated in the Investiture Struggle, had been a constant conflict.

In the late medieval and early modern times, various civil and religious wars killed off many of the feudal nobility and did a great deal toward reducing the power of the feudal lords, which were especially illustrated by the Hundred Years' War, English Wars of the Roses, the French religious wars, and the later Thirty Years' War. But this self-destruction on the part of the feudal lords was not sufficient. What was needed for kings was a large independent source of income. With the Great Discovery and expansion, the monarchs now were able to meet their financing demands through various sources of income from oversea trade and colonization. These included some income from the discovery of precious metals, some from their share in piracy or privateers, some from fees from chartering commercial companies and granting of monopolies, and some from customs duties on the increased foreign trade. At the same time came the Protestant Revolution that broke up the unity of Roman Catholic Church and removed the ecclesiastical barriers to nationalism and royal dominance.

1. Theory of Absolutism

In the 17th and 18th centuries, absolutism appeared superior to other forms of government for very practical reasons: Despots were able to check civil strife within their realms, and in the struggles with competing rulers, they could command the full resources of their states. However, the absolute monarchs had to seek ideological justification for their rule. Although they might have turned to the absolutist theory of Machiavelli who had viewed politics as a purely secular art and science, monarchs preferred a higher justification for their authority, and they found it in the doctrine of divine right.

However, this was not the same with the divine right in the Middle Ages when all authorities were thought to be sent from heaven. Authorities were believed to be distributed and limited. Since Charlemagne the Great was anointed by Pope Leo Ⅲ at Christmas in 800, the relationship between the State and the Church had been defined. With the Pope as the donor in the superior position and Charlemagne under obligation, it gave force to later claim that the papacy had a right to withdraw what it had given. But the theorists of the 17th century had their own explanation. By reconciling absolutist concepts and practices with traditional Christian doctrine, they linked the absolute monarchy directly with God himself. Jacques Bossuet (1627–1704), a favored bishop of the court of Louis ⅩⅣ, was one of the chief theorists of divine-right monarchy. Referring to the Bible as the ultimate truth, he supported his points with appropriate quotations. He claimed that royal authority was sacred, fatherly, and absolute. The king's judgment was subject to no appeal on earth, and the king must be obeyed for reasons of religion and conscience. Whoever resisted the king's command in reality resisted God. For, as Bossuet declared, "The royal throne is not the throne of a man, but the throne of God Himself."

Bossuet was not the only French advocate for absolute monarchy. Another important theorist before him was Jean Bodin (1529–1596). Surrounded by the bloodshed of the Huguenot wars in France, Bodin realized that the salvation of his country lay in the strong rule of a central power, and as a direct consequence, produced his doctrine of sovereignty. In his theory, a government should have a strong power so that it could always outweigh the special interests of regional autonomy and of religious persuasion, because the state was, above all, to preserve order. This did not mean that the sovereign could do as he pleased. He had to abide by natural law, fairness, and by God's law. As he stated, "This sovereignty (of the state) is unassailable. 'He is sovereign who recognizes nothing greater than himself save only Immortal God...The prince or people who possess sovereign power cannot be called to account for their actions by anyone but Immortal God.'"[1] Though fanatical, his system

---

1　Peter Watson, *Ideas: A History of Thought from Fire to Freud*, London: Weidenfeld & Nicolson, 2005, p.500.

deliberately excluded religious issues, and clearly forbade religious issues to govern the policies of the state and be settled by force.

2. Absolutism in France: Louis XIV

Of all the 17th-century absolute monarchies, the most powerful and successful was that of France. Given the vicious civil wars that tore France apart in the 16th century, it is no wonder that France was the first to embrace the idea of a strong centralized government. Faced with such widespread demoralization and the collapse of all civilized standards, and with religious fanaticism on all sides, humanists everywhere came to the view that any system of government that put an end to civil wars was preferable to continual fighting.

There were two ministers who played crucial roles in maintaining monarchical authority. Cardinal Richelieu, a chief minister of Louis XIII, strengthened royal authority by eliminating the private armies and fortified cities of the Huguenots. He crushed the provincial and aristocratic revolts, and fashioned an effective instrument of royal power. His aim, as he stated, "was to make the king supreme in France and France supreme in Europe". When Louis XIV succeeded to the throne, he was only four years old. Cardinal Mazarin, Richelieu's trained successor, was designated by Anne of Austria, wife of the dead king, to dominate the government. Mazarin attempted to carry on Richelieu's policies until his death in 1661. The most important and perhaps the last challenge to the monarchical power before the French Revolution was a revolt known as the Fronde. The resentful nobles allied with the members of the Parliament of Paris and the masses of Paris in opposing the new taxes levied by the government to pay the costs of the Thirty Years' War. The Fronde broke out twice and were both crushed. With the end of the Fronde, the vast majority of the French concluded that the best hope for stability lay in the crown. When Mazarin died in 1661, Louis XIV took over the supreme power.

The early personal reign of Louis was highly successful in both internal and foreign affairs. At home, the parliament lost its traditional power to obstruct legislation; the judicial structure was reformed by the Codes of Civil Procedure (1667) and Criminal Procedure (1669), although the overlapping and confusing laws were left untouched. Urban law enforcement was improved by creation (1667) of the office of Lieutenant General of police for Paris, later imitated in other towns. Under Jean-Baptiste Colbert (1619–1683), Louis' Controller-General of finance, commerce, industry, and overseas colonies were developed by state subsidies, tight control over standards of quality, and high protective tariffs. Colbert was successful in sharply reducing the annual treasury deficit by developing economy and imposing more equitable, efficient taxation.

Colbert and the king shared the idea of glorifying the monarch and monarchy through the arts. Louis was a discriminating patron of the great literary and artistic figures of France's classical age. His state established or developed in rapid succession academies for painting and sculpture (1663), inscriptions (1663), French artists at Rome (1666), and science (1666), followed by the Paris Observatory (1667), and the academies of architecture (1671) and music (1672). The literary Academie Française also came under formal royal control in 1671. Money was lavished on buildings. In Paris, the Louvre was essentially completed with the classical colonnade by Claude Perrault. In Versailles, Louis XIII's hunting lodge was transformed into a remarkable palace and park, which were copied by Louis' fellow monarchs across Europe.

Louis XIV had a great proclivity for war. The increase in royal power led the king to develop a standing army subject to the monarch's command. However, his ends soon outstripped his means, as his ambitions roused much of Europe to form coalitions that even he could not overcome. In 1667, Louis invaded the Spanish Netherlands to his north and the Franche-Comté to the east. But a Triple Alliance of the Dutch, English, and Swedes forced him to sue for peace in 1668 and accept a few towns in the Spanish Netherlands. In 1672, Louis invaded the United Provinces. His initial success led Brandenburg, Spain, and the Holy Roman Empire to form a new coalition that forced Louis to end the Dutch War by making peace at Nimwegen in 1678, receiving Franche-Comté from Spain. Encouraged by the lands he obtained, Louis for the third time invaded the Holy Roman Empire eastward, which only led to an even wider coalition known as League of Augsburg, consisting of Spain, the Holy Roman Empire, the United Provinces, Sweden, and England. This bitterly eight-year struggle brought economic depression and famine to France. The Treaty of Ryswick ending the war forced Louis to give up most of his conquests in the empire, although he was allowed to keep Strasbourg and part of Alsace. The aging ruler was almost immediately drawn into the disastrous War of the Spanish Succession (1701–1714). Charles II left the throne of Spain in his will to a grandson of Louis XIV. The suspicion that France and Spain would finally be united in the same dynastic family caused the formation of a new coalition to prevent a Bourbon hegemony that would mean certain destruction of the European balance of power. The war dragged on 11 years, and came to an end with the Peace of Utrecht. France retained most of its earlier conquests, and the Spanish empire was divided between Philip V, Louis' grandson, who received Spain and its overseas colonies, and Holy Roman Emperor Charles VI, who acquired the Spanish Netherlands and Spain's Italian possessions. Louis was forced to agree that the crowns of France and Spain would remain separate despite the dynastic connection.

Louis held firm control for half a century, laboring ceaselessly at perfecting his royal image and performing his royal tasks. His governing style became the model for all Europe, as did the French army, language, manners, and culture.

3. Absolutism in Germany: Prussia and Austria

The Peace of Westphalia, which officially ended the Thirty Years' War in 1648, first gave the general Europeans a recognition of the growing national state system and the existence of independent national sovereignty. It brought diversity rather than unity, however, to Germany and helped to postpone German unification until the latter part of the 19th century. After 1648, the Holy Roman Empire was largely a nominal existence: as Voltaire said in the 18th century, the Holy Roman Empire was neither holy, nor Roman, nor an empire. Three hundred or more principalities in this land were virtually autonomous and sovereign. Of these states, two emerged as great European powers in the 17th and 18th centuries.

There appeared the dynasty and the state that were ultimately to bring unification to Germany, namely, Prussia under the Hohenzollerns. The Hohenzollerns came to the north European stage through the purchase of the Mark of Brandenburg by Frederick Hohenzollern from the bankrupt emperor Sigismund in 1415. Through fortunate marriage arrangements, they secured possessions of Prussia in 1618. The basis of the Prussian bureaucracy and military system was laid by Frederick William, the Great Elector (1640–1688). To sustain the army, William established the General War Commissariat to levy taxes for the army. The Commissariat soon evolved into an agency for the civil government as well. One important success of William was his winning over the nobles, whose support derived from the tacit agreement between them. In order to eliminate the nobles' power, William made a deal with them. In return for a free hand in running the government, he gave the nobles almost unlimited power over their peasants, exempted them from taxation, and awarded them the highest ranks in the army and the Commissariat on condition that they would not challenge his political authority. By 1688, when Frederick William died, Brandenburg-Prussia had become the most efficient state in Germany. His successor Frederick III (1688–1713) joined the coalition against Louis XIV in the War of Spanish Succession, and the Holy Roman Emperor awarded him the title of "King in Prussia." Elector Frederick III was transformed into King Frederick I, and Brandenburg-Prussia became simply Prussia. In the 18th century, Prussia emerged as a great power on the European stage.

The Austrian Habsburgs had long played a significant role in European politics as Holy Roman emperors. However, by the end of the Thirty Years' War, which was mainly battled in the land of Germany, the German princes won recognition as independent sovereigns, and the Holy Roman Empire was reduced to a shell. In the 17th century, the House of Austria made an important transition: to create a new empire in eastern and southeastern Europe in place of the lost German empire. After the Spanish branch of their dynasty died out, they spent many years on war and finally had to yield Spain to the Bourbon dynasty. But they were able to take over some of the Spanish Habsburg possessions in the Netherlands and Italy, and they held their own hereditary lands in central and eastern Europe in spite of rebellions by Protestant nobles and peasants. Leopold Ⅰ (1658–1705) encouraged the eastward movement of the Austrian empire, but he was sorely challenged by the Turkish power in the 17th century. Having moved into Transylvania, the Turks eventually pushed westward and laid siege to Vienna in 1683. Only a dramatic rescue by a combined army of Austrians, Saxons, Bavarians, and Poles saved the Austrian city. The European army counterattacked and decisively defeated the Turks in 1687. By the Treaty of Karlowitz in 1699, Austria gained territory from the Turks in Hungary and the Balkans. Together, these Habsburg lands formed a large block of territory, establishing an Austrian Empire in southeastern Europe.

The Austrian monarchy, however, never became a highly centralized, absolutist state, primarily because it included so many different national groups. Another reason was that it was a collection of divided territories held together by a personal union. Each of the areas had its own laws, Estates-General, and political life, and no common sentiment tied them together other than a common bond of services to the House of Habsburg. Nevertheless, at the beginning of the 18th century, Austria was a populous empire in central Europe with great potential military strength.

4. Emergence of Russia

The rise of Russia in the 17th century was perhaps the most striking change in eastern Europe. At the end of the Middle Ages, the principality of Moscow, from which modern Russia originated, had been a tributary state of the Asiatic Tartars. The Russians were Orthodox Christians with strong religious and cultural ties to Constantinople. After the Turkish capture of that city and the end of the Byzantine Empire in 1453, the Muscovite ruler Ivan the Great married Sophia, the last emperor's niece. Ivan assumed the title of tsar as the legitimate successor of the Byzantine rulers.

In the 16th century, Ivan's successors first threw off the overlordship of the Tartars, and then expanded their territory farther east into the wilderness of Siberia. The death of Ivan in 1598 was followed by a period of anarchy known as the Time of Troubles. In 1613, Michael Romanov was chosen as the new tsar, beginning a dynasty that lasted until 1917. From the accession of the Romanov dynasty, the tsars began to look to the West. They fought with two main competitors, Poland and Sweden, for control of the territories between the Black and the Baltic Seas. By the end of the 17th century, they had reached the coasts of the Black Sea, and were pressing forward to the Baltic Sea. In the 18th century, Peter the Great, the most energetic and ruthless of the Romanov tsars, at last broke through.

Peter the Great (1689–1725) was the first tsar to put Russia along the path of westernization.

Peter gained a firsthand view of the West when he made a trip there in 1697–1698 and returned home with determination to westernize Russia. What he admired first and foremost was European technology which he desired to transplant to Russia. Peter's reform unfolded in multiple fields. In order to make Russia a great power, he first built a standing army of 210,000 men and formed the first Russian navy. He then reorganized the central government, partly along Western lines. He created a Senate to supervise the administration of the state. To impose the rule of the central government more efficiently throughout the land, he divided the country into eight provinces, and later into 50. To obtain the enormous amount of money needed to sustain the army, he adopted the Western mercantilism to stimulate economic growth, that is, increasing exports and developing new industries, as well as raising taxes.

The object of Peter's domestic reform was to make Russia a great state and a military power. His primary goal was to open a window into the West, which could only be achieved on the Baltic. Russia's rival in the Baltic area was Sweden. By the 16th century, the Swedish monarchy had succeeded in making itself the dominant power of the Baltic region. After a long war, in 1721, Peter took from Sweden the eastern Baltic provinces of Karelia, Estonia, and Livonia. In this region, he built a new capital, St. Petersburg, his window on the West and a symbol that Russia was looking westward to Europe.

5. England and the Emergence of Constitutional Monarchy

In England, the whole 17th century saw the struggle between the kings and the Parliament for which road the government should go to—an absolute monarchy or a constitutional monarchy. By the end of the century, the Parliament had the final victory, and a constitutional monarchy was sealed once and for all.

5.1 The Early Stuarts

When Elizabeth I died, she was succeeded by James I (1603–1625), the Stuart King of Scotland and son of Queen Mary. James was a pedantic monarch who believed in unrestricted monarchy. His life was a sorry tale of high aspirations and deplorable failures. His son, Charles I (1625–1649) carried forward his father's absolutist ambitions. He dispatched the Parliament when it refused to grant him the taxes he wanted and managed to govern without Parliament. A rebellion of the Scots broke out and Charles was compelled to call Parliament back into session after an 11-year interval. The Parliament promised to grant him the necessary funds on condition that the king abandon his absolutist and anti-Puritanical policies. The civil war broke out in which Parliament joined the Scots to fight against the royalist Cavaliers. In 1648, Charles became the prisoner and was executed in the following year.

It was now Parliament's turn to establish an effective government upon the basis of a republic or commonwealth. Oliver Cromwell, the army commander, became the monarch of England in all but name. However, the revolutionaries divided among themselves as to religious and political issues. Cromwell found that he could maintain an orderly government only through strong personal rule backed by the army. When Cromwell died, the monarchy in the person of Charles Ⅱ, the eldest son of the Charles Ⅰ, was re-established.

5.2   The Glorious Revolution

Charles Ⅱ, when on route home, promised that he would respect the religious freedom of the British peoples and govern with Parliament and under the law. However, he had his own purposes. These were to govern by prerogative as much as possible and to prepare the way for the restoration of Catholicism as the state religion, or at least to win toleration for Catholics. The indication of Charles' fondness for Catholicism, his efforts to achieve toleration, and the conversion of his brother James to the Roman faith led to an upsurge of anti-Catholic feeling in the 70s and 80s of the 17th century.

Despite opposition, James succeeded to the throne after the death of Charles Ⅱ because the latter had no legitimate children. More radical than Charles Ⅱ, James Ⅱ suspended the anti-Catholic laws and named Catholics to leading positions. By expanding the use of prerogative, James Ⅱ was moving strongly in the direction of absolutism. At first, the Tories did nothing more than to wait out the reign of James Ⅱ primarily because his two daughters were both good Protestants. However, when James married an Italian woman and a son was born to them in 1687, the situation changed.

To prevent the establishment of a Catholic monarchy, the Tories joined with the Whigs. James's nephew and son-in-law William Ⅲ, Prince of Orange in the Netherlands was invited to England in 1688 with a fleet and a small army. James fled to France and the Parliament gave the throne to William and his wife in 1689 under conditions set down in the Bill of Rights, reaffirming the character of England as a constitutional monarchy. The reign of William saw the consolidation of the principles of constitutionalism in England, the permanent abandonment of absolutism, and the close collaboration among all parties in the work of government. The central political issue, viz., whether the sovereignty lay in king or Parliament, was thus decided once and for all.

(After the English Revolution in 1688, the Parliament passed a Bill of Rights that specified the rights of Parliament and laid the foundation for a constitutional monarchy.)

Bill of Rights

And thereupon the said Lords Spiritual and Temporal and Commons, pursuant to their respective letters and elections, being now assembled in a full and free representative of this nation, taking into their most serious consideration the best means for attaining the ends aforesaid, do in the first place (as their ancestors in like case have usually done) for the vindicating and asserting their ancient rights and liberties declare:

That the pretended power of suspending the laws or the execution of laws by regal authority without consent of Parliament is illegal;

That the pretended power of dispensing with laws or the execution of laws by regal authority, as it hath been assumed and exercised of late, is illegal;

That the commission for erecting the late Court of Commissioners for Ecclesiastical Causes, and all other commissions and courts of like nature, are illegal and pernicious;

That levying money for or to the use of the Crown by pretence of prerogative, without grant of Parliament, for longer time, or in other manner than the same is or shall be granted, is illegal;

That it is the right of the subjects to petition the king, and all commitments and prosecutions for such petitioning are illegal;

That the raising or keeping a standing army within the kingdom in time of peace, unless it be with consent of Parliament, is against law;

That the subjects which are Protestants may have arms for their defense suitable to their conditions and as allowed by law;

That election of members of Parliament ought to be free;

That the freedom of speech and debates or proceedings in Parliament ought not to be impeached or questioned in any court or place out of Parliament;

That excessive bail ought not to be required, nor excessive fines imposed, nor cruel and unusual punishments inflicted;

That jurors ought to be duly impaneled and returned, and jurors which pass upon men in trials for high treason ought to be freeholders;

That all grants and promises of fines and forfeitures of particular persons before conviction are illegal and void;

And that for redress of all grievances, and for the amending, strengthening and preserving of the laws, Parliaments ought to be held frequently.

Key Terms

theory of absolutism → divine right → absolutism in France → absolutism in Germany → emergence of Russia → Peter the Great → England and constitutional monarchy → the early Stuarts → the Glorious Revolution → the Bill of Rights

Exercises

① Vocabulary Building

❧ Fill in each blank with a synonym to the word in the brackets.

1) After the religious disputes and wars, the _____ (credibility) of Christianity had been _____ (irrevocably) weakened and the idea of a united Christian Europe gave way to the practical realities of a system of _____ (secular) states since now state took _____ (precedence) over the salvation of souls.

2) The feudal system had become a huge _____ (obstacle) to centralized government. Another element that _____ (hampered) the origins of nationalism was the power of the international _____ (ecclesiastical) state—the Roman Catholic Church. The struggle for the supremacy of power between popes and secular kings, _____ (culminated) in the Investiture Struggle, had been a constant conflict.

3) Given the _____ (vicious) civil wars that tore France apart in the 16th century, it is no wonder that France was the first to embrace the idea of a strong centralized government. Faced with such widespread _____ (demoralization) and the collapse of all civilized standards, and with religious _____ (fanaticism) on all sides, humanists everywhere came to the view that any system of government that put an end to civil wars was _____ (preferable) to continual fighting.

② Translation

❧ Translate the following sentences into Chinese.

1) The early personal reign of Louis was highly successful in both internal and foreign affairs. At home, the parliament lost its traditional power to obstruct legislation; the judicial structure was reformed by the Codes of Civil Procedure (1667) and Criminal Procedure (1669), although the overlapping and confusing laws were left untouched.

Urban law enforcement was improved by creation (1667) of the office of Lieutenant General of police for Paris, later imitated in other towns.

2) In order to eliminate the nobles' power, William made a deal with them. In return for a free hand in running the government, he gave the nobles almost unlimited power over their peasants, exempted them from taxation, and awarded them the highest ranks in the army and the Commissariat on condition that they would not challenge his political authority.

3) Peter the Great created a Senate to supervise the administration of the state. To impose the rule of the central government more efficiently throughout the land, he divided the country into eight provinces, and later into 50. To obtain the enormous amount of money needed to sustain the army, he adopted the Western mercantilism to stimulate economic growth, that is, increasing exports and developing new industries, as well as raising taxes.

❸ Questions

❧ Answer the following questions.

1) What hindered the development of nationalism during the Middle Ages?

2) What are the causes of political absolutism in the 17th-century Europe?

3) How did other states in Europe deal with Louis XIV's proclivity for war?

4) Why did the Austrian monarchy never become a highly centralized, absolutist state?

5) What did Peter the Great admire first and foremost about Europe?

6) What event marked the permanent abandonment of absolutism in England?

❹ Topics for Discussion

❧ Below are two topics related to this chapter. Read them and finish the discussion.

1) The differences between absolutism and constitutional monarchy.

2) Read more about Peter the Great, and find out what the life story of Peter the Great inspires you most and the quality which moves you most.

❺ Writing

❧ Read the following direction and finish the writing.

If you were a king in the 17th-century Europe, which system would you like to choose to run your country, absolutism or constitutional monarchy? Based on what you have learned from this chapter and other resources you can search for, make a rational choice and write a short essay with the title of "My Way to Run My Country."

Chapter 17

The Beginning of Modern Capitalism

Capitalism was certainly the outstanding economic feature of the modern and contemporary eras and more than any other element serving to differentiate the period since 1500 from the economy that prevailed in antiquity and the Middle Ages. Some of the more fundamental attributes of capitalism may be summarized as the following: (1) the desire for private profit rather than the service of the community or the mankind; (2) the estimation of social status and success in terms of relative monetary resources; (3) the evaluation of goods and services in terms of prices set by bargaining in the market rather than by considerations of justice or intrinsic worth; (4) the accumulation of large monetary resources for investment in business ventures; (5) the existence of a free market for the sale of goods; (6) the presence of a sufficient labor market to procure the needed laborers; (7) a credit system adequate to the needs of economic era; and (8) a reasonably thorough development of commercial and industrial life.[1]

The organization before this age which was most like modern capitalism was the Italian financial organization in the Late Middle Ages, but only in some respects. Many of the leading Italian banking houses were family ventures, with archaic tradition and practices, and much less capital than those of modern concerns. It was not until the era of the Great Discovery and overseas expansion, with the remarkable growth of commercial activity and the discovery of precious metals, that modern capitalism was made possible. Associated with this was the increased need on the part of both State and Church for working capital. The Catholic Church had developed a financial system in raising and administering its vast fund. Moreover, the decay of the manorial and guild systems dispossessed large classes of traditional ownership of production and made labor marketable in a new sense.

---

1 Harry E. Barnes, *The History of Western Civilization* (Vol. 2), New York: Harcourt, Brace, and Company, 1935, p.57.

1. New Forms of Business Organization

An outstanding aspect of the rise of capitalism was the new way of doing business—new business organization. Business in the ancient and medieval worlds had been carried on almost entirely by individuals or through family or quasi-family enterprises. Since 1200, commerce was becoming more extensive and complex, requiring a pool of capital and of managerial talent. Gradually, the partnership came into favor as a unit of business organization. The merchants of the port cities of Germany, for instance, achieved a sort of partnership in the Baltic Sea area. They found that by pooling their resources, they could build fleets and win joint trading privileges abroad, and by the 14th century, the leading towns of northern Germany had formed an effective commercial league, the Hanseatic League, which dominated the trade of northern Europe from England to Russia. The cities of the Hanseatic League monopolized the foreign trade of northern Germany and set up outlets in the trading centers of Russia, Poland, Norway, England, and the Low Countries.

The partnership facilitated the accumulation of more capital for investment in business, and increased the opportunities for the profitable investment of surplus wealth. But it had one grave defect, the unlimited liability of partners. In the case of the failure of one partner, the other partners were liable for the full indebtedness. Furthermore, a partnership was ordinarily dissolved upon the death or withdrawal of any of the partners, and thus failed to prove any real permanence of the organization. Accordingly, new and more adaptable forms of business organization began to arise. The first was the regulated company, best developed in England. The regulated company was in reality a form of business association. Take the Merchant Adventurers beginning in the 15th century as an example. It was an association of men engaged in foreign trade, which secured a Royal Charter granting a monopoly of that particular branch of trade. The point is that there was no common pool of actual capital. They acted together and this association enabled them to seek special power and privileges.

It was out of these regulated companies that there developed the joint-stock companies, which became fairly common in the 17th and 18th centuries. This new type of organization was a great improvement over earlier forms. Its shares were split up into relatively small sums, which made the amount of pooling much larger. At the same time, it provided highly centralized control, which was lacking in the regulated company. In general, the joint-stock company possessed many of the advantages of the 19th and 20th-century corporation, but it lacked certain favorable legal characteristics of the latter. The joint-stock company played an important part in the European trade with the East and in the Western Hemisphere as well. One of the first, the East India Company in England, was originally organized in 1600 as a regulated company, but within a few years it had become a true joint-stock company.

2. The Rise of Modern Banking

Intimately connected with the genesis of modern capitalism and the appearance of new forms of business organization was the development of banking. The most important functions of financial agents were the acceptance of money deposits for safe-keeping, the transferring of money from place to place, and the handling of bills of exchange.

Bills of exchange were in common use during the Late Middle Ages. They arose originally only out of commercial transactions, being simply promises to pay at a specified time and place. As both commercial and credit instruments, bills of exchange were in wide use at all the leading fairs and markets of the Late Middle Ages. And dealing in these places and the transferring and lending of money were functions usually performed by merchants. As has been pointed out, it was the merchants of the Italian cities who in the Late Middle Ages became the bankers of Europe. At the start of the 15th century, the Medicis were Europe's greatest banking dynasty, but their political power later distracted them from the highly focused business of making money. After the reign of Lorenzo the Magnificent, the bank's finances were in perilous state. Their role as leading bankers was usurped by a German dynasty, that of the Fuggers. Like the Medicis, the Fuggers amassed vast wealth by massaging the finances of the papacy and of great princes, for instance, providing a huge loan for Charles Ⅵ for his election as the Holy Roman Emperor. A bank was opened at Delft in 1313, one at Calais in 1320, and a third at Genoa in 1345. These institutions, however, must not be thought of as banks in the modern sense: Their chief functions were to accept deposits for safe-keeping and to take over the public debt.

The critical period in the development of modern banking came, however, after the opening of the 17th century. Beginning to feel the impact of overseas trade, all of western Europe were ready for the remarkable development of commerce and industry. Many important banks were established between the 17th and 18th centuries. The Bank of Sweden was founded in 1668, and the Bank of England in 1694.

The development of these banks made possible the systematic accumulation of capital to be put at the disposal of enterprising merchants and manufacturers, facilitated loans and money transfers, and rendered more effective the various financial aids to commerce and industry. Banks also promoted the rise of various types of commercial papers, the use of which has been indispensable to modern exchange, either national or international. Among these were promissory notes, drafts, checks, and bills of exchange. The development of modern double-entry bookkeeping and the rise of various business auxiliaries, such as auditors, agents, and brokers, also played an important role in business operations.

3. Mercantilism and Overseas Colonies

With the combined and parallel growth of world commerce and the national dynastic state, there developed a definite and clear-cut national economic policy—mercantilism. Mercantilism is the name used by historians to identify a set of economic principles that dominated economic thought in the 17th century. It is a complete governmental regulation of economic activities. It was known as mercantilism in England, Colbertism in France, and cameralism in Germany.

The basic assumptions of the mercantilism system run as follows: (1) Precious metals are the most valid measure of the wealth of a nation; (2) aside from mining of ore, trade is the chief means of accumulating these precious metals in the shape of specie; (3) in order that this trade may be profitable and specie accumulated, there must be a favorable balance of exports over imports; (4) to furnish markets for these exports, and thus to create a favorable balance of trade for the mother country, colonies are valuable; (5) colonies serve mainly as the market for finished products from the mother country, and a source of supply of raw materials, and manufacturing must be forbidden there lest they supply their own necessities and exhaust the stock of raw materials; (6) colonies must be looked upon primarily as profitable commercial enterprises of the mother country and colonial trade as a monopoly of the mother country. Fundamental to mercantilism was the belief that the total volume of trade was unchangeable. One nation could expand its trade and hence its prosperity only at the expense of others. To mercantilists, economic activity was a war carried on by peaceful means. As a system of economic principles, mercantilism focused on the role of the state, believing that state intervention in economy was desirable for the sake of the national good.

As we can see, mercantilism theory related directly to colonial policies and practices. With the development of colonies and trading posts in the Americas and the East, Europeans entered into an age of internationalization in the 17th century.

For much of the 16th century, much overseas trade was still carried by the Spanish and Portuguese, the efforts of the English, French, and Dutch to explore, trade, and colonize overseas were overshadowed by the fabulous successes of Portugal and Spain. France and England were powerful national monarchies whose rulers, nobles, and merchants were all eager for land and profits overseas. The Dutch rebelled against Spanish rule in the second half of the 16th century, formed their own independent republic (officially the Netherlands, but commonly known, from the name of its largest province, as Holland), and became the most dynamic commercial nation of Europe. As the 16th century drew to a close, the English, French, and Dutch redoubled their efforts to gain a share of world trade and world empire.

The Dutch East India Company was established in 1602. It was a joint-stock company between the wealthy oligarchy and the government. The Company not only had a monopoly on all Asian trade but also possessed the right to make war, sign treaties, establish military and trading bases, and appoint government officials. Gradually, the Dutch East India Company took control of most of the Portuguese bases in the East and opened trade with China and Japan. Its profits were spectacular in the first 10 years. However, the Dutch West India Company, created in 1621, was less successful. Dutch settlements were also established on the North American Continent. The mainland colony of New Netherlands stretched from the mouth of the Hudson as far north as Albany, New York. In the second half of the 17th century, competition from the English and the French and years of warfare with them led to the decline of the Dutch commercial empire. In 1664, the English seized the colony of New Netherlands and renamed it New York; soon afterward, the Dutch West India Company went bankrupt.

The English East India Company received a Royal Charter from Queen Elizabeth in 1600, making it the oldest among several similarly formed European East India Companies. Wealthy merchants and aristocrats owned the Company's shares. The government owned no shares and had only indirect control. The Company eventually came to rule large areas of India with its own private armies, exercising military power and assuming administrative functions. Initially, the Company struggled in the spice trade due to the competition from the already well-established Dutch East India Company. English traders frequently engaged in hostilities with their Dutch and Portuguese counterparts in the Indian Ocean. After achieving a major victory over the Portuguese in the Battle of Swally in 1612, the Company decided to explore the feasibility of gaining a territorial foothold in mainland India, with official sanction of both countries, and requested that the Crown launch a diplomatic mission. And it succeeded. The Company rose to account for half of the world's trade, particularly trade in basic commodities that included cotton, silk, indigo dye, salt, saltpetre, tea, and opium.

French commercial companies in the East experienced much difficulty. The East India Companies set up by Henry Ⅳ and Richelieu all failed. In 1664, Colbert established a new East India Company that only barely managed to survive. The French had a greater success in North America and Canada became a French province. But due to the all-out involvement in continental wars, they could not provide adequate men or money. In 1715, by the Treaty of Utrecht, the French began to cede some of their American possessions to their English rival.

Key Terms

new forms of business organization → partnership → the regulated company → the joint-stock company → the rise of modern banking → bills of exchange → mercantilism and overseas colonies → the Dutch East India Company → the English East India Company

Exercises

❶ Vocabulary Building

❧ Fill in each blank with a synonym to the word in the brackets.

1) By the 14th century, the leading towns of northern Germany had formed an effective commercial league, the Hanseatic League, which _____ (dominated) the trade of northern Europe from England to Russia. The cities of the Hanseatic League _____ (monopolized) the foreign trade of northern Germany and set up _____ (outlets) in the trading centers of Russia, Poland, Norway, England, and the Low Countries.

2) It was an association of men engaged in foreign trade, which _____ (secured) a Royal _____ (Charter) granting a monopoly of that particular branch of trade. The point is that there was no common _____ (pool) of actual capital. They acted together and this association enabled them to seek special power and privileges.

3) At the start of the 15th century, the Medicis were Europe's greatest banking dynasty, but their political power later _____ (distracted) them from the highly focused business of making money. After the reign of Lorenzo the Magnificent, the bank's finances were in _____ (perilous) state. Their role as leading bankers was _____ (usurped) by a German dynasty, that of the Fuggers.

❷ Translation

❧ Translate the following sentences into Chinese.

1) The partnership facilitated the accumulation of more capital for investment in business, and increased the opportunities for the profitable investment of surplus wealth. But it had one grave defect, the unlimited liability of partners. In the case of the failure of one partner, the other partners were liable for the full indebtedness. Furthermore, a partnership was ordinarily dissolved upon the death or withdrawal of any of the partners, and thus failed to prove any real permanence of the organization.

2) The development of these banks made possible the systematic accumulation of capital to be put at the disposal of enterprising merchants and manufacturers, facilitated loans and money transfers, and rendered more effective the various financial aids to commerce and industry. Banks also promoted the rise of various types of commercial papers, the use of which has been indispensable to modern exchange, either national or international. Among these were promissory notes, drafts, checks, and bills of exchange. The development of modern double-entry bookkeeping, and the rise of various business

auxiliaries, such as auditors, agents, and brokers, also played an important role in business operations.

3) The English East India Company received a Royal Charter from Queen Elizabeth in 1600, making it the oldest among several similarly formed European East India Companies. Wealthy merchants and aristocrats owned the Company's shares. The government owned no shares and had only indirect control. The Company eventually came to rule large areas of India with its own private armies, exercising military power and assuming administrative functions.

Questions

❧ Answer the following questions.

1) Why did the new way of doing business emerge in the ancient and medieval worlds?

2) What were the new forms of business organization?

3) What is mercantilism?

4) What caused the decline of the Dutch commercial empire?

5) Why did France lose power in North America?

Topics for Discussion

❧ Below are three topics related to this chapter. Read them and finish the discussion.

1) Based on what you have learned from this chapter and other resources you can search for, can you expound the important position of the beginning of modern capitalism in the course of the evolution of human society?

2) Do you think mercantilism is suitable to contemporary society? Why or why not?

3) Based on your reading and research, give an account of the factors which contributed to the success of the English East India Company.

Writing

❧ Read the following direction and finish the writing.

As a saying goes, "Business is business." It may demonstrate the fierce competition and the cruelty in business world. On the other hand, corporate culture is highlighted by many companies. Do you think corporate culture is of great importance to companies? Based on your knowledge and study, write a short essay with the title of "My View of Corporate Culture."

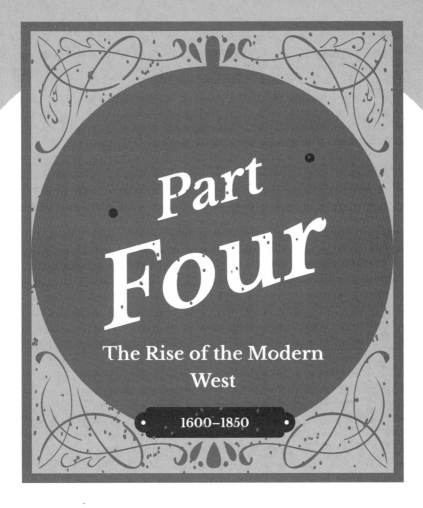

Part
Four

The Rise of the Modern West

1600–1850

The 17th, 18th, and 19th centuries were an era of spectacular shifts in civilization, following upon those that had already altered the medieval pattern. These new shifts eventually brought into being all the basic features of the modern West. It is not easy to summarize concisely the dominating features of this era, but two deep undercurrents were the growing secularism and rationalism.

Secularism manifested itself first in religion. Supernaturalism of the Catholic Church held over without any serious break, and was intensified by the necessity of defense against the assaults of Protestantism. Nevertheless, Christianity itself saw a growing secularism. Protestantism was very closely related to the rise of capitalism.[1] Protestantism, while still predominantly absorbed in the

---

1   Max Weber, *The Protestant Ethic and the Spirit of Capitalism*, London & New York: Routledge, 1992.

matter of salvation of the soul, believed that one means of assuring spiritual as well as earthly salvation lay in industry, thrift, and the accumulation of pecuniary profits. A political basis of secularism was found in the revived prestige and influence of Roman law and in the development of social-contract conception. Both emphasized the secular absolutism and human origins of political institution.

Scientific discoveries, especially the rise of modern astronomy from Copernicus to Newton, were a direct challenge to the orthodox theory of creation and cosmology. Francis Bacon questioned the deductive reasoning of medieval scholastic theology as a tool of scientific research, and called for a more reliable method, inductive reasoning from a mass of observed facts. By refusing to accept anything that cannot be proved to be such, Déscartes brought his own brand of skepticism. Human reason, not divine revelation, was deemed as the proper way to gain knowledge.

The first of the secular ideologies, the Enlightenment belief in reason, progress, and human fulfillment in this world, was developed by 18th-century thinkers impressed by Europe's growth in knowledge, wealth, and power up to their own time. The rise of industrial society was made possible by the technical advances of the Late Middle Ages, the worldwide markets opened up by overseas exploration and empire building, and the financial resources of burgeoning capitalism. As a result of all these changes, a new kind of civilization grew up within the West that was different from all others of its own time and of the past. In this new civilization, the majority of the population lived in cities and worked in factories and offices rather than on farms. Citizens, in turn, were equipped with rights and freedom that enabled them to wield greater power over governments than ever before, above all through more or less democratically elected representative assemblies.

As far as the mental climate of modern times marked a break with that of the Middle Ages, this era may be said to have been characterized chiefly by a growing secularism, tolerance, and freedom, and by an increasing reliance upon the scientific method.

Chapter 18

Scientific Revolution and the Emergence of Modern Science

By tradition, Scientific Revolution refers to historical changes in thought and belief, and changes in social and institutional organizations, which unfolded in Europe between roughly 1550 and 1700; it began with Nicholas Copernicus (1473–1543), who asserted a heliocentric (sun-centered) cosmos, and ended with Isaac Newton (1642–1727), who proposed universal laws and a mechanical universe. These were the discovery of the heliocentric view of the heavens, the identification of universal gravitation, and important advances in the understanding of light, of the vacuum, of gases, of the body, and of microscopic life. If by "revolution," we mean "a change that is sudden, radical, and complete," the Scientific Revolution was not a revolution, for it did not happen overnight, but in a gradual and piecemeal fashion. Nevertheless, its impact and influence were truly revolutionary: It produced a radically different view of the universe and a new mode of thinking. The Scientific Revolution was a key factor in setting Western civilization along its modern secular and material path. The fertile minds of the time produced a stunning intellectual triumph and made the West the teacher of the world.

1. Revolution in Astronomy: Copernicus, Kepler, Galileo, and Newton

The greatest achievements in the Scientific Revolution of the 16th and 17th centuries came in those fields most dominated by the ideas of the Greeks—astronomy, mechanics, and medicine, which had long been dominated respectively by Aristotle, Ptolemy, and Galen. In order to understand the revolutionary nature of the new astronomy, a look at the old Aristotle's system or Ptolemaic geocentric conception is necessary.

Aristotle's scheme placed the solid, immovable Earth at the center of things. The luminous heavenly bodies were rotating around the Earth in perfect circular motion, each embedded in a transparent sphere. Closest to Earth was the sphere that carried the moon; then, at successive intervals, came the spheres of Mercury, Venus, the sun, Mars, Jupiter, Saturn, and the fixed stars. Beyond the sphere of the fixed stars was the Primum Mobile (Prime Mover). Beyond the Primum Mobile was the Empyrean (the highest Heaven). This medieval, geocentric conception of the universe fitted both Christianity and everyone's ordinary observations. It was easy to accept this view into Christian thought, according to which the real mover of the whole system was God himself, located in the highest Heaven beyond the visible universe.

Nicolaus Copernicus revived the ancient view that contradicted the Ptolemaic system. Although not an accomplished observational astronomer, he was a mathematician who felt that Ptolemy's geocentric system was too complicated and failed to accord with the observed motions of the heavenly bodies. He found that the heliocentric system offered the simplest geometrical explanation of observed movements. His major work, *On the Revolutions of the Heavenly Spheres*, was published in the year of his death. In the book, he argued that the universe consisted of eight spheres with the sun motionless at the center and the spheres of the fixed stars at rest in the eighth sphere. Between them were the planets revolving around the sun in the order of Mercury, Venus, Earth, Jupiter, and Saturn. Furthermore, the Earth rotated around its own axis, and that was why the sun and fixed stars appeared to move around the Earth. However, Copernicus did not reject Aristotle's heavenly bodies moving in circular orbits. Objection to Copernicus's theory first came from the Church. The new system seemed to create uncertainty about human role in the universe as well as God's location. Protestant reformers were the first to attack the new ideas and they were not the only one. Objection to his system was not wholly theological. That Copernicus could provide no observational proofs of his belief was also an important reason for his contemporaries to reject. If, as he thought, the Earth revolved around the sun, then the position of fixed stars should show a shift when they were sighted from opposite sides of the Earth's orbit. Moreover, Copernicus could not provide a convincing answer for a problem that baffled the ancients: How could he account for a force sufficient to keep the Earth in rotation? Religious denouncement was not the only obstacle; a great deal of observational work had to be done before its correctness could be checked.

On the Revolutions of the Heavenly Spheres

By Nicolaus Copernicus

4. The Movement of the Celestial Bodies is Regular, Circular, and Everlasting—or Else Compounded of Circular Movements.

After this we will recall that the movement of the celestial bodies is circular. For the motion of a sphere is to turn in a circle; by this very act expressing its form, in the most simple body, where beginning and end cannot be discovered or distinguished from one another, while it moves through the same parts in itself. But there are many movements on account of the multitude of spheres or orbital circles. The most obvious of all is the daily revolution—which the Greeks call *nucqhmeron*; i.e. having the temporal span of a day and a night. By means of this movement the whole world—with the exception of the Earth—is supposed to be borne from east to west. This movement is taken as the common measure of all movements, since we measure even time itself principally by the number of days.

Next, we see other as it were antagonistic revolutions; i.e. from west to east; on the part of the sun, moon, and the wandering stars. In this way the sun gives us the year, the moon the months—the most common periods of time; and each of the other five planets follows its own cycle. Nevertheless these movements are manifoldly different from the first movement. First, in that they do not revolve around the same poles as the first movement but follow the oblique ecliptic; next, in that they do not seem to move in their circuit regularly. For the sun and moon are caught moving at times more slowly and at times more quickly. And we perceive the five wandering stars sometimes even to retrograde and to come to a stop between these two movements. And though the sun always proceeds straight ahead along its route, they wander in various ways, straying sometimes towards the south, and at other times towards the north—whence they are called "planets." Add to this the fact that sometimes they are nearer the Earth—and are then said to be at their perigee—and at other times are farther away—and are said to be at their apogee.

Though Copernicus did not overcome the limitations of traditional science, he inspired later generations to resume the search for a simpler and more satisfying truth. Tycho Brahe (1546–1601), a Danish astronomer, made many accurate astronomical measurements from his Oresund laboratory which included an observatory. These observations were left behind when, in 1599, Brahe quit Denmark and transferred to Prague, where he was appointed chief mathematician to the Holy Roman Emperor, Rudolf II. It was Johannes Kepler (1571–1630), his no less talented assistant who set about the task of trying to marry Brahe's measurements and Copernicus' theories. When that effort yielded a negative result, he tried fitting the data to elliptical orbits. This gave him a positive result, and his finding came to be known as Kepler's First Law. His Second Law, as we know, is in the variant form that Newton later found to be a consequence of his law of gravitational attraction: A line from the sun to the planet traces out equal areas in equal time. Mathematicians were barely able to deal with such a bizarre formulation and they preferred other variants that were mathematically tractable: The speed of a planet is inversely proportional to its distance from the sun. His Third Law established that the square of a planet's period of revolution is proportional to the cube of its average distance from the sun. In other words, planets with larger orbits revolve at a slower average velocity than those with smaller orbits. Kepler was the first to define in precise mathematical terms how the speeds of planets vary according to their distance from the sun. Kepler thus appears as the first man to work in the manner of modern scientists: He first formulated hypotheses and then tried to check the deduced consequences empirically. Kepler's three laws effectively eliminated the idea of uniform circular motion as well as the idea of crystalline spheres revolving in circular orbits. The basic structure of the traditional Ptolemaic system was disapproved and people began to think in new terms of the actual paths of planets revolving around the sun in elliptical orbits.

Though Kepler described the movements of the planets in precise mathematical terms, he was less successful in explaining what made them move. He assumed that some force might be holding the planets in orbits and moving them continuously along their courses. This force he concluded to be the sun. It was left to the Italian genius Galileo Galilei (1564–1642) to complete the overthrow of Aristotle. A contemporary of Kepler, Galileo was less a mathematician and more an observer and experimenter. In 1609, he constructed a telescope that could be used to examine the heavens. When turning his telescope to the skies, he made a series of discoveries: The moon, just like the Earth, is covered by mountains and craters, and four moons revolve around Jupiter. With tens of thousands of stars now under his telescope, Galileo began to believe that there could be more than one center of heavenly orbits. His observations seemed to destroy yet another aspect of the traditional cosmology that the universe was composed of transparent or perfect and unchanging substance.

The Catholic Church was quick to challenge Galileo's proofs and to condemn his conclusions. Because its authority and doctrines were linked to the Ptolemaic system, it regarded the new ideas as a menace to Christian truth and salvation. Galileo fell into trouble after publishing his *Dialogue on the Two Chief System*s. In 1633, he was charged with heresy and brought before the Roman Inquisition; threatened with torture, he formally recanted. However, after the ordeal before the Inquisition, Galileo, though under house arrest, turned to the subject of motion that in itself would not disturb the authorities, but would open the way to the ultimate victory of the new view of the universe. The Aristotelian conception of mechanics held that an object remained at rest unless a force was applied against it. If a force was constantly exerted, then the object moved at a constant rate, but if it was removed, then the object stopped. Based on his experiments with falling bodies and his study of the acceleration of polished balls rolling down frictionless wooden surfaces, Galileo made significant discoveries to the problem of motion. First, if a uniform force is applied to an object, it will move at an accelerated speed rather than a constant speed. Second, a body in motion continues in motion forever unless deflected by an external force, the principle of inertia. Thus, a state of motion is just as natural as a state of rest. Third, the distance covered by any falling body is proportional to the square of its time of descent. Galileo did not quite see that his law of falling bodies was the same law that kept the planets in their orbits. This would be the work of an Englishman who has long been considered the greatest genius of the Scientific Revolution.

The final statement of 17th-century science was left to Isaac Newton, who perfected and refined the new cosmic system first outlined by Kepler and Galileo. As early as 1666, Newton experienced his first burst of creativity: He invented the calculus, began his investigation into the composition of light, and started his work on the law of universal gravitation. In 1669, he accepted a chair of mathematics at the University of Cambridge. During a second intense period of creativity from 1684 to 1686, he wrote his famous *Principia*. He was made president of the Royal Society in 1703 and knighted in 1705 for his great achievements. Sir Isaac Newton was the only English scientist to be buried in Westminster Abbey.

Newton's major work, the "hinge point of modern scientific thought," was his *Mathematical Principles of Natural Philosophy*, known simply as the *Principia* by the first word of its Latin title. In the book, Newton demonstrated the universal law of gravitation with mathematical proofs. His famous Three Laws of Motion include: Every object continues in a state of rest or uniform motion in a straight line unless deflected by a force; the rate of change of motion of an object is proportional to the force acting upon it; and for every action there is always an equal and opposite reaction. By applying these laws to the problems of astronomy, Newton integrated them into his universal law of gravitation: Every object in the universe is attracted to every other object with a force (gravity) that is directly proportional to the product of their masses and inversely proportional to the square of the distances between them. The universal law of gravitation could explain why the planetary bodies did not go off in straight lines but continued in elliptical orbits about the sun.

The implications of Newton's discovery were enormous. He demonstrated the fact that human beings have means to achieve a far greater understanding. At the same time, the Newtonian synthesis created a new cosmology in which the world was seen largely in mechanistic terms.

2. Advances in Medicine

In 1543, the year in which Copernicus finally published *De Revolutionibus Orbium Coelestium*, Andreas Vesalius (1514–1564) presented to the world his book on the structure of the human body. Vesalius' extremely meticulous study of anatomy also raised philosophical speculation about man's purpose. His advances have to be placed in context. Late Medieval medicine was dominated by the teachings of the Greek physician Galen who had lived in the 2nd century A.D. But since human anatomy was proscribed at his time, Galen had relied on animal, rather than human, dissection to arrive at a picture of human anatomy that was quite inaccurate in many instances. It was during the reign of Frederick Ⅱ, the Holy Roman Emperor, that things began to change. Out of a general concern for his subjects and combined with a genuine interest in knowledge, Frederick issued a decree in 1231 that "no surgeon should be admitted to practice unless he has learned in the anatomy of the human body." Early in the following century, the college of medicine for Venice, which was located at Padua, was authorized to dissect a human body once every year. In the early decades of the 16th century, Vesalius traveled to Padua for his training. In his work, Vesalius corrected more than 200 anatomical errors of Galen. For example, he showed that the jawbone in man is a single bone, not divided as it is in the dog and other lower mammals. He proved that the thigh bone is straight, not curved as it is in the dog. He proved that the sternum is made up of three bones, not eight, as was thought. Theologians also remained unconvinced. "It was a widely accepted dogma that man had one less rib on one side, because from the scriptural account Eve was formed from one of Adam's ribs." Vesalius, however, found an equal number of ribs on each side. He did not hesitate to correct Galen's assertion that the great blood vessels originated from the liver; instead, he claimed that they came from the heart. Nevertheless, Vesalius still clung to a number of Galen's erroneous assertions, including the Greek physician's ideas on the ebb and flow of two kinds of blood in the veins and arteries. It was not until the Englishman William Harvey's work on the circulation of the blood that this Galenic misperception was corrected.

William Harvey (1578–1657) attended Cambridge University and later Padua where he received a doctorate of medicine in 1602. His reputation rests upon his book *On the Motion of the Heart and Blood*, published in 1628. The book is only 78 pages long, but much more clearly written than either Newton's or Copernicus' masterpieces, and its argument is plain enough for even the layman to grasp: All the blood in the body moves in a circuit and the propelling force is supplied by the beating of the heart. Although Harvey's work dealt a severe blow to Galen's theories, his ideas did not begin to achieve general recognition until the 1660s, when the capillaries were discovered, which explained how the body's blood passed from the arteries to the veins. Harvey's theory of the circulation of the blood laid the foundation for modern physiology.

3. Scientific Societies and Organizations

The story of science since Newton has been one of continuous acceleration in the growth of knowledge. Discoveries were proceeding in numerous fields. Findings in one subject suggested and aided investigations in others and discoveries in one country were known to other countries, and some even came out simultaneously. Newton and Leibniz, for instance, are now believed to invent calculus without knowing each other's work. These developments reflected the growing interdependence of scientific investigators and their investigations. The advance of science was now an international achievement that depended on generally accepted procedures and continuous communication among investigators. Curiously, while religion and politics were breaking down into national and subnational units, science took the opposite direction.

One important contributing factor in the dissemination of science and research was the scientific society. The earliest scientific society was founded in Italy. Rome set up an academy (the Academy of the Lynx-Eyed) in 1603, of which Galileo was the sixth member; a half-century later, the Medicis established a scientific institution in Florence. More influential and longer lasting, however, was the Royal Society of London. Formally founded in 1662, the Royal Society consisted of scientists and mathematicians as well as interested merchants, nobles, and clerics. The Society aided experiments, listened to learned discussions, corresponded with foreign societies, and published a scientific journal, *Philosophical Transactions*. It was the Fellows of the Royal Society who developed the familiar form of scientific publication. Fellows, and other scientists, had begun writing to the Society with their discoveries and in this way the Society became a clearing house and then a publisher of *Philosophical Transactions*, which formed a model for subsequent scientific communication. In their hard-headed, practical way, the Fellows demanded good English in these papers, even going so far as to appoint the poet John Dryden to a committee to oversee the writing style of scientists. It became a prototype for later scholarly journals and a crucial instrument for circulating news of scientific and academic activities. In France, at the suggestion of his finance minister, Colbert, Louis XIV approved the Academy of Science in 1666. The French journal *Journal des Savants*, published weekly beginning in 1665, printed results of experiments as well as general scientific knowledge. The Dublin Philosophical Society was founded in 1684 in imitation of the Royal Society. Similar institutions were founded in other European states. German princes and city governments encouraged the foundation of small-scale scientific societies of their own, such as the Scientific Academy created in 1700 by the elector of Brandenburg and in 1700 Leibnitz founded the Berlin Academy. Most of them were sponsored by the governments and were mainly devoted to the betterment of the state.

Universities also made a contribution, though not very dramatic or striking. The Lucasian Chair of Mathematics was founded at Cambridge in 1663 and the Savilian Chairs of Mathematics and Astronomy were also founded in Oxford at much the same time. John Bainbridge, an early Savilian professor of astronomy, undertook expeditions to see eclipses and other phenomena. Newton was a Cambridge man, Galileo a professor at Pisa, and Harvey and Vesalius both developed their ideas in a university context.

The Scientific Revolution represents a major turning point in modern Western civilization. The medieval, Ptolemaic-Aristotelian view of the universe was overthrown; a new conception of the world was invented. The scientific methods created by Bacon and

Descartes left Europeans with the separation of mind and matter and the belief that by using only reason, they could understand and dominate the world of nature. Most important of all, theology, once queen of all the sciences, is not allowed on the premise any more. A once Christian culture has become a scientific one, which would lead to further emancipation of human beings in this world.

Key Terms

Copernicus and heliocentric theory → Kepler and his theory of the elliptical orbits of the planets → Galileo's Three Laws of Motion → Newton and his gravitation theory → Vesalius and the development of human body anatomy → William Harvey and circulation of the blood → scientific societies and organizations

Exercises

❶ Vocabulary Building

❧ The words and phrases in the columns are all selected from this chapter. Match pairs of words and phrases that are antonyms.

secular	motion
fixed stars	wandering stars
perigee	geocentric
circular	religious
rest	negative
contradict against	apogee
heliocentric	accord with
motionless	elliptical
positive	recant
cling to	moving

✷ Translation

✎ Translate the following sentences into Chinese.

1) Kepler's three laws effectively eliminated the idea of uniform circular motion as well as the idea of crystalline spheres revolving in circular orbits. The basic structure of the traditional Ptolemaic system was disapproved and people began to think in new terms of the actual paths of planets revolving around the sun in elliptical orbits.

2) Nevertheless, Vesalius still clung to a number of Galen's erroneous assertions, including the Greek physician's ideas on the ebb and flow of two kinds of blood in the veins and arteries. It was not until the Englishman William Harvey's work on the circulation of the blood that this Galenic misperception was corrected.

✷ Questions

✎ Answer the following questions.

1) What was Copernicus' new discovery about the heavenly bodies? Where was his theory flawed?

2) What were the objections to Copernicus' theory?

3) Who effectively eliminated the idea of uniform circular motion?

4) What was the Aristotelian conception of mechanics?

5) What were Galileo's discoveries of motion?

6) What were the implications of Newton's discovery?

✷ Term Explanation

✎ Explain the meaning of the following terms in your own words.

1) Kepler's three laws

2) Newton's Three Laws of Motion

✷ Topic for Discussion

✎ Below is a topic related to this chapter. Read it and finish the discussion.

How is Galileo's law of falling bodies related to Newton's law of gravity that keeps the planets in their orbits?

⑥ Writing

Newton in his notebook had written: "*Amicus Plato; amicus Aristoteles; magus amica veritas.*" ("Plato is my friend, Aristotle is my friend, but my best friend is truth.") Based on your knowledge and study, write an essay with the title of "My Best Friend Truth."

Chapter 19

Emancipation of Philosophy: Empiricism and Skepticism

Humanism, the new astronomy, the scientific revival, and the overseas discoveries brought about notable changes in philosophic thought. Empiricism as a new scientific method in gaining knowledge arose and with it the skepticism on religious beliefs and certainties occurred. The most representative of them were the writings of Michel Eyquem de Montaigne, Francis Bacon, René Descartes, John Locke, and David Hume.

1. Michel Eyquem de Montaigne: Skepticism and Religious Tolerance

Michel Eyquem de Montaigne (1533–1592), better known as Montaigne, was born to a devout Catholic father and a Jewish mother who converted to Protestantism later. He was considered by many scholars as the first French skeptic. He broke with the medieval theology and scholastic philosophy in his whole attitude toward the fundamental problems of life and human existence. He repudiated the supernatural and otherworldly perspectives of the Christians and adopted a predominantly secular outlook. He held that man's body is fully as important as the soul, a view contrary to the typical religious view of life which is prone to associate the "higher" things with the soul and the "lower" things with the body. Similar to that of the Greeks, his philosophy suggested a complete revolution in the whole perspective of medieval philosophy by advocating the characteristic Epicurean thought. This gave Montaigne a great tolerance for others and for different ways of thinking, and together these provided the basis for his complete rejection of one of the central tenets of Christianity. For the Christians in the world where Montaigne grew up, the chief purpose of someone's intellectual life was to secure salvation in the world to come. Philosophy's main function in such a world, as the handmaiden of theology, was likewise "the preparation of man for a safe death." Montaigne thought this was nonsense and reversed the proposition, arguing that the purpose of knowledge is to teach men how to live more adequately, more productively, more happily, right here on Earth.

Montaigne was also known for his religious tolerance. His background made it next to impossible for him to accept that any faith had a monopoly of divine revelation and he applied this thinking not just to beliefs but also to morality. The two main intellectual influences that helped to shape his thinking were ancient classics and overseas discoveries which were just getting under way during his lifetime. The overseas discoveries brought sharply to Montaigne's attention the great diversity of customs and ideas among both savage and civilized peoples scattered over the world's surface. Here was a very direct challenge to the prevailing Christian idea that there could be only one right way of living and thinking. Montaigne was impressed by the huge variety in both physical nature and human conducts. This led to his idea of religious tolerance. While people tended to construct conceptions of God in terms of their own attitudes and experiences, Montaigne, at least, conceived of a God as broad-minded and tolerant. He held that if variety and diversity were characteristic of nature and mankind, God must be responsible for this situation. Otherwise, people would have to divorce God from both nature and society, or imagine both to be expressing itself in a manner repugnant to the will of God.

Montaigne was thus a forerunner of the great French rationalistic philosophers, such as Bayle, Voltaire, and Montesquieu. Although not an active crusader of the type of Voltaire, he had a wide influence on promoting tolerance and humanity because of the vast popularity of his essays.

2. Francis Bacon: New Approach to Knowledge

Like Montaigne, Francis Bacon (1561–1626) was secular and social rather than otherworldly and religious. He was likewise greatly influenced by the Renaissance humanism and overseas discoveries. He added a warm appreciation of the scientific attitude to these, for which he is most known. As mentioned in Chapter 18, Bacon was considered as the founder of empiricism in scientific research. While Aristotle's ideas were being upset by Kepler and Galileo, Bacon struck at the root of his system—its deductive methodology. A similar and popular form of deductive reasoning was syllogism where people began with two statements, found a common term in these statements, and then drew from this a conclusion in which the common term was absent. An example used by the Christians was Paul's statement in Romans 10:18 that the gospel had been preached "to the ends of the world," then a second statement that the apostles never went to the ends of the world, i.e. the antipodes or Australia; therefore it was concluded that there were no people living "at the ends of the world" for them to preach to. Feeling that the deductive method was inadequate to the task of discovering new knowledge, Bacon advocated the inductive or experimental method.

Another important contribution Bacon made to the knowledge was his ingenious argument designed to overcome people's unreasoning admiration for ancient knowledge. The Christian scholars of the Middle Ages understood that since man had continued to fall from a noble beginning, wisdom was to be found by looking back to the writings of the "ancients," notably Scripture and the early Church Fathers. Renaissance, when rediscovering the classic Greek culture, also strengthened this fashion of looking back. However, Bacon rejected this vintage style head on. In his famous summary, "We are the ancients," he meant that the accumulated fund of knowledge becomes older and richer with each generation. If we go back to remote antiquity, we find that knowledge is both scantier and more unreliable. Bacon thus presented the most powerful of all general arguments against the exclusive worship of intellectual authority and reverence for the knowledge of antiquity.

In the analysis of the obstacles to clear scientific thinking was his conception of the four "Idols." The "Idol of the Tribe" means those defects which are inherent in the thinking of the human race as a whole, i.e. man's limited intellectual capacity, the dominion of emotion over reason, the tendency to jump at conclusions, etc. This is the first handicap. The "Idol of the Cave" represents the special handicap which is peculiar to the thinking of any given individual, namely, the prejudices that have arisen from the circumstances of his social surroundings, education, and experience. Next comes the "Idol of the Market-Place." By this, he meant that men are impeded in thinking through the necessity of putting out thoughts into words. It is often difficult to find the right words even if one has clear and defensible ideas. The final obstacle is the "Idol of the Theater." Men tend to be fond of a given system of thoughts or particular intellectual hobbies. Their notions will revolve around these special or personal formulations. This last "Idol" produces the single-track mind and promotes emotional embrace of particular bodies of thought or types of social reform. All of these make it very hard for one to approach a problem in an unbiased and open-minded fashion characteristic of science.

Bacon did not doubt human's ability to know the natural world, but he thought that human reason had been employed in a wrong direction. His new direction was the use of inductive principles, a revolt against Aristotle's deductive principles. He viewed deduction as mere manipulation of words, while induction required repeated experiments that would lead to a general statement or conclusion. Bacon shared the view of many contemporaries that knowledge could only be built up by the observation of nature (rather than through intuition or "revealed" knowledge), starting from concrete data rather than abstractions that had just occurred to someone.

3. René Descartes

While Bacon despised or ignored mathematics, the eminent French mathematician and philosopher, René Descartes (1596–1650) proposed a different approach to scientific methodology by emphasizing deduction and mathematical logic. In his *Discourse on Method*, he set forth an admirable body of principles. He held that the first step is to wipe away all earlier and accepted authorities and to start out with a clear and unbiased mind. The philosopher must never accept anything as truth, which cannot be proved to be such. Everything must be stated at the outset in the most simple and clear form, gradually and logically advancing to the more complex and more involved problems. Each specific problem must be divided into as many parts as possible in order to solve it. Thoughts and propositions must be arranged in an orderly sequence of ideas. In the end, there must be a complete analysis and a sufficiently comprehensive review of the whole problem. His philosophy was in fact much influenced by the then-current vogue for skepticism. Descartes brought his own brand of skepticism. And when he looked about him, he realized that one thing was clear. The one thing that could not be doubted—because he was certain of it—was his own doubt. Hence comes his famous saying, "I think, therefore I am."

As Richard Tarnas has pointed out, there have been three great epochs in Western philosophy. During the classical era, philosophy was a largely autonomous activity, mainly as a definer and a judge of all other modes of activity. Then, with the advent of Christianity, theology assumed a pre-eminent role and philosophy became subordinate to that.[1] With the coming of science, however, philosophy transferred its allegiance from theology and began to define itself in relation to science. Bacon and Descartes were the main figures in bringing about this latest phase. Finally, after a long night of 2,000 years, since ancient Greece, the twin forces of empiricism and rationalism were back at the forefront of human activity. After Newton, science reigned as the authoritative definer of the universe. The universe out there was devoid of human or spiritual properties, nor was it especially Christian. After Bacon and Descartes, the world was set for a new view of humanity: That fulfillment would come, not from the revelations of a religious nature, but from an increasingly fruitful human engagement with the natural world.[2]

4. John Locke: Tabula Rasa

John Locke (1632–1704) was the foremost apostle of that 17th-century mechanical conception of experience—known as empiricism. According to this doctrine, all concepts

---

1   Richard Tarnas, *The Passion of the Western Mind*, London: Pimlico, 1991, p.272.

2   Peter Watson, *Ideas: A History of Thought from Fire to Freud*, London: Weidenfeld & Nicolson, 2005, p.491.

originate in experience—all concepts are about or applicable to things that can be experienced, or all rationally acceptable beliefs or propositions are justifiable or knowable only through experience. This broad definition accords with the derivation of the term *empiricism* from the ancient Greek word *empeiria*, "experience." Locke set forth this empirical doctrine in *An Essay Concerning the Human Understanding*, which has been called by an eminent historian of philosophy "the inaugural lecture of the 18th century."

In terms of epistemology, or the theory of knowledge, Locke vigorously assaulted the doctrine of innate ideas, contending that man is not born with any apprehension of universal truth. Instead, he put forward the famous Tabula Rasa theory. The mind at birth, said Locke, may be likened to "white paper, void of all characters, without any ideas." The ideas that come to be written on this paper come from but one source: experience. It not only means the direct sense of perceptions (sensation), but the consciousness of the operation of the mind in sorting and arranging those perceptions (reflection). These are the two sources of human knowledge. By basing knowledge on experience rather than on innate ideas or revelations, Locke separated himself from existing philosophical tradition and theological dogma.

5. David Hume: An Outright Skeptic

David Hume (1711–1776) possessed the most devastating critical mind in the whole period of Rationalism. His philosophy represented the most extreme development of the skeptical tendency.

Hume was particularly famous for his criticism of the accepted doctrine of causation. He sought to prove that the idea of a "necessary connection," or logical necessity, was no essential part of a working theory of causation. His empirical idea of causation was merely observable "constant conjunction" between things. The observation of this "constant connection" did indeed establish a workable notion of causal relation, but not any "necessary connection." Hume ruled the idea of logical necessity out of the theory of causation, but he was not highly skeptical about the doctrine of a causal order based on observation. Instead, Hume used the notion of a causal order constantly in criticizing miracles and other theological conceptions. What he condemned was inference going beyond observation.

His intellectual battle against theological conceptions may be seen from the range of titles of his works, including *Of Superstition and Enthusiasm* (1742), *Essay on Miracles* (1747) and *Essay on Providence and a Future State* (1748). Hume studied religion historically and this taught him, first and foremost, that it had a lot in common with other areas of human activity. He concluded that there wasn't anything special about religion, that it had emerged as just another aspect of human activity in ancient civilizations, and that it was kept alive because parents taught it to their young children who grew up unable to think in any other ways. He argued that polytheism was the earliest form of religion. The great natural phenomena, strange happenings, such as earthquakes, lightning, rainbows, and comets, convinced man that these were the actions of a powerful and arbitrary God. Hume observed, accurately enough, that polytheism had been more tolerant than monotheism. In particular, Hume worked hard to show that the alleged proofs of God's existence were no such thing.

Then there were Hume's devastating criticisms of both miracles and the "future state." He did not deny in principle that miracles had ever taken place, but his criteria for accepting the evidence were never met. His chief argument was that, when all has been said and done, there is no unimpeachable evidence for any miracle that would be accepted by a reasonable person. Hume insisted that it was equally absurd to imagine that God would "even the score" in a future life, making up for all the injustices in this one.

Hume's general position regarding God was the order in the universe does offer some slight evidence that the universe has or had a creative force remotely analogous to human intelligence. But he held that we certainly cannot affirm anything about the moral qualities of the creator; and we cannot derive guidelines for our own actions from speculating about his (its) nature. Hume regarded Christianity as superstition.

Of Superstition and Enthusiasm[1]

By David Hume

That the corruption of the best things produces the worst, is grown into a maxim, and is commonly proved, among other instances, by the pernicious effects of superstition and enthusiasm, the corruptions of true religion.

...

These two species of false religion might afford occasion to many speculations; but I shall confine myself, at present, to a few reflections concerning their different influence on government and society.

My first reflection is, that superstition is favorable to priestly power, and enthusiasm not less, or rather more contrary to it, than sound reason and philosophy. As superstition is founded on fear, sorrow, and a depression of spirits, it represents the man to himself in such despicable colors, that he appears unworthy, in his own eyes, of approaching the divine presence, and naturally has recourse to any other person, whose sanctity of life, or perhaps impudence and cunning, have made him be supposed more favored by the Divinity. To him the superstitious intrust their devotions: to his care they recommended their prayers, petitions, and sacrifices: and by his means, they hope to render their

---

1   David Hume, *Selected Essays*, Oxford: Oxford University Press, 1993, pp.38–41.

addresses acceptable to their incensed Deity. Hence the origin of priests, who may justly be regarded as an invention of a timorous and abject superstition, which, ever diffident of itself, dares not offer up its own devotions, but ignorantly thinks to recommend itself to the Divinity, by the mediation of his supposed friends and servants. As superstition is a considerable ingredient in almost all religions, even the most fanatical; there being nothing but philosophy able entirely to conquer these unaccountable terrors; hence it proceeds, that in almost every sect of religion there are priests to be found: but the stronger mixture there is of superstition, the higher is the authority of the priesthood.

On the other hand, it may be observed, that all enthusiasts have been free from the yoke of ecclesiastics, and have expressed great independence in their devotion, with a contempt of forms, ceremonies, and traditions. The Quakers are the most egregious, though, at the same time, the most innocent enthusiasts that have yet been known; and are perhaps the only sect that have never admitted priests among them. The independents, of all the English sectaries, approach nearest to the Quakers in fanaticism, and in their freedom from priestly bondage. The Presbyterians follow after, at an equal distance, in both particulars. In short, this observation is founded in experience; and will also appear to be founded in reason, if we consider that as enthusiasm arises from a presumptuous pride and confidence, it thinks itself sufficiently qualified to approach the Divinity, without any human mediator. Its rapturous devotions are so fervent that it even imagines itself actually to approach him by the way of contemplation and inward converse; which makes it neglect all those outward ceremonies and observances, to which the assistance of the priests appears so requisite in the eyes of their superstitious votaries. The fanatic consecrates himself, and bestows on his own person a sacred character, much superior to what forms and ceremonious institutions can confer on any other.

My second reflection with regard to these species of false religion is, that religions which partake of enthusiasm, are, on their first rise, more furious and violent than those which partake of superstition; but in a little time become more gentle and moderate.

Key Terms

Montaigne and his religious tolerance → Francis Bacon and empiricism → René Descartes and rationalism → John Locke and the Tabula Rasa theory → David Hume, the outright skeptic

Exercises

1 Vocabulary Building

❧ The words in the box are all selected from this chapter. Find out pairs of words that are either synonyms or antonyms.

secular	reverse	repudiate	otherworldly
broad-minded	apprehension	deductive	handicap
unbiased	advent	empiricism	conjunction
void	coming	preeminent	devoid
fruitful	scanty	reign	rich
sorting	experimentalism	understanding	inductive
obstacle	arranging	open-minded	predominant
exclusive	doctrine	connection	rule
unimpeachable	prejudiced	tenet	productive

synonyms: _____

_____

_____

antonyms: _____

_____

_____

❧ Fill in the blanks with proper prepositions to complete the following sentences.

1) _____ particular, Hume worked hard to show that the alleged proofs of God's existence were no such thing.

2) Bacon did not doubt human's ability to know the natural world, but he thought that human reason had been employed _____ a wrong direction.

3) Everything must be stated _____ the outset _____ the most simple and clear form.

4) Finally, after a long night of 2,000 years, since ancient Greece, the twin forces of empiricism and rationalism were back _____ the forefront of human activity.

5) He broke with the medieval theology and scholastic philosophy _____ his whole attitude toward the fundamental problems of life and human existence.

6) He did not deny _____ principle that miracles had ever taken place, but his criteria for accepting the evidence were never met.

7) His philosophy suggested a complete revolution _____ the whole perspective of medieval philosophy _____ advocating the characteristic Epicurean thought.

8) Montaigne was impressed by the huge variety _____ both physical nature and human conducts.

9) Then, _____ the advent of Christianity, theology assumed a pre-eminent role and philosophy became subordinate to that.

❷ Translation

❧ Translate the following sentences into Chinese.

1) Montaigne held that if variety and diversity were characteristic of nature and mankind, God must be responsible for this situation. Otherwise, people would have to divorce God from both nature and society, or imagine both to be expressing itself in a manner repugnant to the will of God.

2) However, Bacon rejected this vintage style head on. In his famous summary, "We are the ancients," he meant that the accumulated fund of knowledge becomes older and richer with each generation. If we go back to remote antiquity, we find that knowledge is both scantier and more unreliable.

3) Hume did not deny in principle that miracles had ever taken place, but his criteria for accepting the evidence were never met. His chief argument was that, when all has been said and done, there is no unimpeachable evidence for any miracle that would be accepted by a reasonable person. Hume insisted that it was equally absurd to imagine that God would "even the score" in a future life, making up for all the injustices in this one.

❸ Questions

❧ Answer the following questions.

1) What were the two intellectual influences that helped to shape Montaigne's thinking?

2) What contribution did Francis Bacon make to human's intellectual history?

❹ Term Explanation

❧ Explain the meaning of the following terms in your own words.

1) Four Idols theory

2) Tabula Rasa theory

Chapter 20

The Intellectual Enlightenment

The Scientific Revolution in the 17th century, especially that in astronomy, did not just prove that the Earth moved around the sun, but developed a whole new understanding of the universe as a vast self-regulating entity, whose rules of operation could be discovered by observation and experiment, and described in the language of mathematics. This new understanding of the natural universe in turn helped lead to a new understanding of humanity and God—that of the 18th-century Enlightenment.

The philosophers were so dazzled by Newton's brilliance that they considered themselves to be living in an unprecedented "age of light." It was this notion that gave rise to the term "Enlightenment" as a name for the century from 1687, the publication of Newton's *Principia*, to 1789, the start of the French Revolution.

In 1784, Immanuel Kant in his essay "Answering the Question: What is Enlightenment?" defined the Enlightenment as "man's leaving his self-caused immaturity." Kant proclaimed the motto of the Enlightenment: "Dare to Know! Have the courage to use your own intelligence!" For Kant, Enlightenment was mankind's final coming of age, the emancipation of human consciousness from an immature state of ignorance. The Age of Enlightenment was a cultural movement of intellectuals beginning in late 17th-century western Europe emphasizing reason and individualism rather than tradition. It spread across Europe and to the United States, continuing to the end of the 18th century. Its purpose was to reform society using reason, to challenge ideas grounded in tradition and faith, and to advance knowledge through the scientific method.

The scientists themselves had little to do directly with the new way of looking at life that took shape during this era. Nor did professionally trained philosophers play a very significant role. The shift in thinking was mainly the work of gifted amateurs—"literary" persons, such as Pierre Bayle, Montesquieu, Voltaire, and Denis Diderot. Most of them were French, and although they did not establish any formal system of philosophy, they came to be known in their country and eventually in the English-speaking world as the philosophers.

1. The Growth of Doubt

The growth of doubt occurred in four stages. These were rationalistic supernaturalism, deism, skepticism and, finally, full-blown atheism.

1.1　Rationalistic Supernaturalism

The first of the four stages of doubt, rationalistic supernaturalism, was especially popular in England. Its basic tenets were laid down in the writings of John Locke, especially in *The Reasonableness of Christianity*. The underlying contention was that nothing in religious dogma should be accepted by an intelligent man that did not square with reason. According to Locke, there are certain general religious principles that can be deduced from the very nature of things and are thus acceptable to reason. These basic tenets are: (1) There is one God who is the Ruler of the universe; (2) He demands that men lead a virtuous life in conformance with His will; and (3) there is a future life in which evil conduct will be punished and good conduct rewarded. For Locke, they made good sense. He argued that miracles may be "above reason," but cannot be contrary to reason.

Rationalistic supernaturalists differentiated themselves from deists and atheists in their response to revelation and miracles. Since rationalistic supernaturalists argued that historical Christianity was fundamentally the same as the natural religion of the deists, then, if natural religion can be discovered by intellect, why should its truth need such reinforcement as revelation and miracles? They argued that man can lose sight of God in spite of the fact that the intellect leads one to Him. Secondly, most men had a rather inadequate idea of their moral duty. Thirdly, worship needed simplification and purification. Lastly, miracles were deemed necessary as God's exceptional encouragement to virtue. However, they also differentiated themselves from the traditional believers in that they demanded that the deductions derived from miracles should square with the claims of reason. They could not be entirely irrational. Locke's contemporary, John Tillotson (1630–1694), archbishop of Canterbury, argued that any religion must be considered as a series of rational propositions supported by logic. Tillotson's main concern was with miracles. He said, miracles, to be miracles, must be performed for a logical reason, not simply as a display of magical ingenuity. On this score, he said, the miracles of Jesus conformed to reason: They were performed for a purpose. But not all the alleged miracles of the post-Apostolic saints fell into this category. Another more passionate follower was John Toland (1670–1722), whose important work was *Christianity Not Mysterious*. As a professed disciple of Locke, Toland took Locke's suggestion seriously that the Bible might well be investigated to see if any of its statements failed to conform to reason. He found that many did fail. He recommended that all such statements should be rejected, since anything that the Deity did not care to reveal clearly could hardly be worth knowing. Among them were many miracles, including the virgin birth of Christ.

Toland's words created a storm of protest, even impelling Locke to repudiate the more radical conclusions of his disciple. But the book had a wide influence on the Continent. Voltaire, for one, was attracted by it and gave it much publicity.

1.2   Deism

The "enlightened" concept of the universe raised disturbing questions about religious convictions. Many scientists and intellectuals found it extremely difficult to bring together the Newtonian system and Christian theology. This did not mean that they necessarily gave up the idea of God, because it was still difficult for people to think of something as existing that had not been made. They tended to believe that since God created the world, He left it to run on its own. Since God had removed Himself from the affairs of the physical universe, only nature remained—so it was nature that must be understood and respected. This was a religion of sorts, which was labeled "deism." In a word, deism is the view that God created the world but thereafter left it alone.

The overall impact of the deists was to achieve a major transformation in the concept of God. Instead of the jealous, petty-minded, and arbitrary tribal God of the Israelites, God was now regarded as a law-making and law-abiding deity. The shared belief and activities among the deists were that they rejected both revelation and miracles, and claimed that the natural religion of reason was in itself sufficient to sustain human virtues.

Deism came into existence in England, from where it spread to both the Continent and to America. It found its earlier exponent in Lord Herbert of Cherbury (1583–1648), an English historian and philosopher. He posed five basic truths as common to the foremost religion of the world: (1) belief in the existence of God; (2) encouragement of the worship of God; (3) the view that the promotion of better living is the chief end of worship; (4) the contention that better living must be preceded by the repentance of sins; and (5) the belief in a world to come, in which man will be dealt with in accordance with his daily life here on the earth. While this list contains nothing controversial in itself, it is groundbreaking nevertheless since Herbert maintained that these principles are the sole foundations of true religion. There is no divinely inspired Scripture; the true message of God comes to all of us through natural reason instead of revelation; a religion with doctrines going beyond these five should be viewed as fabrications.

The discoveries in America, Africa, and elsewhere, and their religious activities only proved that all men had a religious sense, but on the other continents there was no awareness of Jesus. The deists therefore used this as evidence to argue that religion requires no supernatural elements to support it, and that prophecy and miracles have no place in a "scientific religion." Most deists insisted that the extensive superstitions and elaborate machinery of worship in the Church were simply concoctions dreamt up by the priesthood to satisfy their own selfish and political ends. The worst of these elements was that of intercession, which placed the priesthood between man and God, maintaining a set of privileges that had no basis in Scripture and were all too easy to see through. The Bible was attacked by individuals such as William Whiston and Anthony Collins: They examined carefully the prophecies of the Old Testament and found scant support for the idea that they had predicted the coming of Jesus. Peter Annet, in his *Resurrection of Jesus Considered* (1744), came out boldly with an argument that the apostolic accounts of the Resurrection were fabricated, while Charles Blount was equally blunt about original sin, the concept of which he found was unreasonable. He said heaven and hell had been invented by priests "to increase their hold over the terror-stricken and ignorant masses." The most influential French deist was Voltaire (1694–1778). He derided everything about Christianity, from the idea that the Bible is a sacred book to the miracles. "Every man of sense," he wrote, "every good man, ought to hold the Christian sect in horror. The great name of theist, which is not sufficiently revered, is the only name one ought to take. The only Gospel one ought to read is the great book of nature, written by the hand of God and sealed with his seal. The only religion that ought to be professed is the religion of worshipping God and being a good man."

In Germany, Immanuel Kant, while accepting the basic tenets of Christianity as a loving religion, was implacable in opposing the supernatural elements—prophecy and miracles—calling them "wholly evil." In America, both Benjamin Franklin and George Washington were deists and so were Thomas Jefferson and John Adams. Franklin was an out-and-out deist. We can find a most concise summary of the fundamentals of deism in his response to a request from the president of Yale University: "I believe in one God, the Creator of the universe. That he governs it by his providence. That he ought to be worshipped. That the most acceptable service we render him is doing good to his other children. That the soul of man is immortal, and will be treated with justice in another life respecting its conduct in this." Washington was also cordial to deistic doctrines. He never received communion. Jefferson was an aggressive deist. He extolled reason and declared that men should follow wherever it leads, even if they must, as a result, deny the existence of God. Adams was an advanced Unitarian, a kind of belief called "respectable deism."

In both Europe and America, however, deism eventually foundered and it did so because it fell between two stools. It was too adventurous and too abstract to comfort the devout, the traditional, and the orthodox, while at the same time it was seen as too timid to appeal to the truly skeptical.

1.3 Skepticism

By the close of the 18th century, many people had decided that there was really no need even for a Creator. Newton had shown that motion is as natural as non-motion. Is matter, then, not as natural as non-matter? Was it not old-fashioned to think that things must be created? The universe and its motion had always been and always would be like that. This line of reasoning led some people to deny God absolutely (atheism); others said they could not or did not know whether God existed (skepticism or agnosticism).

Skepticism was already evident in earlier writings by Montaigne, Thomas Hobbes (though he never called himself a skeptic), and David Hume. The most important figure in French skepticism was Pierre Bayle (1647–1706), who attacked the Old Testament with all the gusto with which Hume had demolished miracles. Bayle attacked superstition, religious intolerance, and dogmatism. Individual conscience, he argued, should determine one's action. Bayle was one of a number of intellectuals who believed that the new rational principles of textual criticism should be applied to the Bible as well as secular documents. He demonstrated his own criticism in his most famous work *Historical and Critical Dictionary*. Through textual analysis, he portrayed the Israelite king David as a sensual, treacherous, cruel, and basically evil man instead of the traditional picture of the heroic David. His work, which attacked traditional religious practices and heroes, was well known to 18th-century philosophers.

Historical and Critical Dictionary

By Pierre Bayle

"Of the Sexual Form of Adam"

A great number of the rabbis believed that Adam's body was created double, male on the one side, and female on the other; and that the two bodies were joined together by the shoulders; the heads looking directly opposite, like the heads of Janus. Thus they pretend that when God made Eve, he only divided the original body into two: the part which was of the masculine sex forming Adam, and that which was of the feminine sex Eve. Manesseh-Ben-Israel, the most learned rabbi of the 17th century, maintained this fantastical opinion, if we may believe Heidegger. The learned Maimonides, the honor and glory of the Jewish nation, had already maintained a similar notion; and Antoinette Bourignon pretends, that before Adam sinned, he had the principle of both sexes in himself, and the virtue to produce his likeness without the help of woman. The necessity that each sex has at present to unite to each other for multiplication, is (she says) a consequence of the alterations that sin has made in human bodies. Men think that they have been created by God as they are at present, but it is not true, seeing that sin has disfigured the work of God in them, and instead of men as they ought to be, they are become monsters in nature, divided into two imperfect sexes, unable to produce their like alone, as trees and plants do, which in that point have more perfection than men or women, who are incapable to produce by them.

"Good and Evil"

How detestable so ever the opinion of two principles hath constantly appeared to all Christians, they have nevertheless acknowledged a subaltern principle of moral evil. Divines teach us that a great number of angels having sinned, made a party in the universe against God. For brevity's sake this party is denoted by the name of devil, and he is acknowledged as the cause of the fall of the first man, and as the perpetual tempter and seducer of mankind. The devil having declared war against God from the moment of his fall, hath always continued in his rebellion, and there has never been any peace or truce. He continually applies himself to usurp the rights of his Creator, and seduces his subjects, in order to make them rebels and engage them to serve under his banner against their common master. He succeeded in his first hostilities with regard to man; in the Garden of Eden he attacked the mother of all living, and vanquished her; and immediately after he attacked the first man, and defeated him. Thus he became master of mankind. God did not abandon this prey to him, but delivered them out of their bondage, and recovered them out of that state of reprobation by virtue of the satisfaction which the second person of the Trinity undertook to pay to his justice. This second person engaged to become man, and to act as a mediator between God and mankind, and as a Redeemer of Adam and his posterity. He took upon him to combat the devil's party; so that he was the head of God's party against the devil, who was the head of the rebellious creatures. The design was not to conquer all the posterity of Adam; for they were all by birth, in the power of the devil, but to preserve, or recover the country which had been conquered. The design of Jesus Christ, the Mediator, the Son of God, was to recover it; that of the devil was to hold it.

The victory of the Mediator consisted in leading men into the paths of truth and virtue; that of the devil in seducing them into the road of error and vice. So that in order to know whether moral good equals moral evil among men, we need only compare the victories of the devil with those of Jesus Christ. Now in history we find but very few triumphs of Jesus Christ: *"Apparent rari nantes in gurgite vasto"*; and we every where meet with the triumphs of the devil.

1.4   Atheism

There were some men who, unlike the skeptics, flatly stated that they did not believe in God. The first outright atheist in this modern sense was probably Lucilio Vanini (1585–1619), an Italian scientist. He was the first literate proponent of the thesis that humans evolved from apes. He was arrested for heresy, and after having his tongue cut out, he was burnt at the stake.

More reasoned atheists arose in England and France in the wake of Newton's discoveries. There was a street called "Atheists' Alley" near the Royal Exchange in London. Bookshops began to teem with pamphlets and tracts dealing with atheist scare. Theaters were homes to atheist satires, which taught men "how they might live without a Creator; and how, now they are, they may live best without any dependence on his Providence. They are called to doubt the existence of God". In France, one of the more prominent atheists was Julien de La Mettrie (1709–1751), who wrote a book called *Man a Machine*, in which he offered a thoroughgoing mechanistic analysis of man and the universe. There was no room left for God. His view was that human nature and animal nature were part of the same continuum, that human nature equated with physical nature, and that there were no immaterial substances, thus casting huge doubt on the existence of the soul. He was supported by another downright atheist, Baron d'Holbach (1723–1789), a German émigré who had moved to Paris. He was much more radical, openly admitting that concepts of God and supernaturalism had been invented by primitive man who simply did not understand natural phenomena. He argued that the universe could be adequately accounted for on the basis of materialistic determinism, a system in which God had no essential place. Everything from the cosmos to human conduct was a product of causal necessity. There was no place for arbitrary free will. He insisted that morality was not dependent on religion. Holbach was also one of the first to argue that man was really no different from other living creatures in the universe, neither better nor worse. It followed that man had to work out his own morality, not deriving it from any supernatural authority. This was an important insight and, decades later, would help lead to the theory of evolution.

The Enlightenment is similar to Christianity in the humanitarian and ethical goals. The essential differences may be summed up as follows: Christianity rests its faith in the power of God as known through revelation; the Enlightenment puts its trust in nature as understood through reason. The supreme goal of Christianity is heaven (spiritual bliss after death); the goal of the Enlightenment is progress (physical happiness in life on the earth). Respect for the harmonious motions of the heavenly bodies led some philosophers to an unscientific, sentimental attitude toward all objects in nature.

2. Vision of Progress

One of the more conspicuous results of the rise of science and the growth of rationalism was the gradual rise of the idea of progress. Progress was a new idea in history. The ancient Jews, holding the doctrine of the Fall of Man, believed perfection to be found in the past rather than in the future. The Christians, taking over the Jewish notion, thought men could never expect any utopia here on the earth. They did believe in blessedness in the future, but only in the world to come. The ancient pagans shared to some degree a comparable notion, namely, the dogma of a decline from a golden age. Even the humanists of the Renaissance, for all their high estimate of human capacity, had looked backward to Greece and Rome as the time when perfection had been most fully realized.

However, there arose gradually a conviction that better things might be in store for humanity here on this earth. Back in the 13th century, Roger Bacon had a vision of what science might do for man. Montaigne had a glimmering of a new idea when he suggested that philosophy should be concerned with human happiness on the earth rather than with salvation. Francis Bacon contended that the moderns were superior to the ancients and suggested that utopia might be secured through applying science to human problems. But 17th-century science at last broke the spell of antiquity. Scientists felt that it was the Greeks and Romans who were "children" in time. Science thus dissolved the myth of classical superiority in knowledge and, with its new tools, pointed the way toward a grander future.

The doctrine of progress, as it is conventionally understood, began with men like Bernard de Fontenelle (1657–1757). In *Digression on the Ancients and the Moderns*, he believed that the ancients and the moderns are essentially alike in a biological sense, there being no progress in this respect. The same is true with the fine arts. In the fine arts, there seem to be no law of progress, because they are chiefly a spontaneous expression of the human spirit. On the other hand, in science and industry, there has been vast progress since antiquity and even greater things may be looked for in the future. Moreover, Fontenelle proceeded to state that unreasoning admiration for the past is a major obstacle to progress. In the first half of the 18th century, Giovanni Battista Vico (1668–1744), an Italian, worked out his conception of progress. He held that human progress does not take place in a straight line. Rather, it takes the form of a spiral. There may seem to be cycles of development, but they never go back to the original starting-point. Even more optimistic was the distinguished writer of the French Revolution period, the Marquis de Condorcet (1743–1794). He not only stated his belief in progress but divided the history of civilization into ten periods. There are other men who also contributed to the notion of progress. The German philosopher Johann Gottfried Herder divided history into five periods, Georg Wilhelm Hegel divided it into four, and Immanuel Kant sought to prove the reality of moral progress and believed that progress had gone through nine stages. Henri de Saint-Simon (1760–1825) believed that a definite social science must be provided to guide human progress. These notions culminated in Auguste Comte (1798–1857). He worked out a comprehensive system of laws concerning intellectual progress and formulated an expansive philosophy of history, embodying the division of the past into a large number of periods and subperiods, each characterized by some phase of cultural advance.

3. Culture

The intellectual adventures launched by the philosophers were accompanied by both traditional practices and important changes in the 18th-century world of culture, mainly in art, literature, and music.

3.1 Art

In the 18th century, the grandeur and drama of the Baroque in painting was no longer in fashion. In France and elsewhere, royal and aristocratic patrons preferred the elegance, charm, and grace of the Rocco style.

Unlike the Baroque, which stressed majesty, power, and movement, Rocco emphasized grace and gentle action. Rocco rejected strict geometrical patterns and tended to follow the curving lines of natural objects. It made much use of interlaced designs colored in gold with delicate contours and graceful curves. Highly secular, its lightness and charm spoke of the pursuit of pleasure, happiness, and love. The Belgian master Antoine Watteau (1684–1721) was the finest representative of this style. Watteau caught the spirit of refined ease and gallantry associated with the aristocratic ideal.

In landscape painting, the leading master was a Dutch, Jacob van Ruysdael (1628?–1682). He was an extreme realist, reproducing natural scenes as they were. His chief rival in landscape painting was a Frenchman, Claude Lorraine (1600–1682). Different from Ruysdael's realism, he painted imaginary landscapes in a conventional style to serve as backgrounds for classical or mythological episodes and scenes. Another capable imaginary landscape painter was Nicolas Poussin (1594–1665). He was the leading painter of the classical French Baroque style, although he spent most of his working life in Rome. His works are characterized by clarity, logic, and order, and favor line over color. Themes of tragedy and death are prevalent in Poussin's works.

Portrait painting reached a far higher degree of popularity and perfection in this period than in any earlier age. The most famous painter of portraits was the Flemish master, Anthony van Dyck (1599–1641). He combined naturalness, dignity, and refinement to a remarkable degree. In the 18th century, there were two great English painters of portraits, Sir Joshua Reynolds (1723–1792) and Thomas Gainsborough (1727–1788). Reynolds idealized the English generals, statesmen, and ladies with classic dignity, while Gainsborough excelled him in delicacy of touch and skillful use of color.

3.2 Literature

The 18th century is credited with an age of the development of the novel. Growing out of the medieval romances and the picaresque stories of the 16th century, the modern novel was becoming the chief vehicle of fiction writing.

The English were credited with the establishment of such genre. Two English writers stood out in the 18th century. Samuel Richardson (1689–1761) was a skilled letter writer. He is best known for his three epistolary novels: *Pamela: Or, Virtue Rewarded* (1740), *Clarissa: Or the History of a Young Lady* (1748), and *The History of Sir Charles Grandison* (1753). Richardson had a faith in the act of letter writing, and believed that letters could be used to accurately portray character traits. In his first novel, *Pamela*, he explored the various complexities of the title character's life, and the letters allow the reader to witness her growth and progress over time. The novel was an experiment, but it allowed Richardson to create a complex heroine through a series of her letters. When Richardson wrote *Clarissa*, he had more experience in the form and expanded the letter writing to four different correspondents, which created a complex system of characters encouraging each other to grow and develop over time. By the time Richardson wrote *Grandison*, he transformed the letter writing from telling personal insights and explaining feelings into a means for people to communicate their thoughts on the actions of others and for the public to celebrate virtue. The letters are no longer written for a few people, but are passed along in order for all to see.

Henry Fielding (1707–1754) was a novelist and dramatist. Almost by accident, in anger at the success of Samuel Richardson's *Pamela*, which extols how virtue is rewarded, Fielding took to writing novels in 1741 and his first major success was *Shamela*, an anonymous parody of Richardson's melodramatic novel. Most of his novels are about people without scruple who survived by their wits. His greatest work is *Tom Jones*, a meticulously constructed picaresque novel telling the convoluted and hilarious tale of how a foundling came into a fortune.

3.3　Music

Music has always been a vital part of life and an expression of Western culture. It has been used for both sacred and secular purposes. From the ancient Greeks to the troubadours, music had been monophonic, consisting of a single tune, without harmonizing chords. Polyphony ("part" music, in which singers or players perform different but harmonizing notes or tunes) had its beginnings in the 10th century and during the Renaissance reached its full development in both sacred and secular music.

The 17th and 18th centuries were the formative years of classical music and saw the rise of opera, oratorio, sonata, concerto, and symphony. The transformation of music to its "modernity" reached full force during the Baroque era of the 17th century. In contrast to the even-tempered, complex themes of traditional polyphony, Baroque compositions were marked by a heavier stress on a dominant melody. Larger numbers and types of instruments were used: flutes, oboes, trumpets, and bassoons, as well as violas, violins, and the harpsichord. More importantly, composers now began to write instrumental music for listening, not just for dancing. Perhaps the most important cultural development of the time was the appearance of a new art form: opera. Originated in Italy, the opera's chief creator was Claudio Monteverdi (1567–1643). A great contributor to the popularization of opera was a German composer George Frideric Handel (1685–1759). Handel spent much of his youth in Italy before settling in England early in the 18th century. Endlessly prolific and versatile, Handel could express in music almost any situation and emotion, ranging from sensual passion, through the magnificence of his works for royal occasions, to the religious grandeur of his sacred music. Another prolific German composer Johann Sebastian Bach (1685–1750) could write in every form except opera. A giant of the Baroque period and one of the great musicians of all time, Bach composed profound and inspiring scores for religious texts (cantatas and oratorios), Masses, and Passions, as well as secular music. He is notable for the power and grandeur of his expression and for his mastery of polyphonic themes.

However, if we use the term "classical" in a narrower sense, it applies to the 18th century only. The music of that century, as we shall see, echoed the general accent on order, balance, and restraint. Among the most gifted of all the classical composers were Franz Joseph Haydn (1732–1809) and Wolfgang Amadeus Mozart (1756–1791), both Austrians. Haydn brought the chamber and symphonic forms to a high point of perfection and in doing so created works of enduring appeal. Mozart, a child prodigy, composed serious works before the age of five. He was a master of all types of composition and displayed the clarity and grace of classicism at its best. But his ultimate triumph was in opera. Among his most popular operas today are *Don Giovanni*, *The Marriage of Figaro*, and *The Magic Flute*.

Key Terms

Enlightenment → rationalistic supernaturalism → deism → skepticism → atheism → Rocco → landscape painting → portrait painting → literature → modern novel → Samuel Richardson → Henry Fielding → music → Baroque era → opera

Exercises

❶ Vocabulary Building

🔖 Fill in each blank with a synonym to the word in the brackets.

1) Toland's words created a storm of _____ (protest), even _____ (impelling) Locke to _____ (repudiate) the more radical conclusions of his _____ (disciple). But the book had a wide influence on the Continent. Voltaire, for one, was _____ (attracted) by it and gave it much publicity.

2) Francis Bacon _____ (contended) that the moderns were superior to the ancients and suggested that utopia might be _____ (secured) through applying science to human problems. But 17th-century science at last broke the _____ (spell) of antiquity. Scientists felt that it was the Greeks and Romans who were "children" in time. Science thus _____ (dissolved) the myth of classical _____ (superiority) in knowledge and, with its new tools, pointed the way toward a grander future.

3) Handel spent much of his youth in Italy before settling in England early in the 18th century. Endlessly _____ (prolific) and _____ (versatile), Handel could express in music almost any situation and emotion, ranging from sensual passion, through the _____ (magnificence) of his works for _____ (royal) occasions, to the religious _____ (grandeur) of his _____ (sacred) music.

❷ Translation

🔖 Translate the following sentences into Chinese.

1) The ancient Jews, holding the doctrine of the Fall of Man, believed perfection to be found in the past rather than in the future. The Christians, taking over the Jewish notion, thought men could never expect any utopia here on the earth.

2) The 18th century is credited with an age of the development of the novel. Growing out of the medieval romances and the picaresque stories of the 16th century, the modern novel was becoming the chief vehicle of fiction writing.

3) The 17th and 18th centuries were the formative years of classical music and saw the rise of opera, oratorio, sonata, concerto, and symphony.

❸ Questions

❧ Answer the following questions.

1) How did Immanuel Kant define the Enlightenment?

2) What are the four stages of the growth of doubt?

3) What are the basic tenets of rationalistic supernaturalism?

4) Who are the representatives of skepticism?

5) What are the essential differences between Christianity and the Enlightenment?

6) What caused the gradual rise of the idea of progress?

7) What are the differences between the Baroque and the Rocco styles?

❹ Topics for Discussion

❧ Below are two topics related to this chapter. Read them and finish the discussion.

1) During the Enlightenment, people formed a new way of looking at life and there are many representatives, such as Pierre Bayle, Montesquieu, Voltaire, Denis Diderot, etc. Whose view do you support? Support your views with substantial evidence and sound argumentation.

2) Do research on the important changes in the 18th-century world of culture, mainly in art, literature, and music, and exchange your findings with your classmates.

❺ Presentation

❧ In groups, make a presentation on the following topics.

1) Enlightenment

2) rationalistic supernaturalism

3) deism

4) skepticism

5) atheism

Chapter 21

The Secularization of Political Theory: Social Contract

With the rise of the secular national state, philosophical justifications of its supremacy had to be forthcoming. Apart from the doctrine of Roman law, the theory of the divine right of kings which had justified more or less the supremacy of kingship, the conception of social contract was the most important invention of this age. Roughly, the social-contract theory of political origins ran as follows: Men originally lived in a pre-social state of nature without law or order. This condition was full of inconveniences and dangers because of avarice and struggles over property. Hence, the more sensible people decided to leave this state of anarchy and institute a well-ordered community life. The agreement to do so constituted the social contract. Next, they decided upon the form of government and entered into a second or governmental contract between rulers and subjects, defining the right and power of each and the relations between the two. If rulers violated this contract, then subjects possessed the right to rebel, drive out their oppressive rulers, and install a new set. Such was the essential doctrine of the social contract as it appeared in a well-developed form with Locke, Pufendorf, and Rousseau. Hobbes was an exception, because he refused to sanction the right of revolution at all.

Several factors may have contributed to the need of social-contract theory. The rise of business and capitalism made private property far more significant than in earlier ages. Those who possessed private property desired public protection and assurance against confiscation and robbery. The new political theory therefore laid special stress upon the duty of the state to safeguard private property. Finally, the development of rationalism and religious liberalism, together with the rise of Protestantism, tended to destroy the vitality of the old struggle between the political State and the Roman Catholic Church. Philosophers went into history and psychology rather than into divine revelation and approval for the foundations of political philosophy. The Protestants took the side of the State in most cases and favored political control of the Church. Most of the bourgeois political philosophers were rationalists, and they would accept none of the old arguments that relied primarily upon supernatural sanctions. By the end of the 18th century, the modern psychological and historical interpretations of political origins had been firmly established and political philosophy was thoroughly secularized.

1. Thomas Hobbes

The first thoroughgoing exposition of the social-contract idea was put forward by Richard Hooker, a famous English ecclesiastic. However, it remained for the English philosopher Thomas Hobbes (1588–1679) to give the first statement of that conception.

Thomas Hobbes lived during the English civil war. It is said that his mother when bearing the child was so frightened by the news of the civil war that she labored, so fear was the twin to Hobbes. Hobbes' name was associated with the book *Leviathan* where he advocated the state's claim to absolute authority. Leviathan is a mythical sea monster or dragon mentioned in Job 41 that describes it as a fire-breathing sea monster or dragon. "Smoke pours from his nostrils" and his breath is so hot that it "sets coals ablaze" with the "flames (that) dart from his mouth." In the book, Hobbes contended that by nature people were so unsocial that if they had to live without an effective government to check them, they would find themselves in a "war of all against all." In such a war, everyone's life would be "solitary, poor, nasty, brutish, and short." This alternative was so horrible that life under any effective government would be preferable to it, no matter what the form of that government was. The same features of human nature made it impossible for any government to be effective if it did not possess absolute power. To try to limit the power of government by a constitution or by dividing authority among different branches of government was to invite anarchy and misery of the state of nature. So, the subjects of an absolute government should prefer that form of government to any other and give it "simple obedience." For Hobbes, it therefore followed that, to avoid this primitive condition of perpetual war, men must submit to a common authority. Since the main law of nature was self-preservation, it followed that men were obliged to confer all their power and strength upon one man, or upon one assembly of men that they may reduce all their wills to one will.[1] This is what he meant by the great Leviathan, a form of mortal God (as he put it) who alone has the power to enforce contracts and obligations.

1　Peter Watson, *Ideas: A History of Thought from Fire to Freud*, London: Weidenfeld & Nicolson, 2005, p.518.

2. Samuel Pufendorf

The German statesman and philosopher Samuel Pufendorf (1632–1694) had a political theory, mainly Hobbesian. He held that the social instinct in man would account for the existence of the family and lesser social groups, but a contract was necessary to bring into being the state and the government. Though beginning the analysis of the state of nature as a state of peace, Pufendorf, nevertheless, came to the same conclusion as that arrived at by Hobbes. His conception of contract was two-fold: First, there was a social contract that embodied the agreement to unite; then a vote was taken to determine the form of government desired. Finally, a governmental contract was established between the governors and the governed regarding the principles and limits of political administration.

3. John Locke

Every political theory which sets out to justify or advocate a particular system of government must rest on an explicit or implicit theory of human nature. Unlike Thomas Hobbes who claimed that in the state of nature, before society was organized, human was guided by animalistic instincts and a ruthless struggle for self-preservation, John Locke believed that human lived then in a state of equality and freedom rather than in a state of war. In this state of nature, human had certain natural rights—to life, liberty, and property. Since there was no impartial judge in the state of nature, people agreed to establish a government to protect their rights. The chief and immediate cause of men's leaving the state of nature was the increase of private property, the desire to use and preserve it in safety. This emphasis on the preservation of private property might have been expected from the apologists of the Bourgeois Revolution of 1688. Locke frankly maintained that the chief end of government was the protection of property.

Locke differentiated clearly between the political community formed by the social contract and the government to which it delegated the functions of political control. By doing so, he was able to show how the government might be dissolved without destroying the civil society itself. Locke held that this dissolution or revolution was justifiable when the terms of contract were violated by those in power. Locke thus laid the philosophical foundations for the American and French revolutions.

4. Baruch Spinoza

According to his political theory, the Jewish philosopher Baruch Spinoza (1632–1677) was a member of the contract school. He agreed with Hobbes on the existence of a pre-social state of nature that was one of war and universal enmity. Society, he maintained, was basically utilitarian, favoring mutual aid and the division of labor. To secure this advantageous association, it was necessary for this utilitarian basis to be supplemented by a contract to give it a legal foundation and thus to guarantee the rights that he had possessed as an individual prior to the contract.

In order to understand Spinoza's political theory, it would be helpful to first have a look at his ethics. Three of the most striking and important claims of Spinoza's *Ethics* are that: (1) All things come to exist and act necessarily from the laws of God's nature; (2) nature does not act on account of some end or purpose; and (3) nature is everywhere and always the same. Collectively, these three claims entail that human behavior, like the behavior of everything else, is fully necessitated by, and explicable through, the immutable—and non-providential—laws of God or nature. This forms a significant part of the metaphysical backdrop against which Spinoza developed his political theory. The view that is constituted by these three theses is called naturalism by some scholars. This naturalism led him to adopt radical views regarding the source and status of rights, obligations, and laws, distinguishing his works from other 17th-century political theorists. Spinoza's naturalism excluded transcendental conceptions of God. Of course, on Spinoza's account, God is not a transcendent legislator; God is nature itself. Spinoza's naturalism entailed that all claims of entitlement deriving from God's will are specious. This is a direct rebuke not only of defenders of the divine right of kings, but also of most accounts of natural rights as entitlements that were embraced by many 17th-century theorists.

Spinoza differed from Hobbes in that he always preserved the natural right in its entirety and that the sovereign power in a state had a right over a subject only in proportion to the excess of its power over that of a subject, whereas Hobbes insisted on the transference of one's natural right. The transferability or alienability of one's natural right to judge how to defend oneself serves as the foundation of Hobbes' political theory; it allowed him to explain the formation of the commonwealth and the legitimacy of the sovereign. In Spinoza's view, however, Hobbes violated naturalism here.

The difference between Hobbes and Spinoza on natural right bears directly on their distinct accounts of obligation. Hobbes thought that men incur binding obligations when they make pledges under the appropriate conditions. By contrast, Spinoza maintained that "the validity of an agreement rests on its utility, without which the agreement automatically becomes null and void." Whereas Hobbes argued that the sovereign is always vested with nearly absolute legislative authority, Spinoza claimed that "since the right of a commonwealth is determined by the collective power of people, the greater the number of subjects who are given cause by a commonwealth to join in conspiracy against it, the more must its power and right be diminished." If a sovereign is to maintain its right, it must legislate wisely, so as not to incite insurrection.

As Curley rightly pointed out, to deny that there is a transcendental standard of justice is not to deny that there is any normative standard by which we can evaluate action.[1] The goodness of an action is to be judged in relation to whether the action aids one's striving to preserve and augment one's power. This striving which constitutes one's actual essence, provides a standard for moral judgments: Things are good or bad to the extent that they aid or diminish one's power of acting. And just as the individual ought to do those things that maximize his or her own power or welfare, Spinoza took it as axiomatic that the state ought to do those things that maximize the power of the people as a whole.[2]

5. Jean-Jacques Rousseau

The last representative of the classical contract school was the French Jean-Jacques Rousseau (1712–1778). As for man's state of nature, Rousseau in his *A Discourse on the Origin of Inequality* took the position in opposition to Hobbes by claiming that the condition of man in the state of nature was almost ideal in its rude simplicity. It was the whole progress of civilization that mainly contributed to physical and moral degeneration of the race and the growth of inequality and corruption. In his later work *The Social Contract*, however, he abandoned this ecstatic praise of the natural state of man and took the same position of Locke; namely, while this natural condition of man was not one of war, its inconveniences made the institution of civil society imperative. The only way in which civil society could be instituted, and united power and general protection secured, was through the medium of social contract. Rousseau like Locke also distinguished between the state and the government, because he thought that the contract gave rise to the state or the civil community instead of the government, and that the sovereign power was the prerogative of the state and the governmental power was purely delegated.

Rousseau's definition of sovereignty as the absolute power in the state, growing out of an expression of the general will, was probably his outstanding contribution to political philosophy. It had much influence on representative government and democracy which became prevalent in the 19th century.

1　Edwin Curley, "Kissinger, Spinoza, and Genghis Khan," *Cambridge Companion to Spinoza*, Cambridge: Cambridge University Press, 1996, pp.315–342.

2　Steinberg Justin, "Spinoza's Political Theory," April 15, 2019, retrieved from Stanford University website.

Key Terms

social contract → Thomas Hobbes → Samuel Pufendorf → John Locke → Baruch Spinoza and naturalism → Jean-Jacques Rousseau

Exercises

❶ Vocabulary Building

❧ Fill in each blank with a synonym to the word in the brackets.

1) For Hobbes, it therefore followed that, to avoid this _____ (primitive) condition of perpetual war, men must _____ (submit) to a common authority. Since the main law of nature was self-preservation, it followed that men were _____ (obliged) to _____ (confer) all their power and strength upon one man, or upon one _____ (assembly) of men that they may reduce all their wills to one will.

2) Since there was no _____ (impartial) judge in the state of nature, people agreed to establish a government to protect their rights. The chief and _____ (immediate) cause of men's leaving the state of nature was the increase of private _____ (property), the desire to use and _____ (preserve) it in safety. This emphasis on the preservation of private property might have been expected from the _____ (apologists) of the Bourgeois Revolution of 1688.

3) Society, he _____ (maintained), was basically _____ (utilitarian), favoring mutual aid and the division of labor. To secure this advantageous association, it was necessary for this utilitarian basis to be _____ (supplemented) by a contract to give it a legal foundation and thus to _____ (guarantee) the rights that he had _____ (possessed) as an individual prior to the contract.

❷ Translation

❧ Translate the following sentences into Chinese.

1) The rise of business and capitalism made private property far more significant than in earlier ages. Those who possessed private property desired public protection and assurance against confiscation and robbery.

2) This naturalism led him to adopt radical views regarding the source and status of rights,

obligations, and laws, distinguishing his works from other 17th-century political theorists.

3) The only way in which civil society could be instituted, and united power and general protection secured, was through the medium of social contract.

Questions

ॐ Answer the following questions.

1) Who first put forward the social-contract idea?

2) What are the fundamental features of social-contract theory?

3) What is Samuel Pufendorf's conception of contract?

4) How does Thomas Hobbes differ from John Locke in their political theories?

5) What is John Locke's contribution to the American and French revolutions?

6) What are the most striking and important claims of Baruch Spinoza's *Ethics*?

7) How does Thomas Hobbes differ from Baruch Spinoza on natural right?

8) What is Jean-Jacques Rousseau's definition of sovereignty?

Topics for Discussion

ॐ Below are two topics related to this chapter. Read them and finish the discussion.

1) The social-contract theory has been well developed by political theorists, such as Thomas Hobbes, Samuel Pufendorf, John Locke, Baruch Spinoza, and Jean-Jacques Rousseau. Whose view do you support? Support your views with substantial evidence and sound argumentation.

2) Do research on the social-contract theory, and exchange your findings with your classmates.

Presentation

ॐ In groups, make a presentation on the following topics.

1) social contract

2) naturalism

Chapter 22

New Developments in Law and Legal Philosophy

The new developments in law and legal philosophy during the early modern period were dominated by the same note which affected the course of political theory—secularization.

This secularization was first the triumph of Roman law. The revival of Roman law in the Middle Ages promoted royal power and the prestige of the State at the expense of the Church and other rivals of the secular arm. This movement arrived at its culmination in early modern times, when secular absolutism gained defining dominion in political affairs. The Protest revolt, which favored the power of the prince at the expense of the Church, encouraged this tendency. Another effective secularizing influence was derived from the common law of England. It opposed the doctrine of revealed law, since it was admittedly the collective legal wisdom of the nation as derived from the experience of its various communities in dealing with all manners of cases over centuries.

1. The Doctrine of Natural Law

However, perhaps the most influential type of legal development during this period was the doctrine of natural law. The notion of law of nature is an old one: It goes back to Heraclitus and the Stoics. But in this period, the conception was clarified and related more closely to specific political and legal application. The law of nature was regarded as the body of rules and principles that governed men in pre-political days. Natural law was the norm to test the soundness of civil law. The state should not terminate the law of nature, but rather provide for the enforcement of its benign principles. Instead of restricting human's natural freedom, the state should free people from the terrors and anarchy of unorganized pre-political society. Hobbes, Pufendorf, Spinoza, and others contributed to the development of the doctrine of natural law, but it was John Locke who gave it great significance in legal history. He claimed that the major tenet of the law of nature was the sanctity of personal liberty and private property. It was the state's supreme duty to assure their protection and perpetuity. This notion was seized upon by later revolutionaries and written into the constitution. John Locke's natural law and consent of the governed were the foundation of American Declaration of Independence, Constitution, and Bill of Rights. In the Declaration of Independence, it was laid down in the beginning paragraph, "When in the Course of human events, it becomes necessary for one people to dissolve the political bands which have connected them with another, and to assume among the powers of the earth, the separate and equal station to which the Laws of Nature and of Nature's God entitle them, a decent respect to the opinions of mankind requires that they should declare the causes which impel them to the separation."

2. The Rise of International Law

In early modern times, the growth of commercial relations, the rise of national state, and the numerous bloody wars of the period, all combined to create the necessity for a conception of equity rising above the laws of particular states. It was Hugo Grotius (1583–1645), a Dutchman who systematized the subject for the first time. His book *The Law of War and Peace* was published in 1625, which marked the emergence of international law as an "autonomous legal science."

Grotius' truly distinctive contribution to jurisprudence and philosophy of law (international law or law of nations in particular) was that he "secularized" natural law, and therefore was known as "the father of natural law." Grotius had divorced natural law from theology and religion by grounding it solely in the social nature and natural reason of man. When Grotius, considered by many people to be the founder of modern natural law theory (or secular natural law), said that natural law would retain its validity "even if God did not exist," he was making a clear break with the classical tradition of natural law.

In terms of the source of the law, Grotius underwent a change from voluntarism to nature. Voluntarism was a well-established tradition of natural law theories. By an act of volition, God determines the full and exact content of all normative categories—justice, goodness, and so forth. In *The Law of War and Peace*, he declared, "What God has shown to be His Will, that is law. This axiom points directly to the cause of law, and is rightly laid down as the primary principle." In later works, however, Grotius departed from it. For example, in the *De Summa Potestatum*, he declared that normativity of any kind "arises from the nature of the action itself, so that it is right per se to worship God and it is right per se not to lie." Instead of emerging from or being otherwise dependent on God, the fundamental principles of ethics, politics, and laws obtain in virtue of nature. As he said, "The mother of right—that is of natural law—is human nature." Somewhat later, he clarified why it was human nature that produced the natural law: "The law of nature is a dictate of right reason, which points out that an act, according as it is or is not in conformity with rational nature, has in it a quality of moral baseness or moral necessity; and that, in consequence, such an act is either forbidden or enjoined." If an action agrees with the rational and social aspects of human nature, it is permissible; if it doesn't, it is impermissible. That is to say, the source of natural law is the compatibility of actions with our essences as rational and social beings.

Grotius set out two principles of nature to decide whether a war is legal or not: (1) the principle of individual self-preservation; (2) the conformity of things with reason, which is superior to the body. Conformity with moral goodness becomes the principal object. He further distinguished the public war from the private war, and attempts were made to civilize and regulate the conduct of nations in wartime. It was held that international law embodies ideals of right conduct which have a moral authority over the sovereign states, even though international law cannot be imposed by the force of any common superior. This served to mitigate somewhat the then popular conception that the state was wholly an end unto itself and owed no obligations whatever to humanity at large.

After Grotius, the science of international law split into two groups, the naturalists and the pure positivists. Samuel Pufendorf was the leader of the first group, the first German professor of natural and international law at the University of Heidelberg. He recognized the law of nature as the sole source of international law and denied the existence of any rule of positive international law, because there was no common superior over the states from which it could proceed. Whereas the former Christian defenders of natural law, including Grotius, had quoted passages from the Holy Scripture, Pufendorf distinguished between rights and obligations founded in the actual corrupted human nature (after the Fall) and those arising from revelation. Pufendorf's aim was the development of a system of natural law based solely on reason. But reason for him was only a means of examining human nature with its dispositions, and of recognizing the ends to which human nature aspired and from which the norms of natural law could be deduced. For him, there was no doubt that the objective basis of natural law was the fact that a man, in order to be safe, must be sociable, and the laws of sociability are the natural laws.

Another figure in this school is Christian Wolff (1679–1754). Wolff followed Grotius in many respects, but his philosophical basis was that of Gottfried Wilhelm Leibniz, namely, the idea that men are obliged by their nature to aspire to their perfection as well as to further the perfection of others. According to him, international law has its origin in four classes: (1) natural law, also called necessary international law; (2) voluntary international law; (3) conventional law; and (4) customary law. Natural or necessary international law is originally nothing except the law of nature applied to nations. However, since these rules cannot be completely applied to international relations, Wolff introduced "voluntary law." By "voluntary law," he meant that the voluntary law of nations does not depend upon the free will of nations, but upon the purpose of the supreme state. A supreme state is not only a society of all nations, but a world-state with the purpose of promoting the common good with its combined powers. Hence, the supreme state is sovereign over the individual nations, having its own laws which ought to prescribe the means by which its good is maintained. It should follow naturally that the supreme state, being composed of individual states, must have a kind of democratic form, in which the majority has the power to act in the name of whole. However, Wolff rejected this logical conclusion, because he thought all nations "cannot assemble together." Instead, he said what had been approved by the more civilized nations was the law of nations.

The last natural law thinker is Emeric de Vattel (1714–1767). In *The Law of Nations*, Vattel generally followed the system and teachings of his master Wolff. However, he made his own contributions. It was especially Vattel's doctrine of the independence and sovereign equality of states that has deeply influenced people's thought until present time. The principle of sovereign equality of states is now firmly established in the United Nations Charter. Vattel declared that all states are obligated not to intervene in foreign affairs by other means than by good services, unless they are authorized to intervene by a special title. The principle of non-intervention is by now generally recognized. Vattel also dedicated a chapter in his system of international law to the interpretations of treaties. His exposition is much larger and clearer than what had been previously written on this subject. Some of his expositions were accepted not only by arbitral tribunals, but also by the former Permanent and present International Court of Justice.[1]

3. Other Legal Philosophies

Much more accurate and more illuminating than the application of natural law was the rise of comparative jurisprudence in the work of Montesquieu. In his famous work *The Spirit of the Laws* (1748), he made a comparative study of governments. He distinguished three basic kinds of governments, republic, monarchy, and despotism. Montesquieu used England as an example of monarchy and believed that England's system, with its separate executive, legislative, and judicial powers limiting and controlling each other, provided the greatest freedom and security for a state. These ideas had a direct impact on the writing of American Constitution.

Montesquieu had been concerned with the laws of all peoples, but there was another school, the historical school of jurisprudence, which was mainly interested in the evolution of the law within boundaries of their particular state. Most of them, notably Edmund Burke, regarded law as an outgrowth of organic culture of the nation.

1　R. St. J. Macdonald and D.M. Johnston (Eds.), *The Structure and Process of International Law*, Dordrecht: Martinus Nijhoff Publishers, 1983, pp.28–40.

Rationalism had a decisive but by no means uniform influence upon legal evolution. Many rationalists were prone to stress the artificial character of sound law and regard it as the product of the dictates of reason applied to specific social problems. According to them, human legislation was the only valid source of law. There was also a tendency to lay special stress upon the responsibility of law to ensure equal rights to enjoy life, liberty, and property. It was natural that this group should be in favor of the codification of law while the historical school was opposed to such a notion.

The utilitarian school of law also relied heavily upon human reason. Utilitarian jurisprudence was merely a further development of the rationalistic doctrine. Bentham, its chief exponent, held that rational jurisprudence must be a science of social reform, designed in every part to increase the happiness of the largest possible number of men. However, there was still a strong strain of individualism in it. Bentham believed that every man was the best judge of his own happiness. Hence, there should be no restrictions on the acts of anyone except those necessary to secure freedom.

The Enlightenment brought a new vision of the future, which forecast the end of absolute monarchy. Philosophers of the Enlightenment thought they had discovered a simple formula for perpetual human happiness. They sought to deliver individuals from restraints so that they could act freely in accordance with their nature. On the one hand, the formula promised that the pursuit of self-interest would benefit society; on the other, it promised that a free human reason would produce sound moral judgments. In other words, individual freedom permitted the operation of natural law. Believing they had learned the law, 18th-century rationalists thought they had found the secret of never-ending progress.

Rational philosophy undermined absolutism in all of its phases. Deism questioned the necessity of state Church and clergy. The physiocrats, Adam Smith, and other early economic liberals demonstrated the futility of mercantilism. Political theory in the Enlightenment substituted the social contract for divine right and emphasized natural human rights of political freedom and justice. Each of these ideas denied the absolute authority of monarchs.

Key Terms

secularization → natural law → international law → Hugo Grotius → legal war theory → Samuel Pufendorf → Christian Wolff → Emeric de Vattel → Montesquieu → rationalism → utilitarian school of law

Exercises

1 Vocabulary Building

⮞ Fill in each blank with a synonym to the word in the brackets.

1) This movement arrived at its _____ (culmination) in early modern times, when secular absolutism gained _____ (defining) _____ (dominion) in political affairs.

2) The state should not _____ (terminate) the law of nature, but rather provide for the _____ (enforcement) of its _____ (benign) principles.

2 Translation

⮞ Translate the following sentences into Chinese.

1) He claimed that the major tenet of the law of nature was the sanctity of personal liberty and private property. It was the state's supreme duty to assure their protection and perpetuity. This notion was seized upon by later revolutionaries and written into the constitution.

2) When in the Course of human events, it becomes necessary for one people to dissolve the political bands which have connected them with another, and to assume among the powers of the earth, the separate and equal station to which the Laws of Nature and of Nature's God entitle them, a decent respect to the opinions of mankind requires that they should declare the causes which impel them to the separation.

3 Questions

⮞ Answer the following questions.

1) What is the doctrine of natural law?

2) How did international law come into being?

3) What are Grotius' distinctive contributions to jurisprudence and philosophy of law?

4) What are the two groups of the science of international law?

4 Term Explanation

⮞ Explain the meaning of the following terms in your own words.

1) voluntarism

2) supreme state

⑤ Writing

> Read the following direction and finish the writing.

Saint Thomas Aquinas in the 13th century gave a general outline of what becomes the traditional just war theory as discussed in modern universities. According to him, there are seven principles to judge a just war:

- Last Resort: A just war can only be waged after all peaceful options are considered. The use of force can only be used as a last resort.

- Legitimate Authority: A just war is waged by a legitimate authority. A war cannot be waged by individuals or groups that do not constitute the legitimate government.

- Just Cause: A just war needs to be in response to a wrong suffered. Self-defense against an attack always constitutes a just war; however, the war needs to be fought with the objective to correct the inflicted wound.

- Probability of Success: In order for a war to be just, there must be a rational possibility of success. A nation cannot enter into a war with a hopeless cause.

- Right Intention: The primary objective of a just war is to re-establish peace. In particular, the peace after the war should exceed the peace that would have succeeded without the use of force. The aim of the use of force must be justice.

- Proportionality: The violence in a just war must be proportional to the casualties suffered. The nations involved in the war must avoid disproportionate military action and only use the amount of force absolutely necessary.

- Civilian Casualties: The use of force must distinguish between the militia and civilians. Innocent citizens must never be the target of war; soldiers should always avoid killing civilians. The deaths of civilians are only justified when they are unavoidable victims of a military attack on a strategic target.

Based on what you have learned about the theory of just war and what you have known about the wars happening in the world today, write a short essay with the title of "What Is a Just War."

Chapter 23

An Era of Revolution

To the end of the 18th century, the world saw two revolutions, which were followed by many more in the 19th century. The American and French revolutions were the outcome of conflicts arising from the shifts in civilization. Increasing power in central government often provoked resistance on the part of wealthy and educated people whose interests and authority were harmed. Meanwhile, thanks to the Reformation and the Enlightenment, people who did not share the religious beliefs or ideological views of their rulers regarded governments illegitimate. In England, the turmoil of its 17th-century revolution ended in a compromise: constitutional monarchy. Impressed by this new pattern of British government, Enlightenment thinkers developed theories on rational patterns of government for individuals to secure the earthly goals of life, liberty, and property. According to them, rulers were agents of society who could be resisted if they overstepped their limits; and checks and balances between different branches of government were necessary to protect the liberty of the people. In the late 18th century, the American Revolution put these ideas into effect in a more far-reaching way than ever before. The French Revolution has long been considered as the beginning of modern history of Europe, because it destroyed the old regime, and created a new order based on individual rights, representative institutions, and a concept of loyalty to the nation rather than the monarch.

1. American Revolution

The overseas expansion of Europe had brought English settlers to the North American continent in the 17th century. By 1750, the white population of these colonies amounted to about two million. In accordance with the economic doctrine of mercantilism, colonies were considered valuable chiefly as a source of raw materials and as a market for exports, both of which would be monopolized by Britain. Not surprisingly, the colonists resented British efforts to collect existing taxes or to impose new ones. Parliament passed various new taxes and then repealed them in the face of American protests, with the exception of a tax on imports of tea, which it retained for symbolic reasons—to emphasize its right to tax

British subjects everywhere. But the Americans, who sent no members to the distant British Parliament, refused to admit that right. "No taxation without representation!" became the rallying cry of colonial protests. The Americans at first sought redress for their grievances, but gradually they began to think of seizing control of their own destiny through self-rule. Thomas Paine, a shrewd revolutionary propagandist, using the language of the Enlightenment, declared that America's subjection to England was "contrary to reason."

1.1 War and the Declaration of Independence

By 1774, the colonists had begun to commit acts of violence and sabotage (notably the Boston "Tea Party"), and the British responded with tough measures in the hope of bringing the colonists back to senses. Protests and opposition grew in Massachusetts, and shortly thereafter, representatives from all the colonies assembled at a Continental Congress in Philadelphia. The first clash of arms occurred in April 1775, when British troops set out from Boston to destroy a reported supply of rebel weapons stored near Concord. The war for independence was on. A continental army was established under the leadership of George Washington. Of great importance to the colonies' cause was the assistance provided by foreign countries that were eager to gain revenge for earlier defeats at the hands of the British. The French supplied arms and money to the rebels from the beginning of the war. Spain and Holland followed, swinging the European balance in the Americans' favor. The Treaty of Paris, signed in 1783, recognized the independence of the American colonies and granted the Americans control of the western territory from the Appalachians to the Mississippi River.

The most memorable achievement of the Continental Congress was its adoption of the Declaration of Independence (1776) drafted by Thomas Jefferson. Thomas Jefferson formed a direct intellectual link between the English and American revolutions, for he expressed many of the ideas of John Locke and the Enlightenment, and gave them wider circulation. The Declaration of Independence is a masterpiece of revolutionary literature in the world. The ringing sentences of "We hold these Truths to be self-evident, that all Men are created equal, that they are endowed by their Creator with certain unalienable Rights, that among these are Life, Liberty, and the Pursuit of Happiness" remind us of the ideal of John Locke, but they were paraphrased by Jefferson with greater simplicity, clarity, and power.

Declaration of Independence

By Thomas Jefferson

We hold these Truths to be self-evident, that all Men are created equal, that they are endowed by their Creator with certain unalienable Rights, that among these are Life, Liberty, and the Pursuit of Happiness—That to secure these Rights, Governments are instituted among Men, deriving their just Powers from the Consent of the Governed, that whenever any Form of Government becomes destructive of these Ends, it is the Right of the People to alter or to abolish it, and to institute new Government, laying its Foundation on such Principles, and organizing its Powers in such Form, as to them shall seem most likely to effect their Safety and Happiness. Prudence, indeed, will dictate that Governments long established should not be changed for light and transient Causes; and accordingly all Experience hath shewn, that Mankind are more disposed to suffer, while Evils are sufferable, than to right themselves by abolishing the Forms to which they are accustomed. But when a long Train of Abuses and Usurpations, pursuing invariably the same Object, evinces a Design to reduce them under absolute Despotism, it is their right, it is their Duty, to throw off such Government, and to provide new Guards for their future Security.

1.2   The Federal Constitution

After independence, the most pressing need of the former colonies was to agree on a plan for self-government. That is how the federal Constitution (1787–1788) came into being. Approved after bitter debates in the 13 states, the Constitution followed Jefferson's maxim, "That government is best which governs least." They thought the best protection against possible tyranny by one person or one body, was to establish separate political authorities and to leave them in jealous competition. Thus a division of executive, legislative, and judicial powers was established. Although the Constitution provides defenses against the invasion of individual rights, fears of an overly strong central government continued to be voiced. Therefore, at the insistence of many citizens, the Bill of Rights (1789–1791) was added to the Constitution in 1791. Every person is now guaranteed freedom of worship, expression, petition, and assembly; the right to keep and bear arms; security of person and home; and due process of law.

The Declaration of Independence, the Bill of Rights, and the Constitution are regarded as three "founding documents" of the United States. They were first created to perform distinct, complementary functions. The Declaration of Independence was a revolutionary manifesto that proclaimed and justified the end of British rule over America; the Bill of Rights stated the basic rights of the American people; and the Constitution created a new federal government that would secure those rights.

2. French Revolution

At the end of the 18th century, Europe's most powerful absolute monarchy collapsed in France, and in the next quarter century, the turmoil of revolution eventually spread through much of the mainland of Europe. The French Revolution of 1789 proved to be the most violent and far-reaching upheaval so far. It brought about drastic changes in the legal, social, and economic order of France. Even more than the English or American revolutions, the French Revolution was a watershed in the flow of Western history. Not until 1917 was the Russian Revolution an uprising to have such an impact on the Western world. What, then, were the main causes, phases, and consequences of the movement that began in 1789?

2.1　The Three Estates

The status of all French people depended on which of three "orders" or "estates" they belonged to: the First Estate, made up of about 100,000 Catholic clergy; the Second Estate, consisting of 400,000 nobles; and the Third Estate, which included the rest of the 26 million people in France. The members of the First and Second Estates enjoyed various privileges over those of the Third Estate, the most important of which was exemption from the *taille*, a tax on land and other property that was one of the government's main sources of revenue. However, in the 18th century France was undergoing gradual changes that caused pressure to the society. The result would be an explosion of unprecedented suddenness and violence. The existing order would in the 1790s come to be seen as a thing of the past—the "Old Regime."

As we know, absolute monarchy depended very much on the character of the monarch, and France's 18th-century kings didn't have such dominating personalities as Louis XIV. To cover the growing cost of war, France had been increasing taxes and borrowing heavily, but by the middle of the 18th century, both sources had reached their limit. Crippling government debts, oppressive taxation, and shifts in power within the partnership of kings, nobles, and the Church were nothing new, but this time the traditional order was under pressure in other ways as well. A group outside the traditional ruling partnership, wealthy and well-educated business and professional people who belonged to the Third Estate, was outgrowing its traditional humble position in the government and in the social order. At the same time, the new ideology of the Enlightenment was throwing many traditional beliefs and values into doubt.

In 1763, King Louis XV was faced with the problem of paying for a worldwide war that had ended badly for France. Instead of peasants and bankers who had been usually levied, the government announced a tax on lands belonging to nobles this time. The nobles protested fiercely of course. This particular conflict ended in a compromise that enabled the government to raise enough new revenue to avoid bankruptcy. The basic problems remained, however, and for the next quarter of a century, the nobility and the monarchy struggled indecisively over the reform of the public finances, which inevitably raised questions about the reform of the government system in general.

2.2　The Overthrow of the King and the Nobles

The final crisis came after the absolute monarchy fought another expensive war against Britain, this time in support of American independence. The war was successful, but the debts were overwhelming. In order to pass a permanent tax on lands on all subjects, the government was asked to convene the Estates-General.

In 1789, as planning for the meeting went ahead, a split opened between the nobles and the bourgeoisie. Traditionally, the three Estates met and voted separately, and the First and Second Estates usually dominated the proceedings. Now, however, in the age of the Enlightenment and bourgeois self-confidence, lawyers and other professional men who emerged as spokesmen for the Third Estate wanted it revised. They argued that there should be twice as many representatives of the Third Estate as of the other two, and that all three Estates should meet in a single assembly. The King granted the demand for double representation of the Third Estate, but the Parlement of Paris, to which the issue was referred, ruled in favor of the traditional voting method.

After the session opened, conflicts broke out. The representatives of the Third Estate (most of them were lawyers) decided to walk out of the Estates-General. Stating that they were the only true representatives of the people, they then declared themselves to be the "National Assembly" of France. They met at an indoor tennis court nearby the hall where they were supposed to meet. There the members swore the "Tennis Court Oath," pledging not to return home until they had drafted a new constitution for France. Within a few days, the National Assembly was joined by many priests from the First Estate and by some of the nobles. Having failed to persuade the rebels to back down, Louis next tried to intimidate them by a show of force. Toward the end of June, he called some 20,000 soldiers to Versailles.

The National Assembly was rescued by the people of nearby Paris, who were now aroused by the threat to the Third Estate. Excited by rumors of troop movements, crowds began to roam the streets of the capital in search of weapons, and on July 14, they demanded arms from the Bastille, a hated symbol of despotism. After an exchange of gunfire, in which about a hundred of the crowd were killed, the commander agreed to surrender.

The final blow to the Old Regime came from the largest social group in France, the peasants. While many of the nobles were away at the capital, the peasants seized the initiative. During the "Great Fear" of late summer, they vandalized the manor houses of the nobles and destroyed the hated records of their required payments and services. Trying to quiet the peasants, the National Assembly at a single night session (August 4), removed all special privileges in landed property. Reform-minded noblemen led the way by forsaking their historic rights to peasant fees and labor, hunting on farmland, tax exemptions and advantages, and special courts of law for the nobility. A final decree declared that "feudalism is abolished." Thus, a drastic overturn in property rights was the first major reform of the National Assembly.

2.3 The Declaration of the Rights of Man and the Citizens

Drafted as a preface to a new constitution, the Declaration was the French counterpart of the English and American Bills of Rights. It went beyond them, however, in setting forth specific principles of government.

After stating the "natural, inalienable, and sacred rights of man," the Declaration defined the duties of individuals in a society. It stated that every citizen ought to obey the law instantly, but at the same time law must be an expression of the "general will." This emphasis on the "general will" reflected in large measure the influence of the French-Swiss philosopher Jean-Jacques Rousseau, who was the first to use this term. Though having died in 1778, 11 years before the French Revolution, his political ideas had stimulated it. For Rousseau, the "general will" meant the collective will of a community, in which every individual has a share. Since all individuals contribute to the general will, they must obey it because it is their own will; and for the same reason, even if they do obey it, they are still free. Rousseau's ideas were raised against all political institutions that rested on a divine or historical right rather than on the general will. His arguments gave philosophical support to the French Revolution and served to justify the National Assembly's claim to sovereign authority.

(One of the important documents of the French Revolution, the Declaration of the Rights of Man and the Citizen was adopted in August 1789 by the National Assembly. The Declaration affirmed that "men are born and remain free and equal in rights", that government must protect these natural rights, and that political power is derived from the people.)

The Declaration of the Rights of Man and the Citizen

The representatives of the French people, organized as a national assembly, considering that ignorance, neglect, and scorn of the rights of man are the sole causes of public misfortunes and of corruption of governments, have resolved to display in a solemn declaration the natural, inalienable, and sacred rights of man, so that this declaration, constantly in the presence of all members of society, will continually remind them of their rights and their duties...Consequently, the National Assembly recognizes and declares, in the presence and under the auspices of the Supreme Being, the following rights of man and citizen:

1. Men are born and remain free and equal in rights; social distinctions can be

established only for the common benefit.

2. The aim of every political association is the conservation of the natural and imprescriptible rights of man; these rights are liberty, property, security, and resistance to oppression.

3. The source of all sovereignty is located in essence in the nation; no body, no individual can exercise authority which does not emanate from it expressly.

4. Liberty consists in being able to do anything that does not harm another person...

6. The law is the expression of the general will; all citizens have the right to concur personally or through their representatives in its formation...

7. No man can be accused, arrested, or detained except in cases determined by the law, and according to the forms which it has prescribed...

10. No one may be disturbed because of his opinions, even religious, provided that their public demonstration does not disturb the public order established by law...

2.4　From Monarchy to Republic

From the beginning, there was sharp disagreement on what government to build. Some people wanted the new government modeled after that of England, with an upper and a lower house, and a king with executive and veto power. Others, fearing that this arrangement would give undue power to the nobility, wanted a single legislative chamber and a figurehead king.

The growing fear for the fate of the revolution put increasing power in the hands of radical factions, of whom the most influential were members of the Jacobin Society. Drastic measures were taken in 1790: Monastic orders were suppressed, properties of the Church were confiscated as a means of financing the revolutionary government, and the clergy were placed under a "Civil Constitution." These measures provoked not only the anger of most clerics but widespread popular opposition, particularly in the devoutly Catholic western and southeastern parts of the country. Far from acting as the agent of the "general will," the revolutionary government was becoming the leader of one side in an increasingly divided nation. The constitution completed in 1791 provided a unicameral legislature and a suspensive veto for the king. The National Assembly managed to limit the right to vote.

Louis XVI in 1791 made an attempt to escape from France. Captured near the northeast frontier and brought back to Paris in humiliation, he thus destroyed any serious hopes for a successful constitutional monarchy. Soon this government foundered, the king was deposed, and a new assembly was called (1792) to draft another constitution. The new body, named the National Convention, met and proclaimed the (First) French Republic. The Convention governed France during troubled years of reform and war.

2.5　Internal Disorder and Foreign War

The revolution caused great alarm to individuals and groups outside France. Foreign sentiment had led to a military threat in the Declaration of Pillnitz (August 1791). In this document, Leopold Ⅱ of Austria, the Holy Roman Emperor, stated that if the other European powers would join him, he would use force to restore the Bourbon rulers to their full rights. His declaration encouraged the émigrés and alarmed the French leaders. It also strengthened the hand of the more aggressive revolutionists in France. Hoping to carry the banner of "liberation" into neighboring lands and uniting with native radicals to overthrow established governments, the government accordingly declared war on Austria in April 1792, thereby launching a period of continental revolution and war that lasted for 23 years.

The winds of violence, released by the revolution and whipped by nationalist hysteria, now swept across France. King Louis' trial for treason opened a major split between the moderates and the radicals. The seeds of mutual distrust and hostility were thus sown within the revolution, and the rival leaders proceeded to devour one another. By this time, the guiding spirit of the Convention was the radical Maximilien Robespierre. The forces of Prussia, Spain, Britain, the Netherlands, and Sardinia had joined Austria, forming the First Coalition of powers against revolutionary France. Violent uprisings erupted in the strongly Catholic parts of the country. Revolutionary trial courts were set up around the country to limit lynchings and to stifle the rebellions. Probably as many as 40,000 heads fell under the guillotines, usually on charges of treason (aiding the country's enemies) or sedition (rebellion against authority). Thousands more perished during the uprisings in the provinces.

To oppose the First Coalition, the French army, fired by revolutionary spirit, soon showed themselves more than a match for their enemies. By June 1794, they had turned the tide of battle. As the foreign peril declined, internal hysteria declined with it, and within weeks, the foes of Robespierre put an end to his political domination. He was outlawed by vote of the Convention and was executed along with many of his associates. The fall of Robespierre marked the end of "the Terror" and the return to power of the moderates. It was the moderates, chiefly representatives of the well-to-do, who secured the Convention's final approval of the republican constitution of 1795. The government so established was called the Directory. Ruling a mostly hostile or indifferent country, the Directory clung to power only with the aid of the military, a political situation that would soon be grasped by Napoleon Bonaparte, the most successful of France's conquering generals, who would rule for 15 years as a virtual dictator.

Unlike the revolutions of England and North America, the French Revolution ended not in compromise but in defeat—its foreign enemies victorious, France itself occupied, and its old rulers restored. But the shifts in civilization that had undermined the partnership of kings, nobles, and the Church in France could not be turned back, and defeat only continued the conflicts of the revolution—not just in France, but to a greater or lesser extent in the rest of Europe as well. The traditional order that had developed 1,500 years before out of the merging of Greco-Roman civilization and the warrior societies of barbarian Europe was coming to an end, but the struggles over a new order were just beginning.

Key Terms

American Revolution → the Declaration of Independence → the Federal Constitution → French Revolution → the Three Estates → the Declaration of the Rights of Man and the Citizen→ the Jacobin Society → internal disorder → foreign war

Exercises

1 Vocabulary Building

✎ Fill in each blank with a synonym to the word or phrase in the brackets.

1) In accordance with the economic doctrine of _____ (mercantilism), colonies were considered valuable chiefly as a source of raw materials and as a market for exports, both of which would be _____ (monopolized) by Britain.

2) Parliament passed various new taxes and then _____ (repealed) them in the face of American protests.

3) _____ (Crippling) government debts, _____ (oppressive) taxation, and shifts in power within the partnership of kings, nobles, and the Church were nothing new, but this time the traditional order was under pressure in other ways as well.

4) Having failed to persuade the rebels to _____ (back down), Louis next tried to _____ (intimidate) them by a show of force.

5) He was _____ (outlawed) by vote of the Convention and was executed along with many of his associates.

❷ Translation

> ✎ Translate the following sentences into Chinese.

1) "No taxation without representation!" became the rallying cry of colonial protests. The Americans at first sought redress for their grievances, but gradually they began to think of seizing control of their own destiny through self-rule.

2) Of great importance to the colonies' cause was the assistance provided by foreign countries that were eager to gain revenge for earlier defeats at the hands of the British.

3) Reform-minded noblemen led the way by forsaking their historic rights to peasant fees and labor, hunting on farmland, tax exemptions and advantages, and special courts of law for the nobility.

4) Far from acting as the agent of the "general will," the revolutionary government was becoming the leader of one side in an increasingly divided nation. The constitution completed in 1791 provided a unicameral legislature and a suspensive veto for the king.

❸ Questions

> ✎ Answer the following questions.

1) Why has the French Revolution been considered as the beginning of modern history of Europe?

2) How had Rousseau's political ideas stimulated the French Revolution?

Chapter 24

Industrial Revolution

The single greatest 19th-century shift in civilization was what contemporaries themselves called the Industrial Revolution. The era known as the Industrial Revolution (1760–1850) was a period in which fundamental changes occurred in agriculture, textile and metal manufacture, transportation, economic policies, and social structure in England. This period is appropriately labeled "revolution," for it thoroughly destroyed the old manner of doing things. The revolution began in 18th-century Britain with the invention of the steam engine and its use as a source of reliable power for machines to mass-produce cotton textiles. In the 19th century, the fast-moving technical advance, leading to new products, new production processes, and the rise and fall of entire industries, became a seemingly permanent feature of Western civilization.

But the Industrial Revolution did not happen overnight. Many developments from the Late Middle Ages onward had also paved the way for it. The rise of capitalism had created a class of merchants and manufacturers who were willing to take risks, as well as new forms of business organization that were adaptable to the needs of large industrial enterprises. In the technical field, waterwheels had accustomed manufacturers to using stronger sources of power than human or animal muscles, printing had set a precedent for complex mass production operations, and clocks had provided an example of accurately functioning automatic machines. The Scientific Revolution had aroused the expectation that scientific discovery would result in practical benefits. The growth of colonial empires had brought much of the world's trade to the countries of western Europe, giving them the wealth to invest in new technology and worldwide markets for their resulting products. And as it happened, by the 18th century, all these developments had gone farthest in one European country: Britain. It was there that the Industrial Revolution began.

1. The Mechanization of Industry and Transportation

By 1750, Britain had built up a globe-circling trading system, and rich profits awaited those who could increase their exports. Among the goods that British merchants traded across the world were cotton textiles, a product of India that was popular in many markets because it was comfortable, decorative, and cheaper than similar cloths, such as fine linen or silk. The first breakthrough, about 1760, was a hand-powered, multi-spindled spinning wheel or jenny. Soon afterward came Richard Arkwright's water-powered spinning "frame," which spun stronger threads than the spinning jenny. Advances in spinning were soon matched by the development of powered weaving looms.

The logic of events led next to the building of factories. It is no wonder that factories could be built only on the banks of swift-running streams, because they required a source of power which at first was supplied by the traditional waterwheels. The greatest boost to the building of factories came from the development of efficient steam engines, which proved to be more powerful than waterwheels and were not confined to riverbanks. The steam engine was initially developed by Thomas Newcomen about 1700 in response to some problem in coal mining. Later, James Watt and other practical inventors made important improvements on Newcomen's machine, greatly increasing its power and harnessing it to turn a wheel. As a result, the steam engine eventually became the chief source of power in the factories and was adapted to both water and land transportation. The steam engine proved so indispensable that the popular saying that "steam is an Englishman" had real significance by 1850. The success of the steam engine led to a need for more coal and an expansion in coal production. Between 1815 and 1850, the output of coal quadrupled. In turn, new processes using coal furthered the development of the iron industry.

As for many economic historians, railroads were the most important single factor in promoting European economic progress in the 1830s and 1840s. The "age of railways" began in 1825 when the steam locomotive pioneer George Stephenson opened a stretch of line between the coal mining town of Darlington and the harbor of Stockton. Within 20 years, steam trains were running between all the principal cities of Britain. By 1850, 6,000 miles of railroad track crisscrossed much of the country. With its cities linked by steam transportation, its coal mines deep beneath the earth, its mechanized cotton industry, and other industries following cotton's example, Britain provided the pattern for future industrialization around the world.

2. The Industrial Factory

The factory became the chief means of organizing labor for the new machines. As the workplace shifted from the artisan's shop and the peasant's cottage to the factory, employers hired workers who no longer owned the means of production but were simply paid wages to run the machines. From its beginning, the factory system demanded a new type of discipline from its employees. Workers were forced to work regular hours and in shifts to keep the machines at work, for factory owners could not afford to let their expensive machinery stand idle. Factory owners, therefore, faced a formidable task, making themselves different from the pre-industrial workers and agricultural laborers who were accustomed to irregular hours: hectic work at harvest time followed by weeks of inactivity. They had to create a system of time-work discipline that would accustom employees to working regular, unvarying hours during which they performed a set number of tasks over and over again as efficiently as possible.

Factory regulations were minute and detailed. Here is a rule for a factory in Berlin in 1844, very typical of company rules everywhere the factory system had been established: "The normal working day begins at all seasons at 6 a.m. precisely and ends, after the usual break of half an hour for breakfast, an hour for dinner, and half an hour for tea, at 7 p.m., and it shall be strictly observed...Workers arriving two minutes late shall lose half an hour's wages; whoever is more than two minutes late may not start work until after the next break; or at least shall lose his wages until then. Any disputes about the correct time shall be settled by the clock mounted above the gatekeeper's lodge." In one crucial sense, the early industrialists proved successful. As the 19th century progressed, the second and third generations of workers came to view a regular working week as a natural way of life. It was, of course, an attitude that made Britain's incredible economic growth possible in that century.

3. Spread of Industrial Revolution

In the middle of the 19th century, Britain's industrial productivity and technical progress were unique, but it did not keep this position for long. In the second half of the 19th century, with astonishing speed, the Industrial Revolution spread to other countries of western Europe, North America, and the Far East. Many countries in these regions possessed more or less the same features that had enabled Britain to pioneer the Industrial Revolution. By the end of the century, Britain was but one among a global spread of industrial countries, and was no longer even the most advanced or productive. In Europe, that position had been taken by German. However, this permanent worldwide Industrial Revolution was far from painless. It led to massive changes, usually accompanied by conflict and hardship, in the way businesses were organized and run and in the patterns of work and life of ordinary people. It gave rise to radical ideologies that promised relief from the evils of capitalism and industrialization, but in practice often brought their own forms of mass suffering. It altered the balance of power in the world, giving dominance to the advanced and productive nations, subjecting non-industrial ones to imperialistic control, and providing the weapons to fight wars more terrible than any other in history.

Key Terms

spinning machines → waterwheels → steam engines → railroads → industrial factories → spread of industrialization

Exercises

❶ Translation

🕭 Translate the following sentences into Chinese.

1) Factory owners, therefore, faced a formidable task, making themselves different from the pre-industrial workers and agricultural laborers who were accustomed to irregular hours: hectic work at harvest time followed by weeks of inactivity.

2) It has altered the balance of power in the world, giving dominance to the advanced and productive nations, subjecting non-industrial ones to imperialistic control, and providing the weapons to fight wars more terrible than any other in history.

❷ Questions

🕭 Answer the following questions.

1) What developments had contributed to the emergence of the Industrial Revolution?

2) Why were the early factories built only on the banks of rivers?

❸ Topic for Discussion

🕭 Below is a topic related to this chapter. Read it and finish the discussion.

Debate still rages over among why the Industrial Revolution began, when it did, and why it began in Britain. Do research and support this idea with strong evidence.

Chapter 25

Utilitarianism and Positivism

Opposite to the idealist direction represented by such German philosophers as Kant, Hegel, and Schopenhauer in the 19th century, some philosophers believed that the empiricists largely got the story correct, and the task of philosophy was to refine empirical methodology. In Great Britain, for instance, there were two such leading figures, Jeremy Bentham (1748–1832) and John Stuart Mill (1806–1873), who rejected the role of rational intuition in man's quest for knowledge. Their most memorable contribution in this regard is in the field of ethics—specifically, the theory of utilitarianism. According to this theory, moral actions are those that produce the greatest good for the greatest number of people. In France, Auguste Comte (1798–1857) refined empiricism and founded the approach known as positivism. According to positivism, man should reject any investigation that does not rest on direct observation.

1. Jeremy Bentham

Bentham lived during a time full of major social, political, and economic changes. The Industrial Revolution (with the massive economic and social shifts that it brought in its wake), the rise of the middle class, and revolutions in France and America, all were reflected in Bentham's reflections on existing institutions.

1.1 The Principle of Utility

In his book *Introduction to the Principles of Morals and Legislation*, Bentham started with this classic statement: "Nature has placed mankind under the governance of two sovereign masters, pain and pleasure." He made it clear that it is a fact that men desire pleasure and avoid pain. He then offered his "principle of utility," a term which he borrowed from Hume. By "the principle of utility," he meant "the principle which approves or disapproves of every action whatsoever, according to the tendency which it appears to have to augment or diminish the happiness of the party whose interest is in question."[1]

In order to prove the validity of the principle of utility, Bentham rejected so-called higher theories, because he thought they were either reducible to the principle of utility or inferior to this principle. Take social contract as an example. First, there is a difficulty in determining whether there ever was such a contract. Second, even the theory itself rests on the principle of utility, for it really says that the greatest happiness of the greatest number can be achieved only if we obey the law. Only pleasure and pain, therefore, give us the real value of actions.

Just as pleasure and pain give us the real values to acts, so do they also constitute the causes of our behavior. Bentham distinguished four sources from which pleasure and pain can come, and he identified these as causes of our behavior, calling them sanctions. A sanction is what gives binding force to a rule of conduct or to a law and he termed the four sanctions the physical, the political, the moral, and the religious.

When Kant argued that the morality of an act depends on having the right motive and not on the consequences of the act, Bentham took the opposite position. He said that morality depends directly on the consequences. Accordingly, he argued that the law can punish only those who have actually inflicted pain, whatever their motive may be. He believed that it is the same with moral obligations, in which case, the external consequences of the action are more important than the motives behind the action.

Bentham admitted that each individual and legislator is concerned with avoiding pain and seeking pleasure. But pleasure and pain differ from each other and therefore have different values. With a view to achieving mathematical precision, Bentham suggested that we should calculate the values by their "intensity," "duration," "certainty," "propinquity" or nearness, "fecundity" or the chances of being followed by more pleasure, and "purity" or the chances of being followed by some pain and "extent," that is, the number of persons to whom they extend or who are affected by the action. What we are going to do is to sum up all the values of all the pleasure on the one side, and those of all the pain on the other. The balance, if it is on the side of pleasure, will give the good tendency of the act; otherwise, the bad tendency will be given. This famous Pleasure-Pain Calculus shows that Bentham was interested chiefly in the quantitative aspects of pleasure; thus, all actions are equally good if they produce the same amount of pleasure.

1.2　Law and Punishment

Bentham's use of the principle of utility in law and punishment is very impressive. He believed that the principle of utility should be the only criterion for governments to decide

---

1　Samuel E. Stumpf and James Fieser, *Socrates to Sartre and Beyond: A History of Philosophy* (8th ed.), Boston: Lisa Moore, 2008, p.320.

which acts should be considered "offenses." Bentham's method of legislation is first of all to measure the "mischief of an act," and this mischief consists in the consequences. Acts that would produce evil must be discouraged. The law is concerned with augmenting the total happiness of the community, and it must do this by discouraging those acts that would produce evil consequences. It is reasonable that in Bentham's theory of law, many illegal acts of his time would become only matters of private morals.

Bentham thought that all punishment is in itself evil, because it inflicts suffering and pain. At the same time, the object of law is to augment the total happiness of the community. If we are to justify punishment from a utilitarian point of view, we must know that the pain inflicted by punishment will in some way prevent some greater pain. The principle of utility would clearly call for the elimination of pure retaliation, since no useful purpose is served by adding still more pain to the total sum that a society suffers.

According to Bentham, punishment should not be given for four particular situations: when it is groundless, when it is inefficacious, when it is unprofitable or too expensive, and when it is needless. Another question is whether a kind of given behavior should be left to private ethics instead of becoming the object of legislation. Bentham answered it simply by applying the principle of utility. The matter should be left to private ethics if it does more harm than good to involve the whole legislative process and the apparatus of punishment, for the main concern of law must be to encourage those acts that would lead to the greatest happiness of the community. There is, therefore, a justification for punishment, which is that through punishment the greatest good for the greatest number is most effectively secured.

There is radicalism in Bentham's theory. He wanted the legislation process to operate on the principle of utility with practically the same rigor with which the planets obey the principle of gravitation. He thus pressed for reforms wherever he found a discrepancy between the actual legal and social order on the one hand, and the principle of utility on the other. He blamed the aristocratic society for the breakdown of the principle of utility. Why were those nobles in power unwilling to give the greatest happiness for the greatest number of people? They were more concerned with their own interests which would be in conflict with the proper end of government. The way to overcome this conflict is to put the government into the hands of the people. If there is an identity of interest between the rulers and the ruled, the greatest happiness of the greatest number of people will be assured. According to him, this identity of interest can only be achieved in a democracy.

2. John Stuart Mill

Influenced by his father, who was closely associated with Bentham's philosophical theory, Mill became one of the ablest advocates of utilitarianism. What impressed him most was Bentham's "greatest happiness principle" that rendered any unnecessary attempts to deduce morality and legislation from concepts, such as law of nature, right reason, moral sense, or natural rectitude. When reading Bentham's book, Mill said that "the feeling rushed upon me, that all previous moralists were superseded, and that here indeed was the commencement of a new era of thought."[1] However, Mill developed certain convictions of his own about utilitarianism—convictions that were to distinguish his approach from Bentham's in a significant way.

2.1 Qualitative Versus Quantitative Approach

Bentham said that pleasure differs only in its amount, and quality counts little. Therefore, the game of a pushpin is as good as poetry. It necessarily follows that all types of behavior would be equally good as long as they produce the same amount of pleasure. He even suggested that there ought to be a moral thermometer. Just as a thermometer measures the different degrees of heat, so could a moral thermometer measure the degrees of happiness or unhappiness. Goodness, for Bentham, is not connected with any particular kind of behavior but only with the amount of pleasure as measured by his "calculus." Inevitably, the utilitarians were accused of being moral relativists who rejected all moral absolutes in favor of each person's subjective opinion about what is good. In the course of his defense for utilitarianism, Mill, however, was drawn into the position of altering Bentham's quantitative approach to pleasure by substituting a qualitative one.

What can best speak of Mill's position is that he said he would rather be Socrates dissatisfied than a fool satisfied. Pleasure, he noted, differs from each other in kind and quality, not only in quantity. In this regard, he took his stand with the ancient Epicureans, because he believed human beings have faculties which are more elevated than the animal appetites, and when one becomes conscious of this, do not regard anything as happiness which does not include his or her gratification. Pleasure of intellect and imagination, therefore, has a higher value than that of mere sensations.

However, Mill's view of qualitative pleasure raises an important problem with the whole notion of the pleasure principle: If we must assess pleasure for its quality, then pleasure itself is no longer the standard of morality. Mill departed even further from Bentham by grounding the qualitative difference between pleasure in the structure of human nature. That is, if only the full use of our higher faculties can lead us to true happiness, the standard of goodness in behavior has to do not with pleasure but with fulfilling our human faculties, wherein the moral value of life is grounded in the higher pleasure of our higher faculties. In this way, it reminds

---

1　Samuel E. Stumpf and James Fieser, *Socrates to Sartre and Beyond: A History of Philosophy* (8th ed.), Boston: Lisa Moore, 2008, p.326.

us of the ancient teachings of Mencius who is famous for the theory of human nature being good. According to Mencius, "The parts of the person differ in value and importance. Never harm the parts of greater importance for the sake of those of smaller importance, or the more valuable for the sake of the less valuable."[1]

2.2   Departure from Bentham

Mill's utilitarianism differed from that of Bentham in three ways. First, he rejected Bentham's central assumption that pleasure and pain can be calculated or measured. He argued that either the quantity or the quality of pleasure cannot be calculated. Rather, he adopted an empirical approach. That is, we prefer one pleasure over the other only when we experience both possibilities. The second difference involves when we should actually consult the utilitarian guideline. It is unnecessary for us to measure the balance of happiness versus unhappiness for each action we take. We rather go about our lives following general moral rules. Only occasionally do we run into problems following these tried and true moral rules. For example, if I am poor and my family is starving, I may want to steal a loaf of bread from the local store. Here I am torn between two moral rules: (1) providing for my family, and (2) not stealing. In this case, I resolve the conflict by determining which course of action would bring about the most happiness. The third difference between Bentham and Mill involves their respective ways of dealing with human selfishness. While Bentham simply assumed that we ought to choose those acts that produce for us the greatest quantity of pleasure, Mill proposed that laws and social arrangements should place the happiness or the interest of every individual as nearly as possible in harmony with the interest of the whole, and that education and opinion should establish in the mind of every individual an indissolvable association between his own happiness and the good of the whole.

2.3   Proving and Reinforcing Utilitarianism

Nowhere is Mill's difficulty with the problem of moral obligation and choice more apparent than when he raised the issue of "proving" utilitarianism. But how can we prove that happiness is the true and desirable end of human life and conduct? Again, Mill's answer was empirical. He said, "The only proof capable of being given that an object is visible, is that people actually see it. The only proof that a sound is audible, is that people hear it; and so of the other sources of our experience. In like manner, I apprehend, the sole evidence that is possible to produce that anything is desirable, is that people do actually desire it." So, we can give no reason why general happiness is desirable except that "each person so far as he

---

1   D.C. Lau, *Mencius*, London: Penguin Group, 2003, p.130.

believes it to be attainable, desires his own happiness."

In addition to the issue of proving utilitarianism, Mill discussed how we might reinforce this moral conviction as well. He noted two sanctions or motivations, external and internal. External sanctions principally involve other people approving of us when we pursue general happiness and disapproving of us when we instead produce unhappiness. But the most important motivation, according to Mill, is internal and involves a feeling of guilt when we go against the sense of duty. How can we develop this sense of duty? He argued that it formed initially through education. If cultivated properly, then, we will all carry with us a strong sense of duty toward others, which will be very difficult for us to resist.

3. Auguste Comte

Although Auguste Comte is called "the founder of positive philosophy," he did not discover this theory, for, as John Stuart Mill said, positivism was the "general property of the age." Comte's chief objective was the total reorganization of society and he realized that this first required the reconstruction of the intellectual orientation of his era. Since the Scientific Revolution, the achievements of science in France had been outstanding, including the work of Ampère and Fresnel in physics, Chevreul and Dumas in chemistry, Magendie in physiology, and Lamark, Saint-Hilaire, and Cuvier in biology and zoology. Science challenged other ways of thinking. This was also an age when the state philosophy in France was being influenced by both internal political events and external systems of thought. The French Revolution, to the eyes of Comte, was a dramatic example of social anarchy. In its wake, French thinkers entertained differing theories of society. Some were strongly anti-revolutionary; others argued for a social-contract theory. Added to these internal complications was the gradual importation of philosophies from other countries, especially German. Kant, Hegel, Fichte, Schelling, Strauss, Feuerbach, and Goethe all found their passionate readers in France. Materialism, idealism, and new metaphysical systems simulated an atmosphere of vigorous debate.

To overcome both political anarchy and the anarchy of ideas, Comte attempted to reform society and philosophy by developing a science of society, namely, positivism. What Comte was concerned with was how to maintain social unity when theological beliefs were no longer accepted as support for political authority. His solution was positivism which, he declared, can guarantee social unity.

3.1 Positivism

Positivism, on the one hand, rejects the assumption that nature has some ultimate purposes, and it gives up any attempt to discover either the "essence" or the secret causes of things. On the other hand, it attempts to study facts by observing the constant relations between things and by formulating the laws of science simply as the laws of constant relations among various phenomena without asking questions about the essential nature of things. A consequence of this spirit is the assumption that knowledge derived from science can also be used in the social realm. This is positivism's great appeal. Mill, counting himself as a positivist and using much of Comte's own language, described the general outlook of positivism in these terms: "We have no knowledge of anything but Phenomena; and our knowledge of phenomena is relative, not absolute. We know not the essence, nor the real mode of production of any fact but only its relations to other facts in the way of succession or of similitude." This was the intellectual attitude that Comte and his followers brought to the study of society and religion. To be sure, this method has its own assumptions, the foremost of them being that there is an order in the nature of things whose laws we can discover. He also believed that we can overcome the pitfalls of subjectivity by transforming the human brain into a perfect mirror of the external order. This optimism came from his interpretation of the history of ideas and from his study of the development of the various sciences.

3.2   The Law of the Three Stages

Comte saw a clear movement of thought in three stages, each stage representing a different way of discovering truth. The first stage is theological, in which people explain phenomena in reference to divine causal forces. The second is metaphysical, which replaces human-centered concepts of divinity with impersonal and abstract forces. The third stage is positivistic, or scientific, in which only the constant relations between things are factored in and all attempts to explain things by references to beings beyond our experience are abandoned. Naming this evolution the "law of the three stages," he believed that this law is at work in the history of ideas, in science, and in the political realm. He even argued that in the structure of a society, the philosophical orientation is defining, since any major change in philosophical thought will bring about a change in the political order. For example, in the theological stage, we find frequent instances of the intervention of gods or God. This has its counterpart in political theory—in the theory of the divine right of kings. In the second stage, the theological approach is superseded by metaphysics, which speaks of a necessary being as the explanation for the existence of finite things. This concept of necessary being is abstract and impersonal. Its counterpart in political thought is the attempt to formulate abstract principles such as natural rights of the sovereignty of the people. Comte rejected the political structures in both of these stages. The theological stage, he argued, results in the slavery and military states. The metaphysical stage involves the assumptions of liberal democracy and unfounded dogmas such as the equality of all people. Comte believed that people are unequal and have different capacities and must, therefore, have different functions in society. To deal effectively with such questions of political order required a carefully worked-out science of society, which he set out to create, calling it "sociology."

Based on his account of the development of knowledge, thought moves from decreasing generality to increasing complexity and from the abstract to the concrete. So, among the five major sciences he noted particularly, mathematics came first; then, in order, came astronomy, physics, chemistry, and biology. In this sequence, he saw the movement from generality and simplicity to complexity and concreteness. A sixth science—sociology—therefore should come out, which deals with the relations of human beings to each other in society and, as such is the necessary outcome of the previous stage of science. Comte considered it as his task to usher in the science of sociology. For him, sociology was the queen of the sciences, the summit of knowledge, for it made use of all previous information and coordinated it all for the sake of a peaceful and orderly society.

Key Terms

Jeremy Bentham → utilitarianism → the principle of utility → Pleasure-Pain Calculus → John Stuart Mill → qualitative pleasure → Auguste Comte → positivism → the law of three stages

Exercises

1 Translation

 Translate the following sentences into Chinese.

1) What impressed him most was that Bentham's "greatest happiness principle" rendered any unnecessary attempts to deduce morality and legislation from concepts, such as law of nature, right reason, moral sense, or natural rectitude.

2) He said, "The only proof capable of being given that an object is visible, is that people actually see it. The only proof that a sound is audible, is that people hear it; and so of the other sources of our experience. In like manner, I apprehend, the sole evidence that is possible to produce that anything is desirable, is that people do actually desire it." So, we can give no reason why general happiness is desirable except that "each person so far as he believes it to be attainable, desires his own happiness."

❷　Term Explanation

❧ Explain the meaning of the following terms in your own words.

1) utilitarianism

2) the principle of utility

3) positivism

❸　Questions

❧ Answer the following questions.

1) According to Comte, how to calculate the values of pleasure and pain?

2) How did Mill differ from Bentham in their accounts of utilitarianism?

3) How would you justify Comte's sequence of the five major sciences in order of mathematics, astronomy, physics, chemistry, and biology?

❹　Topic for Discussion

❧ Below is a topic related to this chapter. Read it and finish the discussion.

Comte divided human history into three stages and we call this system "a tripartite system" organized around three grand ideas, ages, or principles. Apart from Comte, there are other intellectuals who tend to divide the history of human beings or the history of ideas into three, such as Joachim of Fiore, Jean Bodin, Francis Bacon, Giambattista Vico, Anne Robert, Jacques Turgot, William Godwin, Peter Watson, to name but a few. Do research and find out their tripartite systems separately, and exchange the one you argue for with your classmates.

Appendix: Recommended Readings

A Brief History of the Western World, 8th ed., written by Thomas H. Greer and Gavin Lewis. (New York: Harcourt College Publishers, 2002) This book provides a comprehensive view of the development of Western civilization in half the pages of other texts. Not simply an abridgement of a longer book, this text offers students in survey courses a concise, lucid narrative.

A Dictionary of Philosophy, rev. 2nd ed., written by Antony Flew. (New York: St. Martin's Press, 1984) From the classical thinkers through Aquinas, Descartes, Spinoza, Kant, up to the modern age of Russell and Wittgenstein, this comprehensive dictionary spans the personalities, terminology, and vocabulary of hundreds of philosophers over thousands of years.

A History of Greek Philosophy (Vol.6), written by William Keith C. Guthrie. (London: Cambridge University Press, 1990) All volumes of Professor Guthrie's great history of Greek philosophy have won their due acclaim. The most striking merits of Guthrie's work are his mastery of a tremendous range of ancient literature and modern scholarship, his fairness and balance of judgment, and the lucidity and precision of his English prose. He has achieved clarity and comprehensiveness in this work.

A History of Western Political Thoughts, written by J. S. McClelland. (London: Routledge, 1996) This book is an energetic and lucid account of the most important political thinkers and the enduring themes of the last two and a half millennia. Written with students of the history of political thought in mind, this book traces the development of political thought from Ancient Greece to the late 20th century.

Architecture from Prehistory to Post-Modernism: The Western Tradition, written by Marvin Trachtenberg and Isabelle Hyman. (New York: H. N. Abrams, 1986) This book traces the development of architecture from Stonehenge to the new AT&T Building in New York and looks at important movements, architects, and buildings in human history.

Christendom: A Short History of Christianity and Its Impact on Western Civilization: Volume 1: From the Birth of Christ to the Reformation, written by Roland H. Bainton. (New York: Harper Colophon Books, 1966) It is a good book for anybody wanting an balanced and truthful history of the Christian Church and how it evolved into the Church we know today.

Civilization: A New History of the Western World, written by Roger Osborne. (New York: Pegasus Books, 2008) In the book, Mr. Osborne, with great skills, ties his disparate topics together into a coherent narrative, as absorbing as any novel. It would be hard to imagine a more readable general history of the West that covers so much ground so incisively.

Guns, Germs and Steel, written by Jared Diamond. (New York: W. W. Norton & Company, 1999) Jared Diamond presents the geographical and ecological factors that have shaped the modern world. From the viewpoint of an evolutionary biologist, he highlights the broadest movements both literal and conceptual on every continent since the Ice Age, and examines societal advances such as writing, religion, government, and technology. Diamond also dissects racial theories of global history, and the resulting work—*Guns, Germs and Steel*—is a major contribution to our understanding of the evolution of human societies.

Leviathan, with Selected Variants from the Latin Edition of 1668, written by Thomas Hobbes. (Cambridge: Hackett Publishing Company, 1994) Designed to meet the needs of both student and scholar, this edition of *Leviathan* offers a brilliant introduction by Edwin Curley, modernized spelling and punctuation of the text, and the inclusion, along with historical and interpretive notes, of the most significant variants between the English version of 1651 and the Latin version of 1668. A glossary of 17th-century English terms, and indexes of persons, subjects, and scriptural passages help make this the most thoughtfully conceived edition of *Leviathan* available.

Masterpieces of Western Art, written by Ingo F. Walther. (Koln: Taschens, 1996) Unlike conventional publications that merely illustrate a few essentials, this work places 900 paintings taken from every era squarely in the foreground. The ten chapters each feature an introductory essay profiling the age and the achievements of the major artists, and then present selected works accompanied by searching commentaries.

The Cambridge Companion to Spinoza, written by Don Garrett. (Cambridge: Cambridge University Press, 1995) The essays in this volume provide a clear and systematic exegesis of Spinoza's thoughts informed by the most recent scholarship. They cover his metaphysics, epistemology, philosophy of science, psychology, ethics, political theory, theology, and scriptural interpretation, as well as his life and influence on later thinkers.

The History of Astronomy: A Very Brief Introduction, written by Michael Hoskin. (Nanjing: Nanjing Yilin Publisher, 2013) This is a fascinating introduction to the history of Western astronomy, from prehistoric times to the origins of astrophysics in the mid-19th century. The book concludes with 18th- and 19th-century applications of Newton's law, and the first explorations of the universe of stars.

The History of Rome, written by Livy, translated by Valerie M. Warrior. (Indianapolis and Cambridge: Hackett Publishing Company, Inc., 2006) For the general reader, this is a translation of the first five books of Livy's history of Rome, starting with myths and legends about the founding of Rome, then the history of the kings of Rome and the founding of the republic, the conflicts with Rome's neighbors in Italy and culminating in the sack of the city by the Gauls. Although it is a history book, it is a vivid and exciting account of these events and a very enjoyable read.

The Oxford History of Britain, written by Kenneth O. Morgan. (Beijing and Oxford: Foreign Language Teaching and Research Press & Oxford University Press, 2007) This book tells the story of Britain and its people over two thousand years, from the coming of the Roman legions to the present day. Encompassing political, social, economic, and cultural developments throughout the British Isles, the dramatic narrative is taken up in turn by ten leading historians who offer the fruits of the best modern scholarship to the general reader in an authoritative form.

The Oxford History of Western Art, written by Martin Kemp. (Oxford: Oxford University Press, 2000) This book is an innovative and challenging reappraisal of how the history of art can be presented and understood. Through a carefully devised modular structure, readers are given insights not only into how and why works of art were created, but also how works in different media relate to each other across time.

The Portable Renaissance Reader, written by James B. Ross and Mary M. McLaughlin. (New York: The Viking Press, 1953) This book covers the landscape from about 1400 to 1600, focusing on the three major groups of writings: man, nature, and God. With excepts from Galileo, Kepler, Erasmus, Pius II, Teresa of Avila, Luther, Di Vinci, and many other lesser known writers of the age, the writings provide a glimpse (and little more) into the politics and philosophies of the times.

The Second Treatise of Government, written by John Locke. (Indianapolis/Cambridge, Hackett Publishing Company, 1994) This book is one of the most important political treatises ever written and one of the most far-reaching in its influence.

The Tears of the Indians: Being a Historical and True Account of the Cruel Massacres and Slaughters of Above Twenty Million of Innocent People (1656), written by Bartolome De Las Casas, translated by John Phillip. (Montana: Kessinger Publishing, LLC.,

2010) De las Casas does his best to reveal the heartless brutality and savage greed of the Spaniards in the New World. Page after page is an indictment of virtually all the conquistadors. Anyone wishing to fully comprehend the encounter between the Old and New Worlds must read this text.

Western Civilization: A Brief History, Volume II: Since 1500 (8th ed.), written by Jackson J. Spielvogel. (Boston: Cengage Learning, 2013) Professor Spielvogel has won five major university-wide teaching awards. His engaging style of writing weaves the political, economic, social, religious, intellectual, cultural, and military aspects of history into a gripping story that is as memorable as it is instructive.

教师服务

　　感谢您选用清华大学出版社的教材！为了更好地服务教学，我们为授课教师提供本学科重点教材信息及样书，请您扫码获取。

》最新书目

扫码获取 2024 **外语类**重点教材信息

》样书赠送

教师扫码即可获取样书